HEFLING

HOW TO LIVE

American Heritage Press   New York

CHEAP BUT GOOD

by Martin Poriss

Illustrations by Charles C. Hefling, Jr.

Published by American Heritage Press, a subsidiary of McGraw-Hill, Inc.
Published in Canada by McGraw-Hill Company of Canada, Ltd.

Library of Congress Catalog Card Number: 74–142980
07–050522–5 (hard-cover)
07–050523–3 (paperback)

234567890   BPBP   765432

ACKNOWLEDGMENTS

How to Live Cheap But Good could not have been completed without the efforts of many friends and coworkers, to whom I should like to express my gratitude.

Thanks go to friend and cartoonist Chuck Hefling for his wit, skill, and continual good humor. Thanks too to Ann Aylward and Rob Glueck for their many hours of help in researching the manuscript. Special kudos are due Stanley Kanare, Daria Lewis, Bea Sisk, Marie Foley, Joe Steinberg, Pamela Smith, Jan Roysher, Bea Shneider, and Ed and Bea Poriss for their invaluable suggestions and eagle-eyed editing comments.

I am deeply grateful to Tom Crooks, Nina Madden, Sam Spitz, and Andy Foley for the resources they made available to me; to George David for keeping my 1939 IBM electric typewriter alive for two years and 3,000 pages; and to those many students, professionals, and others who took the time to be interviewed or to answer questionnaires.

Acknowledgment and thanks go to the Science and Mechanics Publishing Company, the Hearst Corporation, the SCM Corporation, and the Robertshaw Controls Company for permission to use their charts and articles. Also to Boston University's Student Union and its president Jack Crisp, for permission to reprint passages from their pamphlet "Boston Housing and You."

Finally, thanks and recognition belong to Karen, whose constant patience, support, and help made life and work so much easier.

To Bice Clemow
and Linda Reithner,
who have lived
cheap but good

TABLE OF CONTENTS

To the Reader:

I have attempted, in this book, to compile a systematic guide to the art of living cheap but good. Such a life-style was once a luxury enjoyed mainly by students, Bohemians, and young couples more in love than in money. But nowadays, thanks partly to changing American values and partly to a fickle economic system, the pleasures of a cheap but good existence are becoming increasingly accessible even to the wealthiest of individuals.

Living cheap but good requires both common sense and a sense of humor. It also requires that each of us be willing to share with his neighbors any bit of information or idea that might help grease the bearings of life.

I look forward to receiving your suggestions, both on topics I've discussed and on those that you feel warrant attention—so that subsequent editions and readers of *How to Live Cheap But Good* may profit from your experiences.

Martin Poriss
c/o American Heritage Press
330 West 42nd Street
New York, N.Y. 10036

CHAPTER ONE

HOME IS WHERE
YOU FIND IT

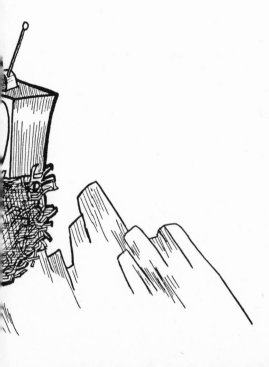

"The following chapter will present the apartment hunter with a nearly foolproof plan of attack on his prey."

Life is filled with entertaining diversions and pleasurable pursuits. Apartment hunting is not one of them, however. He who has a place to live is blessed. But the man in search of a home must ponder, worry, and decide exactly what he wants to live in, where he wants to do it, and how much he is willing to pay for it—"it" being anything from an unfurnished cold-water flat to a Victorian mansion. Once those decisions have been made, the apartment hunter must wander the streets, peer into dingy closets, and manipulate flush toilets—until that moment arrives when exhaustion or a happy discovery brings him and a smiling landlord to a notarized agreement.

Nothing can transform this wearisome odyssey into an after-dinner constitutional. Nevertheless, the following chapter will present the apartment hunter with a nearly foolproof plan of attack on his prey, the apartment, a plan of attack complete in all of its aspects—offensive and defensive.

Remember the first rule of apartment hunting: Don't rush—keep your options open.

SOME A B C'S

The average person, in an average American city, can select among the following to rent and occupy:

1. A single room—generally furnished, with bath and kitchen facilities.
2. A one-room efficiency.
3. An apartment.
4. A house.

He may find all of the above:

1. Furnished—i.e., complete with furniture, appliances, and utensils.
2. Unfurnished—containing only refrigerator, stove, and the artifacts of previous inhabitants.
3. Partially furnished.
   And he may live:

1. Alone.
2. With spouse or mate.
3. With friends.
4. With solicited (or unsolicited) roommates.

THE SINGLE ROOM is invariably the cheapest of living quarters and the easiest to maintain. Furnished simply, though often comfortably, the room may be one of many for rent in a rooming house or guest house or may be a spare room in a house of a family that wishes to supplement its personal income. The latter is common in college communities, where professors and townsfolk invite students to live with them in exchange for a small remuneration and/or light household work. When renting a single room, be careful to find out exactly what bath, kitchen, and parking facilities your money is buying.

Rooming houses vary in atmosphere. Living in one might be a lonely, claustrophobic experience, while another might offer an immediate circle of acquaintances and a communal spirit. Fortunately, amiability combined with respect for individual privacy seems to prevail, especially where good kitchen facilities are shared.

Before opting for a single room, consider what kind of social interaction you want. Remember, you will not be able to entertain guests as comfortably as if you had a living room and kitchen, and your privacy will be less than if you lived elsewhere. On the other hand, if you are new to the area and have few friends, a rooming house is one good way to avoid loneliness.

Shop around, look at local newspaper listings and vacancy signs, and check with college placement bureaus if you are a student. If a room in exchange for service in the home of a local family sounds attractive, consider placing an ad to that effect in the town paper. Finally, remember that single rooms vary in:

A. Size and condition.
B. Furnishings.
C. Facilities offered (private bath, kitchen, parking, linen).
D. Rules and regulations that are enforced. (Beware!)
E. The social atmosphere of the rooming house.
F. Price.
G. Length of rental or lease (week, month, or longer).

THE ONE-ROOM EFFICIENCY—a large room with adjacent bath and kitchenette—is one step away from the furnished room. Efficiency apartments, as they are called, vary from old and dingy to modern and clean. All offer privacy at a rent lower than that of most apartments of similar age and furnishing, but living space is frequently cramped, and appliances often miniature. Like all quarters-for-rent, efficiencies are available in states ranging from the luxuriously furnished to the stark-naked and may be found in a variety of price ranges. Contrary to common myth, the efficiency apartment is not "just right for two." It is often perfect for one, though.

AN APARTMENT, by common definition, is any place for rent that (a) has two or more major rooms in addition to a private bath, and (b) is located in a building containing other apartments. Apartments come in an endless variety of shapes, sizes, and prices, from among which most people who rent living quarters make their selection. For this reason, throughout this book I address myself to "apartments" and "apartment dwellers," although my suggestions are equally applicable to all other sorts of living quarters and their occupants.

HOUSES: In recent years, groups of young people —students and others—have joined together for economic and social reasons to rent houses.*

* Three friends of mine, graduate-school students, "bought" a two-family house. That is, they each contributed three thousand dollars for the down payment, used one-half of the house as their own apartment, and rented the rest to friends. The rent they received from their tenants paid all mortgage, tax, and utilities expenses. At the end of four years my friends sold the house, getting back their initial investment. Thus, by thinking ahead, the three of them had lived rent-free for four years—each of them saving, in total, about four thousand dollars.

Some houses are rented perennially by their owners; others appear on the market when a professor or other professional is planning a sabbatical year. In general, houses-for-rent are most frequently available in suburban areas and at a distance from student centers. Although renting a house involves more upkeep, furnishing problems, roommate searching, and financial juggling, the benefits in terms of money savings and communal living are often attractive. Still, because of varying temperaments, modes of entertaining, and privacy needs, these enterprises have a high mortality rate.

Furnished or Unfurnished?

"Usually, the damage deposit can be considered a gift to the landlord."

For the person whose free time is limited, for whom fixing up and furnishing an apartment holds little appeal, and who can afford a little higher rent, a furnished apartment, room, or house is a good choice. Furnishings, of course, vary with the whim, pocketbook, and conscience of the landlord who supplies them. In every case, however, a higher rent reflects the fact that you have chosen a furnished, rather than an unfurnished, apartment. That is, the identical apartment, rented unfurnished, would have a lower monthly rent.

In addition, most landlords insist upon collecting a damage deposit along with the first month's rent. Usually, this damage deposit can be considered a gift to the landlord, since the tenant can never prove—when he moves out—that he did not do the damage claimed by his friendly landlord. Accepting a damage deposit with no intention to refund it is a common practice. Be wary!

In brief, if furnishings cost the tenant—in added rent—about $15 per month, and if the initial damage deposit amounts to about $100 (a relatively low figure), then the tenant will spend, over a one-year period, about $275 for the privilege of having furnishings that he may neither alter nor keep at the year's end.

If the convenience of a furnished apartment greatly outweighs its cost, perhaps you should consider it. But furniture building and scrounging is easy; an apartment you have furnished yourself is inevitably more creative and homey; and the furnishings so manufactured and obtained may eventually be sold with no loss. And with Chapter 3 of this manual as a guide to apartment decorating and furniture buying, building, and scrounging —how can one possibly go amiss?

Roommates

Even though it is preferred by some who thrive in solitude, living alone is rather lonely and too expensive for most young people. Once the decision to live with others has been made, the problem of finding and choosing roommates is of first importance.

A fact not appreciated by many is that whether you choose to live with boy or girl friend, with long-time friends or acquaintances of your own sex, with a family, with others seeking roommates, or with any combinations of the above, you are married in a very real sense, i.e., you are living in an intensely intimate situation. You may not think so at first, but your roommates' tastes (in music, food, furnishings), habits (in entertaining, conver-

"Your roommates' tastes will affect you directly."

sation, hour of retiring, cleanliness, eating times, television shows), friends (in number, type, and activities enjoyed), financial difficulties (or extravagances), moods and problems (and disposition for sharing them), will affect you directly, just as yours will affect the lives of your roommates.

So, keeping these things in mind, come to an understanding of what you are like and of what you want; and then think and choose your roommates carefully.

If you decide to live with your boy or girl friend, be sure that your relationship is at a stage where day-to-day living will contribute to, rather than harm, what you've already established. Be sure that you will not resent any limitations imposed by such a choice. And finally, consider whether you or your mate will have a place to go if the situation does not prove ideal. "Living together" can be a wonderful experience. But it can also be hell. So think carefully together and discuss frankly all personal likes and dislikes, expectations, habits, and idiosyncrasies.

If you are married, you and your spouse will want to consider such things as whether your apartment will be large enough and attractive enough for entertaining friends or housing a growing family. Be sure your prospective landlord will permit children, should the blessed event occur.

When living with friends, common sense would dictate that you consult each other and decide as a group what you want in terms of an apartment and what types of financial and interpersonal relationships you each envision and desire.

These same issues and more should be discussed by individuals meeting for the first time, drawn together by ads or agencies or at the suggestion of mutual friends. In an interview setting, all questions of taste, habit, friends, and finances should be discussed. And, of course, you must make intuitive decisions about compatibility.

Whether you have rented an apartment and need roommates, or are looking for a room in an apartment already established, avoid feeling pressured by time, money, or individuals; there are always other people and other opportunities—and a mistake can be painful. On the other hand, being overly rigid regarding the types of individuals with whom you opt to live may cause you to miss out on meeting interesting and sometimes wonderful people.

Priorities

Where should your apartment be, and what should it be like? Decide early.

When you have decided:

1. The type of living quarters you want: room, apartment, house;
2. With whom you will live;
3. How many rooms you will need;
4. And the price you can afford for rent and utilities; you and your roommates should discuss the following issues relevant to the location and general nature of the apartment.

Location

A. Distance from campus or job. If you have a car, or if public-transportation facilities are adequate, then an apartment some miles from campus or job will generally prove a cheaper and better deal in terms of upkeep and living space. On the other hand, there will be the added transportation expenses and the time spent in travel. Moreover, friends from work or school will drop by infrequently, or not at all, if the distance is more than a couple of miles. Then there is the issue of personal convenience, which varies according to the temperament of the individual.

B. Convenience of your apartment to laundry, drugstore, supermarket, library, public transportation. If you have no car, convenience is important. Carrying a large bag of laundry even three blocks can be quite an ordeal!

"Friends will drop by infrequently, or not at all, if the distance is more than a couple of miles."

C. Neighborhood. Some areas of town have higher rents than others. You pay extra for lawns, quiet, and a nonslum atmosphere. Think of the following things when you begin your search:

1. Slum, Nonslum, or Borderline Case: Each has its advantages and disadvantages in terms of rent scales, casualness or formality, and ethnic densities.

2. Quietude: Do street noises, including trucks, bother you? Do children's screams and animals on the loose bug you?

3. Danger—a consideration for both men and women: How courageous are you? Do you have possessions attractive to the average thief, a car, for example?

D. Provisions for Children. Are the schools good and easy to get to? Is there an available pool of baby sitters? Is there an outdoor playground? Are there other families with children of the same age?

General Nature of the Apartment

The following considerations may be important to you. If so, know what you need and want.

A. Space. How many rooms do you need? Are you willing to do without a living room in order to avoid paying for a second bedroom? Do you need a study or darkroom?

B. Floor Level.

1. Basement apartments are cheaper, cosy, and subject to humidity and flood damage. They also lack sunlight.

2. First-floor apartments are most convenient. They permit the moving in of large appliances and pianos. But they are also most susceptible to burglary.

3. Top floors combine the joy of continual exercise with lower rents. Generally speaking, apartments on this level have steep stairs leading to them and low ceilings within them, and are unbearably hot in summer. They often have charming windows, however. Noise travels downward in

buildings, so the top floors are usually quieter than those below.

Sometimes, apartments can be found with two levels: living room, kitchen, etc., downstairs, bedrooms upstairs. Lucky is he who finds this treasure, even though his heat bill will be higher.

C. Modernity and Utilities (including air conditioning and type of heating system).
D. Availability of Parking.
E. Permission to Keep Pets.

"Permission to keep pets"

F. Location of Landlord: Does he live in the building, is he nearby, or is he a distant agency? Each has its advantages!

It may seem as though there are a lot of prerequisites to consider. In actuality, thinking about and discussing all the above will not take long, will boil the plan of action down to the simplest course, and will ultimately save time and a good deal of confusion. Moreover, if all your needs and priorities can be enumerated in a clear, succinct list, housing agents will be able to help you more easily, and you will be decisive when the right apartment appears.

THE HUNT

O.K. So you've decided what you want. Now, the quest begins. Where should you search for this Super-apartment of Your Dreams?

Start by looking in the classified and display ads in the real-estate sections of local newspapers. Don't overlook the fact that some towns have more than one paper, and that small weeklies, whose cheaper ad rates can be afforded by smaller landlords, often list better and more unusual bargains. Try to buy the newspaper early in the day that it appears, and make your calls the first thing in the morning. One must be careful about competition.

Look on bulletin boards in supermarkets, churches, Laundromats, and college buildings. Found almost universally, these bulletin boards are frequently used to advertise apartments by landlords and by those who wish to sublet. Ask local residents where their bulletin boards may be found.

Take a walk or drive in the neighborhood you are considering. Sometimes signs saying "Vacancy" or "Apartment to Let" are posted. Go door to door, asking superintendents for clues and advice: if there are no vacancies in his own building, perhaps the man knows of some nearby or of some about to open up. You will discover that superintendents and janitors are very knowledgeable men.

Apply directly to the owners of those buildings that appeal to you. A knock at any door will inform you of the landlord's name. And, if the landlord has no vacancies, his friends might.

If you are a student, consult the student housing office if your college has one. Or, stop by a

"Superintendents and janitors are very knowledgeable men."

club meeting or two and address the assemblage, saying, "Excuse me. I'm John Doe, and I'm looking for an apartment. Do any of you know of anyone who's moving out?" If nothing else, fellow students can direct you to areas of low rent.

Call or stop by the offices of a few real-estate agents. Since the rental agent gets a cut from the landlord, his services may cost nothing. (But be careful. In some cities the *renter* pays a large commission to the agent.) Give your agent the list of wants and needs that you've drawn up and he can check these against his listings and call his many contacts. Let each agent know, tactfully, that you have others prowling around for you and that you will grab the first great bargain that fits your needs.

Finally, let your plight be known! Tell any friends, business associates, and/or relatives you may have in the area that you are apartment hunting. And don't forget to put a note to that effect on those very bulletin boards you are examining for apartment leads.

In summary:

1. Check classified ads of local papers—early.
2. Make a tour of local bulletin boards.
3. Wander the streets and speak with supers and janitors.
4. Apply to the landlords of buildings you like.
5. Consult classmates and student housing offices.
6. Contact several apartment or real-estate agents.
7. Advertise your needs.

If you faithfully execute all of the above, you will rapidly be flooded with leads, hints, and phone calls. Then, it will be time to adjust your tie, comb your hair, and start . . .

EXAMINING APARTMENTS

Examining an apartment is a fine art demanding a sharp eye and a poker face, as well as tact and shrewdness. Dress "respectably" and act in a relatively formal manner. Hunt with your roommates, and carry cash or a check for a deposit. There is nothing casual about choosing a home. Apartment hunting is a serious business that demands as much alertness and attention to details as you can muster. When you visit an apartment, have a notebook with you and a check list like the one at the end of this chapter. Ask the landlord or real-estate agent as many questions as you can think of, and write down all important details, such as rent, descriptions of rooms, condition and appearance of building, specifications of the lease. When you've finished your day's exploration, you'll be able to review your notes quickly to decide which places you should seriously consider and which landlords you should call. Without reasonably explicit notes, details of one apartment soon blur into those of another. Here are a few things to be avoided:

1. Don't take kids, animals, or miscellaneous friends along. Even if they don't get irritable, the landlord or real-estate agent will.

2. Don't be shy. Ask as many questions as occur to you.

3. Don't feel pressured. There are always more apartments.

   If you are a student looking for an apartment in a nonstudent area, go as a person—not as a student. Landlords often stereotype students as loud and irresponsible, so don't advertise your studenthood. In fact, if you hold a part-time job, it might even be preferable to say (if asked), "I work at IBM and go to school part time." A single working girl should indicate that she has a clear source of dependable income, and if it is true, a roommate. All in all, use common sense. First impressions do make a difference, to landlords as well as to others. Make it apparent that you are responsible, honest, and straightforward—and that you expect the same of your prospective landlord.

THE
NEIGHBOR-
HOOD

A. Is it as:
  1. Quiet (check construction sites, steeples, trucks, playgrounds);
  2. Safe (street lights, bars, general appearance);
  3. Convenient (to stores, laundry, transportation)
  as you wanted?
B. Ask your prospective neighbors what they think of the neighborhood, apartment, and landlord.
C. Is overnight on-the-street parking legal? (Note street signs.) Or, is off-street parking available and convenient?

THE
APARTMENT
BUILDING

A. External Appearance:
  1. Peeling paint?
  2. Mailboxes in good repair?
  3. Broken windows?
  4. Locks working?
  5. Sidewalks and grounds cared for?
B. Halls: take a look at how the halls are kept. This gives insight into the type of maintenance services you can expect and also into the type of people living in the building.
  1. Adequate lighting?
  2. Stair treads (and handrails) loose?
  3. Plaster gouged?
  4. Halls cluttered with paper, etc.?
  5. Halls smell bad?
C. Cellar and Back Yard: note general condition.
D. Who are your neighbors?

A TOUR OF THE
APARTMENT
ITSELF

A. Are sinks, bathroom fixtures, and closets clean?
B. What storage facilities are there (including basement/attic)?
C. Do appliances work?
  1. Stove: Do burners and oven light? Do doors close tightly? Are all the broiler pans and racks intact?
  2. Refrigerator: Does door close tightly? Is handle in perfect condition? Are ice trays present?

D. Electricity and Fire Escapes:
   1. Are there light fixtures in each room? Do they work?
   2. Are there at least two electrical outlets per room?
   3. Is there a back exit or fire escape?
E. Noises: Check the noises at dinner time, when kids are around and TV's are going full blast. Also, ask a friend to go into an adjacent room and see if you can hear him talking. Find out who lives upstairs, since that's where the most noise will come from.
F. Plumbing:
   1. Check for roaches, water bugs, etc., under sinks and behind toilet.
   2. Does the toilet flush properly?
   3. Is there plenty of hot water? An independent hot-water system?
   4. Check water pressure in all faucets.
   5. Is there a shower?
   6. Do any faucets leak?
   7. Do all sinks and tubs drain quickly?
   8. Does the bathroom have a window or other ventilation?
G. Garbage Disposal:
   1. What is the system?
   2. What is expected of you?
H. Windows:
   1. Do all windows open and close smoothly?
   2. Does the kitchen have at least one window?
   3. Do screens and storm windows work? (The latter will keep your winter heat bill down.)
   4. Are there pigeon droppings on the window sills? If so, the apartment may be plagued by noisy birds.
I. If Furnished:
   1. Is there enough furniture?
   2. Is the furniture in good condition, or do things wobble and creak?
   3. Are beds and sofas firm and clean?

4. Are there enough kitchen utensils?

J. Sunlight: If being without sunlight depresses you, check the apartment on a sunny day. Check structural overhangs and trees, make a note of adjacent buildings, and determine what compass direction your apartment faces.

Things to Ask the Landlord

A. Are utilities (heat, electricity, water) included in the rent?
1. If they are, have this fact noted in the lease.
2. If not, ask other tenants about the average monthly cost of utilities.
3. If you have to pay for heat in an old building, check for storm windows.

B. If you have a car:
1. Is on-the-street parking both legal and available?
2. If not, does the landlord have available parking space (and at what cost)?
3. If he doesn't, check with the nearest lot or garage for parking rates. And if for one reason or another, you consistently need an extra parking space, rent it! Don't hassle with all of the other tenants.

C. Are pets allowed? Ask rather than avoid the issue, since the landlord may drop by unexpectedly one day, or another tenant may report you.

D. Will the landlord's insurance company insure your personal effects? *This is very important.* Get the phone number and address of the landlord's insurance company. Generally speaking, it is an excellent idea to insure your personal belongings against fire, flood, and theft. The expense is not very great.

Things to Tell the Landlord

A. What date you would like to move in.
B. How many people will be living in the apartment. This makes a difference since in some cities a landlord can raise the rent according to the number of people he discovers living in his apartment.

Things to Remember

A. If you accept an apartment when you see it, you are also tacitly accepting the condition of cleanliness in which you see it. If you are presented with a mess left by former tenants, you can expect to clean it yourself unless you get a written promise to the contrary from the landlord.

B. Any promises made by the landlord in terms of repairs, painting supplies, redecorating, etc., should be stated in writing in the lease.

C. If your landlord asks for a deposit on the apartment, be sure you ask him for a receipt. Remember: The verbal promise that a landlord or rental agent makes to refund a deposit is not legally binding. Be sure that all agreements concerning your apartment are placed in writing!!

Notes on the Rent

A. Your rent = basic rent + cost of all utilities ÷ number of roommates.

B. Pay no more rent per month than you net per week. Or, if you are a student, allocate no more than one third of your income (besides tuition) for your rent.

C. Some cities (notably New York), have apartments under "rent control." Since these invariably have lower rent than comparable apartments that aren't rent-controlled, it is worth the effort to inquire about them.

D. If you think that the apartment you want is too expensive, check the rental rates of apartments in adjacent buildings—and remember that rents vary with maintenance, protection, square feet, and a thousand other variables.

E. Finally, try to evaluate objectively the worth of the apartment and the price of its rent. You should feel that you're getting your money's worth.

A Note on Subletting

Who knows? You might want to sublet your apartment sometime during your leasing period. Before renting an apartment, decide whether it could be easily sublet. Is the location, floor, etc., competitively priced, and does the lease permit you to sublet?

THE LEASE

Having selected an apartment, a formal agreement must be reached with the landlord. There are two ways in which an apartment may be rented. The first is called a "Tenancy-at-Will Agreement." This is a short-term agreement that either party may terminate by giving written notice (certified mail, return receipt requested) at least one rent period in advance. The "Tenancy-at-Will" is usually an oral agreement.

Most people are asked to sign a lease. And if they are under the age of twenty-one, their parents may be asked to co-sign. A lease is a written contract by which the owner of a room, apartment, or house agrees to give possession of his property to another person for a fixed period of time in exchange for a certain sum of money. As long as the tenant pays the rent and follows other rules delineated in the lease, the landlord cannot ask him to leave. On the other hand, under the terms of most leases, the tenant has no right to refuse to pay rent unless he is deprived of possession of all or some portion of his housing.

Remember that the terms of the lease are legally binding and that in no case is the signing of the lease a mere formality. At all times know what you are signing. An application for a lease can sometimes be as binding as the lease itself. Be wary of anyone who pressures you to sign the lease quickly.

Most leases place the tenant at a definite disadvantage. Nevertheless, if the following points are read and followed carefully, these disadvantages will be minimized:

1. Before signing a lease, see several apartments so you can have a basis for evaluating what you are getting.

2. If the landlord advertises one price, and then tries to raise the rent before the lease is signed, be firm. This practice can be fought.
3. If the thought appeals to you, try bargaining with the landlord: he may be willing to lower the rent in exchange for help around the apartment building (e.g., dumping garbage, cleaning halls). If you decide to do this, make certain that all details of the arrangement are put in writing.
4. Be sure that everyone who intends to live in the

"Be wary of anyone who pressures you to sign a lease quickly."

apartment signs the lease. In that way, responsibility is shared by all, and the landlord will have no opportunity to raise the rent on a per capita basis.

5. All promises made by your landlord should be written into your lease. Oral agreements can't change written ones. And supplementary promises are enforceable only if they are written. A landlord feels it necessary to ask for your word in writing; don't feel awkward or embarrassed about doing the same.

6. Some leases contain the notorious "tax-escalator clause." This clause allows the landlord to raise your rent in the event of an increase in local tax rates. If your lease contains this clause, ask your landlord to cross it out and to initial the deletion on both his copy and yours.

7. Make sure that your lease contains no clause making you responsible for all repairs. You should be responsible only for damage due directly to your use and/or abuse.

8. Your lease should contain a clause permitting you to sublet. If it doesn't, have one written in.

9. If your apartment is furnished, have an inventory of furnishings (including a description of the condition of each item) appended to the lease.

10. Be sure to get a signed copy of the lease identical to your landlord's copy. If you can't get such a copy at the time you sign, get a written statement from your agent or landlord promising that he will send you one by a given date.

11. Bring a witness to the signing of the lease.

12. Many landlords demand a "security deposit" in addition to the first month's rent. The amount of this deposit should be noted in the lease, and you should obtain a receipt for it. Do not pay your last month's (or two months') rent; instead, tell your landlord to keep the security deposit. This way you won't have to do the impossible: extract a security deposit from a landlord.

13. Many leases contain an automatic renewal clause. Unless you notify your landlord by certified mail, return receipt requested, before the date of automatic renewal, you will be committed to pay another year's rent. So, note that renewal date on your calendar!!

If You Have Made a Mistake in Signing the Lease

If you have signed a lease too quickly and wish to escape the arrangement, sublet your apartment. It's far easier than trying to break the lease. Furthermore, by subletting, you can avoid losing any deposit you've made. Breaking the lease, when possible, is always costly. (See Chapter 7 for advice on subletting.)

So now you have an apartment. Chapter 2 will tell you everything you need to know about moving in. Chapter 3 discusses cleaning and furnishing your new dwelling and includes information on "convincing" your landlord to provide you with those goods and services to which you are entitled. The remainder of the book attempts to cover, as thoroughly as possible, information dealing with every facet of apartment life, from cooking to home repairs, and finally, to moving out. *Bonne Chance!*

"So now you have an apartment."

APPENDIX 1

APARTMENT HUNTER'S CHECK LIST

Xerox one copy of this check list for each apartment you plan to visit.

A. Address of the apartment:
B. Name of landlord and/or realtor; his phone number and address:
C. Rent: _____. Utilities included: _____heat _____hot water _____electricity. Amount of security deposit: $_____.
D. Date I visited the apartment:
E. Date apartment is available:

Type of Building

1. _____Apartment house _____Two- or three-family house.
2. Mailboxes in good repair?
3. All door locks in good repair? Will landlord change locks in apartment if I move in?
4. Doorbells in good repair?
5. Sidewalks and grounds in good shape?
6. Hallways clean? Well-lit? Is there an unpleasant odor?
7. General condition:
   Miscellaneous comments:

Type of Apartment

1. _____Efficiency, (#)_____Bedroom, _____House, _____Boarding house.
2. Furnished?
   Comments on furnishings:

Location

1. Distance to campus or job:
   Public transportation available? Price:
2. Distance to stores, laundry, etc.:
3. Neighborhood:
   a. Condition:
   b. Street Noise:
   c. Safety:

4. Provisions for children:
   a. Schools:
   b. Playgrounds, etc.:
   c. Other children around:
5. Parking allowed on the street in front of building? Or, nearest available garage and its price:

The Apartment Itself

1. Floor level:
2. Number of bedrooms＿＿: Size of them＿＿: Number of rooms able to be used as bedrooms＿＿: Closet space in each bedroom:
3. Other rooms: ＿＿dining room, ＿＿living room, ＿＿porch.
4. Bathroom:
   a. Clean?
   b. Is there a shower?
   c. Is there a bath?
   d. Check water pressure.
   e. Drain plug close tightly?
   f. Leaky faucets?
   g. Toilet flush properly?
   h. Ventilation: ＿＿window(s) ＿＿fan.

Kitchen

1. Clean? Roomy? Kitchen table and chairs?
2. Refrigerator (size, condition, does it close properly?):
3. Stove:
   a. Everything work?
   b. Oven close tightly?
   c. Pans and racks there?
4. Water pressure in sink:
5. Cooking utensils, if any:

General

1. Comments on condition of decorating: Permission to repaint? Supplies to repaint?
2. Doorbell to apartment functioning?
3. Fire escape or back door?
4. Fireplace? Can it be used safely?
5. Garbage collection system:
6. Insects or rodents (check cabinets and around plumbing fixtures)?

7. Noise:
   a. External (Construction? Trains? Cars? Kids? Dogs?):
   b. Internal (check soundproofing between rooms):
   c. Apartment to apartment (check at dinner time):
8. Pets allowed?
9. Sufficient lights and electrical outlets? Do they all work?
10. Sufficient storage space available?
11. Sunny?
12. Windows open easily? Storm windows and screens available? Are you sure?

Be Sure to Note

1. Name of insurance agent that the landlord uses and recommends:
   Address:
2. Remarks of current occupants and/or neighbors (concerning noise, landlord, cost of heating, etc.):

Signing the Lease

If you decide to rent the apartment, read the section in Chapter 1 on the lease and be sure to get:

A. A receipt for your deposit. Also, write on the check you write for the deposit: "Refundable deposit for apartment, 441 Main Street."

B. A list of present damages, together with the landlord's written promise to make repairs. The list and promise should be appended to the lease.

C. A signed copy of the lease with all of its additions that is identical to the landlord's copy. Do not leave the realtor's office without this.

D. A witness to be present at the signing of the lease.*

* An afterthought: If whoever is showing you the apartment promises repairs, list damages and the promise to repair at the bottom of the Xerox copy of this check list. Your promiser's signature, plus the date, may prove invaluable.

CHAPTER TWO

A MOVING EXPERIENCE

"And thus with His tongue did He move the masses . . ."

For the average individual, not so talented as He, moving house and home presents a variety of decisions, expenses, and inevitable frustrations. Even for the man who owns little, moving can produce the ultimate Excedrin Headache.

Thus, the following chapter is addressed to him who, having read and profited by the remarks of Chapter 1, has somehow procured a place to rest his weary body and dump his worldly belongings.

DECISIONS

O.K., so you have to move in . . . soon. First, two decisions:

1. Whether you will do the moving job yourself or will hire movers.
2. What moving date is best for you and for everyone else.

If you haven't much money for transporting your goods, and if you are aware of the huge expense of nearly all professional moving companies, you will want to make all or most of the moving arrangements, if not carry out all of the work, alone or with the help of friends. This is true even if you live at a great distance from your new home.

For those, however, who adamantly prefer the luxury and outlandish expense of professional movers, the appendix to this chapter, "Preparations and Pitfalls," will make life easier.

Never forget, however:

A. Services such as REA Express, Greyhound Bus Lines, and air freight.*

B. The extremely common, cheap, and feasible practice of renting a truck, arranging personal insurance, and hiring college students as movers and drivers to move your things at a fraction of professional rates.

* REA EXPRESS: All shipping is handled centrally. If delivery is within city limits, it is to the door. Sample rates, per 100 pounds, from Boston to: New York, $11.50; Chicago, $18.32; Los Angeles, $33.34.
AIR FREIGHT: Packages are usually held at the airport, although some companies provide home delivery. Sample rates per 100 pounds from Boston to: New York, $7.10; Chicago, $13.35; Los Angeles, $30.00
GREYHOUND: Service is fast and efficient, but packages must be picked up at the station. Sample rates per 100 pounds from Boston to: New York, $6.30; Chicago, $16.60; Los Angeles, $34.50.

C. Splitting the rental cost of a long-distance truck with other people solicited through an ad in your local newspaper.

Having settled on your method of transport, the date will depend on seven factors:

1. How much work you want to do on your new place before you move in (see Chapter 3).
2. When the landlord, rental agent, or janitor will let you in.
3. If the building is tall and equipped with elevators, when you can reserve the freight elevator (the first of the month is competitive).
4. If you're planning to do the work "yourself," when your friends and relatives can spare time to help you.
5. If you're hiring students, when they can spare the time.
6. If you're using air freight, REA, or bus shipment, when you want your goods to arrive. (Add a few days to whatever they tell you.)
7. If you're hiring professional movers, when both you and they are available (most require reservations four to six weeks in advance).

NOTIFICATIONS

Having made your two crucial decisions, situate yourself next to a telephone, preferably not one of the pay variety. Call:

1. Moving companies for estimates and dates, or truck-rental agencies (see the next section, "Trucks, Trailers, and Equipment Rental").
2. Public utilities, for installation of services:*
   a. Gas, electricity, oil.
   b. Phone: Usually there are several types of service at varying rates. Find out what they are, and get the cheapest. Princess, push-button, and other peculiar types cost more initially and per month. Be prepared to pay a deposit and an installation charge, even if the phone is already installed.
3. Local newspaper, if delivery is desired.

* Avoid placing all utilities in one person's name; this helps distribute responsibility for monthly paperwork and helps prevent one person from being stuck with someone else's debts.

Then, pen in hand, notify:

1. Your current post office of your old and new addresses.
2. Magazine subscription departments of old and new addresses and Zip Codes. Tear off old address labels and send them with your new address. Remember that all post offices have change-of-address cards, free!
3. Your new landlord, by certified mail, of all problems in your apartment and of damaged items. Have three friends sign the letter with you, and keep a copy of it. If anything goes wrong, especially if the problem damages your belongings (e.g., a flood from exploded plumbing, fire, or theft due to bad locks), he will never be able to claim, "I could not have reasonably foreseen the problem."

If possible, do all of the above many weeks before the Great Moving Day. Reservations for moving companies or trucks may have to be made weeks in advance. Subscription departments of periodicals also require several weeks' notice. The utility companies may leave you without light, heat, or means of communication for two or more weeks.

Finally, if moving to a new place entails leaving a place of which you were in charge, be sure to cancel your utilities and finalize your legal-financial-social affairs, according to the dictates of Chapter 7.

You are now ready to make the Big Move. Before tackling the practical aspects of the business, allow me to leave you with one thought: as long as you're moving things, consider what additional things you will want in your new place. If you're considering the acquisition of lumber, beds, piano, bedboards, freezer, furniture, etc., remember that much of the trouble and cost of these things lies in the moving (See Chapter 3, "Purchasing and Scrounging"). Why not do it all at once?

"Utility companies may leave you without light or heat."

TRUCKS, TRAILERS, AND EQUIPMENT RENTAL

If you plan to do your own moving, alone or with the help of friends, rent your vehicles and equipment a couple of weeks in advance. This will prevent last-minute frustrations and allow you to shop around. U-Haul, although the most popular, is not always the cheapest or most practical. Look under "Truck Rental" in the Yellow Pages, and call several companies (including Avis, Hertz, U-Haul, and Ryder).

Obviously, the size of the truck or trailer you need will depend on the quantity of furniture, clothes, rugs, and miscellaneous junk to which you feel attached. Small loads will fit into a U-Haul trailer, which can be attached to almost anyone or anything larger than a Volkswagen. Actually, these trailers—which come roofed or open, in a variety of sizes and colors—can be married to VW's and other foreign chariots, but he who weds them is asking for trouble, not only in terms of driving and handling, but also because of the inevitable strain on the car.

If you are without a car to pull a trailer, or would like something more practical and a little larger, U-Haul rents VANS. These small trucks, somewhat bigger than a VW bus, are easy to drive and convenient if you have relatively little to move. That is, a room of furniture or all of your personal effects or one upright piano and a bicycle or two small motorcycles can be housed conveniently in one of U-Haul's vans. The ride is a bit mind-boggling, but fun.

For the man who thinks big, however, a TRUCK is the solution. Trucks are not nearly so difficult to drive as you might think, especially if you are wary of low-hanging branches, power lines, and bridges. When renting a truck, stay clear of U-Haul, and find a local truck-rental agent who can provide a truck that is equipped with:

1. A standard shift.
2. A hydraulic tail-gate lift.*

* When renting a truck from a franchiser (e.g., U-Haul, Ryder), call several franchise service stations in your area. Prices can vary enormously for the same equipment, destination, and rental duration.

All trucks devour gasoline, but those with automatic transmissions are insatiable. Moreover, automatic-transmission trucks sometimes agonize over hills with which standard shifts can contend quite nicely. So, to save dollars and make things easier, get a standard shift.

A hydraulic tail-gate lift is no luxury. It's a lifesaver—for those who use it carefully. U-Haul discontinued hydraulic lifts because of daydreamers who apparently could not avoid crushing feet, hands, and next-door neighbors, but these lifts are standard equipment on some Avis, Hertz, and Ryder trucks. A hydraulic tail-gate lift allows you to raise furniture, boxes, and people from ground to truck-platform height. For motorcycles, refrigerators, and pianos this is an absolute necessity. And as far as I am concerned, a tail-gate lift is a necessity regardless of what you're moving. It takes half the work out of truck loading and unloading . . . and adds a bit of fun and games as well! *

* U-Haul trucks *do* have long ramps, which are better than nothing.

Having decided what kind of trailer, van, or truck you need, call or visit local truck- and trailer-rental agents. Be prepared to pay a sizable *cash* deposit, and check on the following three items before signing or renting anything:

1. Age: Are you old enough to legally drive this vehicle? Many companies rent only to people over twenty-one years old; if you are younger, you may have to find a friend to drive for you. Is a special license necessary to drive it? Some states have strict regulations for drivers of large vehicles.

2. Insurance: What kind of motor vehicle insurance goes with the rental policy? Make sure it's nondeductible. Also, if possible, arrange for insurance that covers damage to the truck's roof. (Drivers unaccustomed to the height of trucks sometimes "make mistakes.")

3. Duration of rental: Find out the exact date and hour upon which you must return the truck. At the same time, find out what charges you incur if you return it late, and what the procedures are for:

a. Notifying the company that you have been delayed, hours or days.

b. Fixing a flat tire.

"Fixing a flat tire"

c. Having repairs made. Who ultimately pays for repairs? What receipts must you keep?

d. Reporting accidents.

And finally, remember that it is cheaper to rent a big truck and split the space, costs, and driving between two or more people than to rent a smaller truck by yourself.

A Note on Moving Equipment: Most truck-rental companies, U-Haul especially, rent:

A. Furniture pads,

B. Dollies, and

C. Hand trucks (with stair-climbers and straps), all all of which ease considerably the labors of moving. The use of such equipment is described later in this chapter. When reserving your trailer or truck, reserve as many of these items as you might need. They're generally worth the money. U-Haul also rents:

D. Car-top carriers

E. Side-view mirrors.

PACKING Here goes! You've chosen a moving date, rented truck and equipment, and pressured or bribed friends into helping you. You are now ready to pack up and split.

First, raid your local supermarket and liquor store for heavy cardboard boxes—all sizes, as long as they have both tops and bottoms, or at least bottoms. Wardrobe boxes (i.e., tall boxes with wooden rods for hanging clothes) are sold by U-Haul and by most other moving companies. Old foot lockers can be bought for a couple of bucks at pawnshops, used-furniture stores, Morgan Memorial, and the Salvation Army. Bring all these treasure caskets home. Also, buy Manila envelopes for packing letters and papers, a magic marker for labeling packages, masking tape, and twine.

Now. The Poriss Prepacking Preparation Procedures:

1. Search Out.
2. Bring Together.
3. Throw Out.
4. Inventory.
5. Label.

    Bring all your belongings into one, soon-to-be-overstuffed room. All! Look in closets, under floor boards, into cooky jars . . . . then look again, since your eyes will be too bleary to notice the drapes and pictures on the wall.

    Once you bring everything together, decide what things to throw out, give away, or store in the cellar. Books, please note, are comfortable friends to have around. But, if you don't plan to use them, store or sell them.

    Decided what you want? Now, for your own peace of mind, inventory everything—a twenty-minute job. (If professional movers are to be used, this is essential.) And if you are going to have roommates, avoid future hassles by using a laundry marker to autograph books, records, clothing, and linen. Then:

1. Pack CLOTHES in boxes and trunks—the contents of each closet in a separate container. Pack shoes in a separate box.
2. Hang DRAPERIES and CURTAINS on coat hangers, or pack them in drawers.
3. Pack BOOKS and LINENS in cartons (*small* ones, so they'll be liftable), not in drawers. Don't pack breakables with your books.
4. Wrap BREAKABLE ITEMS separately; pack them with the lighter things on top. Stuff towels and socks into spaces, so that nothing within the box or trunk can move, but not so tightly that the box bulges or that things spill over the top.
5. Wrap all PICTURES and MIRRORS within a folder made by taping (use wide masking tape) two pieces of corrugated cardboard together at the bottom. Label "Glass," so that the folder won't be put under heavy furniture or refrigerators. Cover-

ing all glass and mirror surfaces with wide masking tape will help reduce breakage and will minimize damage in the event of breakage.

6. Pack each LAMP SHADE in a separate box.
7. Put jars and bottles containing LIQUIDS in a metal or plastic wastebasket, so that if something spills, everything won't be ruined.
8. Discard FLAMMABLES: paint, alcohol, lighter fluid, and aerosol cans (especially these), and be sure to empty tanks of camp stoves, propane torches, motorcycles, etc.
9. Pack jewelry, current letters and papers, documents, and miscellaneous VALUABLES in a piece of luggage that you can conveniently watch or carry.
10. Pack a small suitcase of items you will need immediately upon arrival in your new home. Include some clothing, toilet paper, a pot or two, and some portable food and drink.

Now for the Big Stuff.

Disassemble as much furniture as possible. This makes carrying easier and greatly reduces chances of damage en route.

1. BEDS: Metal frames are dismantled by loosening and removing nuts and bolts. Sometimes (when wing nuts have been used), no tools are needed. Otherwise, a screw driver or pair of pliers is necessary.

Wooden frames are dissolved with even less effort. No tools are needed. Simply remove the cross braces and pull upward, then apart, on the long beams. Catch the head and foot boards as they fall.

2. TABLES AND DESKS: The legs of many tables and desks can be removed by unscrewing either the legs themselves or the wood screws or nuts and bolts that attach the legs to the desk or table top.

a. Put all nuts, bolts, screws, and hardware in a

heavy envelope. Tape this envelope to the table or desk.

b. Tie the legs together with string so that they won't get lost or separated.

c. Finally, if your desk or table contains drawers, remove them before moving your furniture. Otherwise, while holding your end of the desk and walking down a staircase, you'll find yourself dashing in all directions trying to chase flying drawers.

3. CHAIRS: A few chairs and sofas have removable legs. For the most part, however, there is no way of easing the pain of moving these bulky items.

4. CHESTS OF DRAWERS: Remove the drawers and hope that the stairs won't be steep, that your back will be strong, and that the chest is not of oak.

5. GRAND PIANOS: This feat requires three strong guys and one piano dolly, a screw driver, rubber or wooden mallet, some rubber casters, and an envelope. Place rubber casters or mats under each of the piano legs to prevent rolling or slipping. Then:

a. Remove top or lid of piano by sliding hinge pins (two) out of hinges. Put these pins in a large envelope, and put the piano top where it won't be in the way.

b. Slide the music rest forward on its tracks until it comes off. Put it, too, aside.

c. Remove the lyre, i.e., the unit containing pedals and pedal rods, by pulling out the two pins (or screws) that hold it in place and by removing the bolt holding the rear brace. When all is loose, post one man on one side of the piano and one on the other. Each should hold the piano on the side, but near the keyboard. The third man, underneath the piano, will pull the lyre down and out as the other two lift the piano a few inches.

d. Rest.

e. Ready? Place the piano dolly on the floor, to the left of and parallel with the straight side of the

"Wrap breakable items separately."

piano. While two men support the left front corner of the piano, the third removes the left front leg. This is accomplished in the following manner: Climb under the piano. Loosen, with a screw driver, the wood block that is braced against the leg. Turn this block, once loosened, 90 degrees. (The leg itself may have screws running through it, which must also be removed.) Climb out. Wielding a wooden mallet or a hammer, place a piece of scrap wood against the side of the left front leg and hit the leg sharply from the side while your cronies support the corner of the piano, lifting it a couple of inches above the floor. With any luck at all, the leg will fall off. Catch it and get it the hell out of there, quickly!

f. Hold the dolly in place while your friends, swearing and cursing, lower the left corner of the piano to the floor. Then gently rock the piano onto the dolly.

g. Rest. But don't let the piano topple over!

h. O.K. Remove the other two legs in the same way as you did the first, making sure that the piano is securely held by the two steadfast friends.

i. Drink some lemonade, and thank God you found a truck with a hydraulic tail-gate lift—not to mention two former friends!

6. REFRIGERATORS: Remove shelves and trays. Make sure that the door handle doesn't get knocked off in the moving process! If you remove the refrigerator door, the unit becomes much easier to carry. Refrigerators, like upright pianos, washing machines, freezers, and grandfather clocks must be tilted onto, and strapped to, a hand truck. (Clean a refrigerator before you move it, or fungi and mold will grow.)

7. TYPEWRITER: Bring both margin stops to the center, thereby locking the carriage. Place the typewriter in a heavy box, and pad very, very well with towels, etc. Typewriters, especially electric ones, are delicate and expensive to repair.

"Clean a refrigerator before you move it, or fungi and mold will grow."

8. HI-FI SYSTEMS: Pack all pieces separately and with care. If the turntable is on springs, tighten the nuts on the top side. Then, using lots of masking tape, secure the tone arm to its rest. Put all wires and miscellaneous plugs, clips, and parts into a labeled bag. Pray for good luck and smooth roads.

9. RUGS: For obvious reasons, rugs are packed last. Vacuum them quickly, then roll them up on a bamboo pole (for moving ease), if you can wangle

or bargain a couple of them out of your local rug dealer or cleaner. Roll underpads, if you happen to have them, separately.

All packed? That's what you think! Go back to the kitchen and take the can opener off the wall. Return to the living room and remove the extension cord that's tacked along the molding. Finally, take down that light fixture you spent time choosing and paying for.

Now you are truly packed and ready to get moving. Before broaching the topics of truck loading and driving, a brief digression for a review of certain Poriss Packing Procedural Principles.

1. BOXES:
   a. Many small boxes are easier to move than a few big ones.
   b. Tape the bottoms of all boxes, except those filled with clothing and linens. Or, tie the boxes closed with heavy string.
   c. Using the time-honored magic marker, label all boxes before closing them. This will aid the process of unpacking immeasurably.
2. DELICATE ITEMS: If possible, avoid future heartache by transporting typewriters, hi-fis, and similar delicate items by car, not in the truck.
3. GRUBBY FURNITURE: Don't move saggy beds or lousy furniture. Leave it, junk it, or sell it. You can buy the same sort of thing "wherever you may roam."
4. PACKING PARTIES: When it comes to packing clothing and personal items, do it alone. A group, or even one other person, cannot help you pack. They can only bug you with a constant stream of questions guaranteed to annoy.

FROM APARTMENT TO TRUCK

When it comes to the actual loading of trailer or truck, friends can be a definite asset. Organize a small group of them to help you, remembering that two conscientious friends who know what they are doing work faster and more efficiently than five well-wishers stumbling over each other's feet and bell-bottoms.

Post the most sensible of your friends on the truck, his job being to load all articles according to the rules that follow. The rest of your friends will scurry between truck and apartment, carrying the items you hand them. After a while, to stave off resentment, these roles should be redistributed.

"Well-wishers stumbling over each other's feet and bell-bottoms"

The Relay, or Bucket Brigade, Method of Loading is sometimes a more efficient way of getting the job done—at least it adds a bit of variety to the job.

Finally, there is the man whose friends are all "busy" on the appointed day. His lot is indeed a sad and weary one. But he can ease his burdens tremendously by seating a mother, next-door neighbor, or even a dog by the truck, to keep watch over his goodies and protect them from passing "truck-lifters."

Be sure to:

1. Have everything packed before your "moving squad" arrives.
2. Keep things moving, and avoid jamming the doorway.
3. Follow the old maxim: "Work now, drink later." That is, if you value your belongings.

Lifting and Carrying Techniques

When lifting and carrying objects of any sort, follow two general rules:

1. When lifting things, keep your back straight and perpendicular to the floor. This will, of course, necessitate a deep bending of the knees and a bit of initial awkwardness, but the strain and energy saved by this method is compensation sufficient.
2. Grasp objects low and lift them high. Scientifically speaking, this keeps the object's center of gravity better aligned to that of your body. Effectively speaking, however, it simply makes things one hell of a lot easier.

After reading the above rules twice more, consult the following list for specific techniques.

1. BEDS: Carry mattress, box spring, and dismantled frame separately. For $1.98 you can buy a zip-up plastic mattress cover. This completely encases a mattress and keeps it from getting filthy. When you're finished with it, throw it away —it's well worth the $1.98. When tying a mattress to the top of car or trailer, be careful—all mattresses have an astounding capacity for escaping even the most conscientiously applied knots and tourniquets.
2. BOXES AND TRUNKS: If heavy, grasp the box by its bottom edges; lift and carry at shoulder height, preferably resting it on your shoulder or head. Trunks should be moved by two people, or by one person and a trusty hand truck. When moving by

muscle power alone, hold trunks by their bottom edges (not by their handles)—and carry them as high as possible.

3. CARPETS AND RUGS: If you've been fortunate and wise enough to roll your large rugs on bamboo poles, post a man at each end and carry like a battering-ram, each man resting his end of the pole on one or the other of his shoulders (with both men on the same side of the rug).

If your rugs have not been so skewered, you will soon discover them to be as unmanageable as a twenty-foot eel. In such circumstances, two alternative modes of moving are available:

a. Let one tall, strong male drape the rug around his neck like a horseshoe, supporting, with his

"If your rugs have not been skewered, you will soon discover them to be as unmanageable as a twenty-foot eel."

hands, the rug's ends in front of him as he hobbles along.

b. Post one man at each end of the rug AND a third man in the middle. Carry with care.

Moral: Don't let two people attempt to move a large rug—the result is generally catastrophic.

4. CHAIRS: If they are small and wooden, carry two chairs at a time, one in each hand. Each chair, held upside down, should be grasped by one leg where it meets the seat. Carry large chairs upside down, on your head. The chair's seat will cushion your head, its back, and your back. To manipulate the chair into this interesting position, rest it upside down on the floor; then, with your back straight, stoop down, climb under, and get up.

5. DRESSERS, COUCHES, TABLES, DESKS: Remove legs and drawers. Grasp low and raise high. Couches must sometimes be turned sideways, upside down, on end, backward—or any combination of these positions—in order to fit them

through doorways and narrow corridors. If the furniture is of very good quality, be sure to cover it with furniture pads before moving it out of the apartment.

6. UPRIGHT PIANOS, REFRIGERATORS, AND OTHER MONSTERS should be moved strapped to long hand trucks. The hand truck should be larger

"Upright pianos and other monsters"

than the object to be moved, have four wheels if possible (two will suffice), and be outfitted with straps and stair-climbing caterpillar treads. On staircases, hand trucks are moved up or down, one step at a time, by sliding them along (to avoid bumping) on the treads. On the straightaway, the hand truck is laid flat and rolled along on its four wheels. To turn a corner, press down hard on the handle, and pivot the vehicle on the wheels closest to you. It takes only three strong guys—two at the handle end, one at the other—plus one co-ordinator on the side lines, to move a small upright piano or refrigerator. A large upright piano or mammoth freezer may take two or three more movers, but the job is still fairly easy.

A Last Thought: Prop open all doors before starting the move.

Notes on Loading Trailer and Truck

General:

1. Whether you have a truck or a trailer, load it from floor to ceiling, one quarter of it at a time.
2. More than one half of the weight of your furniture should be placed toward the front of the truck.
3. The weight should be fairly evenly distributed from side to side.
4. Use plenty of clothesline rope to tie things in place.
5. Lastly, pack a hammer and screw driver, together with your hand truck and suitcase of essentials.

Specific:

1. Load appliances and other heavy furniture first, using blankets and rugs to protect them and other furniture.
2. Load chests and dressers with their drawers facing a truck wall or other flat surface. Fill all drawers (which you removed before moving the chest, and have just replaced) with small items, so as not to waste space.
3. Load tables without their legs, or else with legs pointing upward.
4. Fill in spaces with lighter items, placing breakables, padded well, near the top of the load.

Car-Towed Trailers:
1. The combined weight of cargo and trailer should be less than the weight of the empty tow car.
2. Pack your lightest things in the trunk of the car.
   Delicate Machines:
   Try to avoid carrying typewriters, stereo sets, TV's, etc., in a trailer or truck: use a car for these items. Otherwise, pad very well.

Finally:
Have handy a good padlock with which to seal the door of your loaded vehicle.

DRIVING   Driving off with loaded truck or trailer should present no problems if you're careful to allow greater than normal braking distance (because of the truck's weight) and more clearance on corners and overhead to compensate for the length and height of your vehicle. Also, make frequent use of both left and right mirrors, since you will be unaccustomed to the dimensions of your vehicle.

When towing a trailer, start and stop slowly, figuring on twice the normal braking distance. As with trucks, be sure to downshift and use your lower gears when going downhill—thereby using engine compression to hold car, trailer, and load. Finally, try to avoid backing up whenever you are pulling a trailer. If you must back up, do so slowly to avoid the situation known as jackknifing —inevitably, though, you will jackknife. When you find yourself in this predicament, drive forward once more to straighten yourself out, and try again.

Regardless of what you are driving—trailer, van, or truck—check your load (watch out for shifting and/or falling), tires, lights, hookup . . . often. Don't wait until something crashes dramatically, deep within the bowels of your trailer . . . or until something hastily tied to the top of the load extricates itself and glides nonchalantly across a four-lane highway.

Something to remember: When it rains, protect your belongings with a plastic tarp (available at Sears or hardware stores).

Important: Most trucks are fitted with speed governors, allowing you to travel no faster than 45–50 mph. Plan your time schedule accordingly!

MOVING IN, OR THE TENTATIVE BUT EMINENTLY HANDY FLOOR PLAN

By the time you arrive at your new flat, fatigue will undoubtedly have reduced you to a state of complete befuddlement and indecision. Therefore, have handy a scrap of paper, a note written to yourself some days earlier, informing you of what goes where. Even if you are working alone, but especially if others are "helping" you, this bit of five-minute foresight will speed the unloading process a lot.

Be unique!! Defeat the human tendency to dump all your stuff into the first space at hand, which only results in creating an impossibly impassable obstacle course for yourself. Rather, as in painting a floor, fill in the last room, or last corner, first—and work your way out.

It is now late at night. You've moved in, and your friends have left. Unpack quickly. You're probably good for little else at this point, and facing the mess in the morning will be so overwhelming that you may opt to live forever (or at least for weeks) in the not-so-blissful state of unpackedness.

Your odyssey is now completed. Soon you will look back nostalgically upon that trek; for, as we all know so very well, GETTING THERE IS HALF THE FUN.

APPENDIX 2

PREPARATIONS AND PITFALLS FOR THE MAN WHO "MUST" HIRE A MOVING COMPANY

Professional moving companies are generally efficient, reliable, and extremely expensive.

Prices vary from company to company, especially among local movers, so it is a good idea to shop around:

1. Get more than one estimate.
2. Get each estimate in writing.
3. Have each estimate made by a company representative who will visit your apartment and inspect your property.

Remember, however, that the written estimate is neither a bid nor a contract. In fact, it means very little, for the final bill is usually a good deal larger than the initial estimate. Eventually, your moving bill will be based on:

A. The actual weight of your furniture and belongings.
B. The distance your goods were transported.
C. Extra services rendered (packing/unpacking, loading, warehouse storage, insurance).

Thus, no job can be priced with any real accuracy until everything has been packed, loaded, and weighed. And, by that time, there is no turning back.

The RATES of local movers may vary more than those of interstate movers, whose prices are fairly standardized. Often, a small, independent outfit will prove fairly reasonable if you are not moving out of state.

Professional movers bill by the hour (not by the job). On local moves you will be charged from the moment that trucks and men leave the moving office until the moment that, job completed, they arrive back at company headquarters. When the move is long-distance, packing and loading is billed by the hour, and trucking by weight and mileage.

It is therefore to your advantage to do some of the work before the "pros" arrive, and to keep an eye on them while they work. If two men of a six-man crew sit and smoke cigarettes in your attic, your bill will swell in direct proportion to the number of cigarettes consumed.

With these thoughts kept firmly in mind, do the following:

1. Pack as much as you can before the movers arrive. Remember, however, that the moving company is not responsible "for damage resulting from faulty packing you perform." This leaves a lot of room for interpretation, especially by the movers. On local moves items may be left in drawers, since the movers will load chests and bureaus intact.

2. Stoves, refrigerators, and washing machines may need special servicing before shipping. Call an appliance store and arrange to have this work done by one of their servicemen.

3. Take down all curtains, Venetian blinds, mirrors, paintings, and anything else stuck to your walls. If you are taking your carpets with you, pull up the tacks before the movers arrive.

4. Throw out whichever of your belongings deserve that fate. Give the rest to Goodwill, the Salvation Army, etc., or sell them through a classified ad in your local newspaper.

5. Be on hand to make suggestions and to watch the packing and loading. This tends to reduce damage to your furniture, as well as to speed up the operation.

6. Measure large appliances and furniture, and compare their dimensions with those of doors and windows in your new apartment. If a couch, for example, cannot fit through your new door, it will have to be hoisted through a window (a very costly procedure), or simply abandoned. It is better to know such things before the moving job begins.

7. If possible, do some of the moving yourself, especially of delicate and valuable items.

8. When moving interstate, check on the weight ascribed to your goods by the moving company. Too frequently, "errors" are made. As soon as goods are weighed, the mover is required to notify you of the weight of your shipment and of the charges, *if* you request him to do so. If you question this reported weight, ask for a reweighing prior to delivery. Attend the weighing if at all possible.

9. Before your belongings leave for your new home, your moving company should give you what is called a bill of lading. This document contains a description of your property (and its valuation), together with other information. It's an important document to hold on to.

The above advice, if followed carefully, may save you quite a few bucks. Another matter for attention is INSURANCE.

When you contract with a moving company, the price of moving automatically includes some insurance against the loss or damage of your property. Usually, however, this nominal insurance policy is extremely insufficient. Therefore, check the amount of insurance offered—nominally and optionally—and be sure to obtain adequate coverage. Also, before your belongings are moved, insist upon receiving from the mover a document showing the amount of protection you have purchased, its cost, and the risks included and excluded. In the event of loss or damage, this document may prove to be an important piece of evidence.

The End of the Road

Be at your new apartment on the day that your belongings are scheduled to arrive. (Get a delivery date written into your contract, and make sure that you are not charged extra for this service.) Most moving companies will be on time, but if the mover is delayed, the law requires him to give you twenty-four-hour telephone or telegraph notice.* If no one is at your new home when the mover arrives, delivery cannot be made, and your goods will be carted off to a warehouse. Needless to say, this leads to the added expenses of storage and a second delivery.

You are required to pay the bill, in full, before the mover will unload your property. And since a personal check will not be accepted, be prepared with a certified check, money order, cashier's or traveler's check, or cash. Be prepared, also, for charges in excess of the estimate you originally received. Remember, if you can't pay, the truck will drive on to the nearest warehouse.

In return for payment, you should receive a receipt itemizing all charges (weight, mileage, services). This receipt and any papers accompanying it are your written records. Keep them for tax purposes, and in the event of questions or disagreements with the moving company.

When your furnishings are unloaded, have the driver note any damages or losses on the receipt. If he refuses, ask a friend to examine the damage in the presence of the driver. Then, both you and your friend should file a written report to the moving company's home office. Even if the driver does make a record of damage or loss, you should send an estimate of necessary repairs or replacements to the moving company (by certified mail, return receipt requested), which is required to acknowledge your claim within thirty days and to settle it within three months.

Finally, for the sake of convenience to all, prepare a floor plan of your apartment in advance, to direct the movers in their unloading of your furniture and cartons.

HEFLING

CHAPTER THREE

A HABITABLE DOMICILE

OR

SHOVELING OUT, FIXING UP, AND FURNISHING

This chapter concerns itself with the various ecstasies of cleaning, painting, scrounging for furniture, furniture repair, landlord pressuring, and other related activities. It is to be hoped that besides bringing pleasure to the multitudes, it will also ease the burden of "all ye who labour" to make your apartments habitable.

The amount and type of work to be done will depend on the initial state of repair and furnishment of your apartment and on your tastes, your money, and your ambition. But one thing cannot possibly be overstated: *think modestly.* Most people, upon moving into an apartment, immediately envision elaborate paint jobs, curtains, shelves, etc., and after a day or two of hard work, simply quit when they realize how little progress has been made toward the building of a dream world. Think modestly. "Landlord pink" walls can be lived with when graced with appropriate pictures and photographs. Decide early what you can tolerate, keep monetary outlay and painting to a minimum, and concentrate your efforts on adding interesting colors and textures and furnishings that are simple, cheap, and effective. If it is at all possible, clean and paint your apartment before you move into it. If you don't, you'll soon wish you had.

The Preliminary Examination

Case your apartment, testing windows, doors, and plumbing. Scrutinize walls, door locks, and electrical fixtures. Introduce yourself to any rodent or insect roommates you might have inherited. Decide, if you didn't when you first examined the place, what must be fixed and painted, remembering that the appendix to this chapter will aid and abet your attempts to force Monsieur Landlord to fix any problems and to help pay for painting supplies.

For those of you with recalcitrant landlords, Chapter 6 has been included to help you:

a. Fix leaky pipes, faucets, toilets, and clogged drains of all sorts.
b. Fix and replace fuses, electrical cords, plugs, and wall switches.
c. Fix sticky doors and windows.
d. Fix radiators that don't supply heat.

At the conclusion of the preliminary examination, hold a conference with your roommates and decide upon the painting, furnishing, and decorating to be done. Draw up a Grand List of items needed, including mops, brooms, lumber, paints, rugs, and furniture. The list will be of value when the day of scrounging arrives.

CLEANING

The key to cleaning* is not to be overmeticulous. Think in terms of sanitation and relative neatness, and don't get up tight about filthy ceiling moldings in the back pantry.

On the other hand, do a fairly thorough cleaning job upon moving in. You may never get around to doing it again!

* Look in the Yellow Pages under "Cleaning" for a quick, painless, complete, and fairly inexpensive apartment overhaul. Most companies charge twenty to fifty dollars per apartment: several men come in and scrub, clean, polish, and wax.

Purchases

Do not go to your corner hardware store. Instead, go to a large wholesale store, like Woolworth's or Sears and Roebuck, or in some cases, to a grocery store. (By doing so, you've already saved yourself more than the cost of this book.) Buy:
a. Lightweight brooms, mops (with squeezers), toilet brush, scrub brush, many sponges, and—optional —a carpet sweeper. Disposable gauze diapers make excellent cleaning rags.
b. Two or more big plastic buckets and one dustpan.
c. Ammonia, powdered cleanser, refrigerator-defrosting spray (optional), and, perhaps, some carpet cleaner and oven degreaser.
d. A box of 15-amp fuses (or Fusetrons, which indicate whether your fuse has blown because of a short circuit or an overload, an important fact to know), some light bulbs, extension cords, and electrical outlets that screw into light fixtures.

e. Hammer, screw driver, nails, and picture hooks.
f. And, from a gas station passed on the way home, one gallon of kerosene (bring a container).
g. Finally, if you cannot possibly live without a vacuum cleaner, stop by a store that repairs vacuums (and/or small electrical appliances) and find out if they have any unclaimed vacuum cleaners for sale. Often, for the cost of the repairs already made to them, a decent vacuum can be had cheaply.

Getting to Work

Sweep up anything that can be swept. Then wash walls and ceilings with a sponge or clean mop, warm water, and detergent. Wash walls in small sections at a time—from ceiling to floor, overlapping cleaned areas. Before starting, test your detergent on a hidden spot of the wall; once started, finish the entire wall. Floors can be washed with mops and detergent or, for a more potent solution, a mixture of ammonia and water. (Clean wood floors with wood-floor cleaners or waxes instead of water.) Remember, thirty years' worth of previous tenants can deposit many layers of sedimentary artifacts!

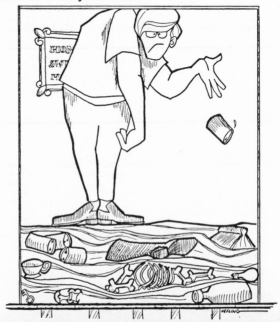

"Thirty years' worth of previous tenants can deposit many layers of sedimentary artifacts."

Use two buckets when washing: one for the cleaning solution, one for rinsing. Protect your hands with gloves of cloth or rubber, and have a step stool or chair handy for reaching high places.

To avoid buying a prepared solution, mix ½ cup kerosene, vinegar, or old tea with a quart of warm water for use on windows. Wipe on with a cloth, wipe dry with a towel. Bathe metal Venetian blinds in the bathtub; wash wooden ones, using a damp cloth, in place on the windows. Curtains should be washed or dry-cleaned (preferably in self-service machines), or at least aired out on a clothesline.

For sinks and bathtubs, hot water plus ammonia plus detergent works wonders. There are also several commercial preparations that are excellent for cleaning sinks, tubs, and other areas of your bathroom. In my opinion, Dow Spray Disinfectant Bathroom Cleaner works best. It will clean absolutely anything from anything, and requires no scrubbing to help it.

Use the same sort of potions on the toilet bowl, scrubbing inner and outer surfaces with your new Sears and Roebuck toilet brush. Scrub shower curtains against the side of your tub with a brush, or put them into an automatic washer which helps remove old soap and mildew. Then rinse by hand.

Finishing Touches

Those fortunate enough to have a fireplace should sprinkle ancient ashes with water—just a dash on top, no flood is needed—and scoop into a cardboard box lined with newspaper. Fold the paper over and dump out the whole mess. The dark stains surmounting the brick tiling of most fireplaces can be eliminated with common vinegar and a stiff brush. Or, use a soldering torch to burn off old carbon stains.

Oven cleaning offers little in the way of rapturous enjoyment to the average individual. Nevertheless, it should be done at least once a year

"The noble refrigerator, majestically cloaked in robes of icy whiteness"

(most people say once a month, but that's most people for you). A spray oven cleaner, like Easy-Off, and steel wool will do the job. (It's a good idea to line the broiler with tin foil when baking things, and as for the top of the stove, "Don't forget to brush after every meal.")

The noble REFRIGERATOR, majestically cloaked in robes of icy whiteness, must next be considered. Defrosting may be accomplished by means of a commercial spray combined with a dash of elbow grease. Alternatively, the following time-honored method may be employed:

1. Unplug the refrigerator.

2. Remove edibles (and other foods, eh?) from freezer and cooling compartment. Place foods, together with some ice, in a Styrofoam ice chest if you have one. Otherwise, use a pot or vegetable bin for your leftovers on the rocks.

3. Put great gobs of newspaper on the top shelf under the freezing unit to ensnare cascading icicles.

4. Fill any receptacle but an ice tray with boiling water—ice trays have a coating destroyed by hot water—and place inside the icy caverns of the freezing compartment. (A second receptacle of water should simultaneously be heating on the stove. By alternating the two, the freezing compartment can be provided with a constant supply of steam.)

5. While the steam is doing its thing, chip away with knife, fork, and great care (so as not to rupture a freezing artery) on the coat of ice. Soon, large boulders will succumb to the two-pronged attack of steam and tools.

6. Dump ice into sink. Be sure to empty the water and ice that has accumulated in the meat drawer.

7. Spray the interior of the freezing compartment with commercial deicing gunk, or with alcohol, which will postpone defrosting for a while and make the job easier when the day arrives once

again. Nearly the same results can be obtained by either lining the freezer with heavy tin foil, which can be pulled out with the ice that has formed on it, or greasing the interior of the compartment with Crisco or margarine (shortening must be unsalted).

8. Plug in the refrigerator, that noble beast, once more.

The simplest method of defrosting, however, is simply to unplug the refrigerator on shopping day, when there is little left in the refrigerator anyway. If you put a couple of pans on the bottom of the main refrigerator compartment, throw out leftover foods or put them in an ice chest or vegetable bin, and then go for a movie and some groceries, you will return to a defrosted refrigerator.

If your refrigerator emanates fragrant "remembrances of things past," exorcise such foul odors in the fouling way: place a small amount of uncompressed charcoal in the freezer and in the refrigerator itself; remove the old charcoal and add a new supply each day until all the bad odors have been absorbed.

The same results can be accomplished by washing refrigerator innards with hot water spiked with baking soda. Empty vegetable bins of their customary assortment of apples, carrots, and the like, and use them (the empty bins, that is) as buckets in which to mix about ½ gallon of hot water with more-or-less ¼ cup of baking soda. Then, using a Sears and Roebuck sponge, start scrubbing.

BUGS, MICE, AND OTHER MASCOTS

Many kitchens nowadays, as always, come equipped with a full assortment of pests eager to greet you. Some carry diseases; all are unappetizing to the eye as well as to the palate.

Here, then, is a bit of preventive and curative advice. But, when all is said and done, the best way to contend with these beasties is to force your landlord (see Appendix) to do the job for you.

The omnipresent COCKROACH, which multiplies at an astonishing rate, is easily pleased: he'll live almost anywhere. But what he really digs is dampness—kitchens, bathrooms, garbage pails, plants, old newspapers, etc.

The moral, of course, is to keep corners and crevices clean of food and water, especially under baseboards, in cabinets and cupboards, and around all sinks and plumbing fixtures. Close shrinkage cracks around sinks with putty, and keep food and garbage in closed containers. Also, be careful of grocery cartons, the transportation vehicle of the average cockroach.

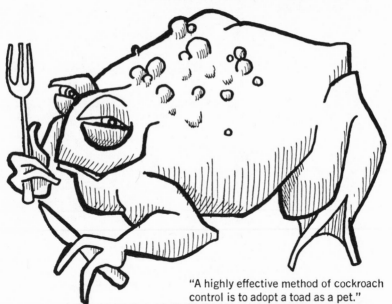

"A highly effective method of cockroach control is to adopt a toad as a pet."

(An additional—and highly effective—method of cockroach control is to adopt a toad as a pet. A friend of mine once tried this; the toad hopped around his apartment at will, staying out of everyone's way, and grew fatter and fatter—despite the fact that no human ever fed him. My friend never again saw a cockroach, or a mosquito, in fact, in his home.)

Finally, spray preventively. Surface sprays are lethal for weeks. Aerosol sprays, for winged insects, are good, but only for the moment. When spraying, cover all food, close windows and doors, and leave the room for at least one-half hour after the job has been done. Follow these guidelines for safety when using insecticides:*

* For toad-haters, best bets for killing cockroaches: House cats eat cockroaches, and small cans of TAT are fairly effective. But if you've *really* got troubles, look up "Exterminating and Fumigating Equipment and Supplies" in the Yellow Pages. From one of the companies listed, buy and use a quart of Diazanon-based liquid (bottled under many brand names) in a sprayer. Cost of reusable sprayer and liquid is $4–$5. This will be far more effective than standard hardware-store sprays.

No spray, however potent, is effective for more than a few weeks. Only a roach-killing powder (Chlordane-based, buy at exterminating supply company) will let you make one application and then sit back roach-free for years. Be forewarned, however, that it takes many hours on hands and knees, using a bulb duster, to blow Chlordane-based powder under all baseboards.

1. Read labels to make sure that contents are right for your particular collection of pests.
2. While using insecticides, take as few breaths as possible.
3. Never spray food or food-related equipment and surfaces. The same goes for pet equipment.
4. Never use insecticides near any type of flame including a lighted cigarette.

After using an insecticide:
1. Wash your hands thoroughly.
2. If you sprayed or spilled insecticide on clothing, wash the clothing.
3. Store insecticides out of the reach of children and pets and away from drugs and food.

MICE seem to be a less common nuisance than cockroaches, but they are a nuisance nonetheless. If you notice one of these critters scurrying across your floor, invest in a couple of small mousetraps. Almost any kind of bait—from sharp American cheese or raw meat to Hershey bars—will seem appetizing to your furry visitors.

If your apartment is in an old building, examine the pipes beneath sinks and radiators. Should you find that the pipes do not fit snugly into walls or floors, pack the cracks with coarse steel wool. Mice and rats often live behind such cracks, but they are unable to eat through steel wool.

A product on grocery-store shelves, D-Con, is supposed to be 100 per cent effective against rats and mice. Give it a try, but make sure there are no pets around when you're using it, unless you wish to put *them* away too.

Having purged your apartment of dust and mini-roommates, you are ready to engage in the pursuit of paint, furniture, and other aids to happiness. But first, a word about the art of:

SELF–DEFENSE

Defense against what? Against fire, flood, power failure, and thieves (landlords are dealt with elsewhere).

Self-defense of this sort lies in preventive research and action. Take a tour of your apartment and of your building's cellar, searching for the location of:

a. Apartment fuses and circuit breakers or main electrical shutoff switch.
b. Light meter.
c. Shutoff valves for gas and water. Know where the main water shutoff valve for your apartment is located (usually in the cellar near the water meter) and know the locations of all the valves (within the apartment) for sinks, tubs, and toilets.

All of the above should be clearly tagged; in an emergency, a flood or gas explosion can ruin your apartment and property before a landlord or plumber arrives.

Self-defense

The guiles of thieves are a bit more difficult to foresee and prevent. First, get a good insurance policy against fire and theft. Also, keep first-floor windows locked and valuables out of view. A TV on a first-floor window ledge can easily be swiped by cutting the window open and quickly removing that tempting morsel.

Finally, make sure that your doors are fitted with good, secure LOCKS. The most common locks are worthless. A great many apartments, for example, have locks with latches like those shown in the diagram. Any amateur crook can open these locks in three seconds, using only a credit card or a dirty comb. Other apartments are locked with interchangeable skeleton keys, which can be purchased anywhere by anyone.

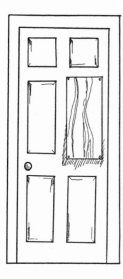

The laws of many towns and cities require landlords to supply you with good locks. Insist on this (see Appendix to this chapter). Hardware stores carry locks of good quality.

Remember, too, that a lock is only as secure as the wood paneling supporting and surrounding it. Plywood panels screwed to thin apartment doors (see diagram) are a cheap means of self-defense.

To conclude the subject of self-defense, three final thoughts about locks:

1. Never make copies of keys from other copies; make them from the original key. Otherwise, they may not work.

2. If you or your landlord is replacing your locks, and if you have more than one, arrange to have "the tumblers synchronized"; that is, have the locks set so that the same key can be used to open all of them.

3. If a lock sticks, lubricate it with graphite ("pencil lead")—never with oil. Graphite powder comes in a spray tube, which allows it to be blown in through the keyhole. Or, if you prefer, blacken a key with an ordinary pencil. Then slip the key in and out of the lock. Both methods work well.

PAINTING

Onward to the joys of painting, a messy, back-breaking job to be avoided or minimized at all costs. It looks easy and fun until you've tried it. From then on, to quote one great author, "Pink walls can be lived with." *

PURCHASES

* Sometimes, simply washing the walls and repainting the woodwork alone (in the same or a different color as the walls) does an amazing job of refinishing a room. Trouble spots on walls can be covered with mirrors or posters.

If paint you must, get your landlord to pay for the various supplies (see Appendix to this chapter). But if all attempts at "convincing" that august personage fail, buy your paint at railroad-salvage or large department stores—where prices are low —not at hardware or paint stores. And remember that prices are higher for the brighter "saturated colors" than for light colors or whites. These two

"Onward to the joys of painting."

hints should reduce your paint expenses considerably.

Despite their slightly higher prices, LATEX PAINTS (water-base) should always be bought. Unlike other paints, they require no mixing or priming and can be applied over wallpaper. They dry many times faster than oil-base paints; messes can be wiped up and brushes cleaned with water (rather than turpentine); and the resulting finish is more washable than that of oil-base paints. Are you convinced?

Buy semi-gloss for walls,* flat for ceilings, and semi- or high-gloss enamels (all latex) for doors, windows, moldings, and baseboards. Use latex floor paint for floors (it doesn't wear as well as other floor paints, but you won't be in your apartment long enough to see it rub off). Remember, if you decide to apply a light color over a dark one, more than one coat will probably be needed.

Before going to the store for your paint, measure the area to be painted. With that information, the salesman can determine the quantity of paint you will need. Once at the store, buy all necessary supplies:

a. Brushes: It's probably wisest to buy the cheapest brushes available, which cost less than half the price of good brushes, and then discard them after the day's work. (The bristles fall out of cheap brushes after they're cleaned once.) This can save you a lot of money if you don't plan to paint more than one day—or if you'd rather not bother with cleaning your brushes. Be sure to buy a small, angled brush for trim, as well as a somewhat wider brush for corners. If you can only afford one, buy a two-inch brush.

b. Rollers: Buy a sturdy roller that can be attached to a roller extension. Buy, also, a roller extension for use on the tops of walls and ceilings. The roll itself should be of a synthetic fabric.

c. Solvents: Turpentine and waterless hand cleaner

(a puddinglike substance that comes in a can), if you've decided not to use latex paints.

d. Sandpaper, putty, Spackling compound (for patching cracks), and a putty knife (two- to three-inch width)—all for preparing the surface.

e. Masking tape and dropcloths (paper or plastic), to prevent paint from going where it's not wanted. Razor blades and Vaseline for windows.

f. Cardboard mixing buckets. Also, sticks and paint trays (Styrofoam trays if you can find them; otherwise, line metal trays with brown paper).

Preparing the Surface

Having returned home, laden with painting supplies, you are now ready to prepare the walls and ceilings. (Floors are dealt with later.)

Move your furniture to the center of the room, and if you can, cover it with paper or plastic dropcloths (available at hardware and department stores) or with old sheets. Use Vaseline to coat the windows and metal hardware with a film that can be easily rubbed off, taking with it any paint that might have splattered.

Using a broom, sweep the more blatant dirt and cobwebs from walls and ceilings. Scrape any flaking paint off with a putty knife. Then, wash down the surfaces (especially the moldings, which have a shiny, difficult-for-paint-to-adhere-to surface) with a damp sponge. If this preliminary cleaning is omitted, your paint won't stick to the walls and the job will have been done in vain.

Patch cracks with Spackle, either the powder or prepared paste. If you are using powder, mix only a little of this quick-drying substance at a time. Remove all loose plaster from the crack by scraping it with a knife or can opener. Blow or rinse out the dust and spread the Spackle over the crack or hole with your handy-dandy putty knife. For a smooth surface use crisscross strokes over the drying Spackle. For super-deep holes a second layer of Spackle may be needed, but that's not too much of a chore, since Spackle is cheap and dries quickly.

Wide cracks and holes (left by removed pipes, prize fighters, etc.) require plastering. This, in turn, demands special tools and knowledge, not to mention (horror of horrors!) work. Get your landlord to do this sort of thing (have a promise to that effect written into the lease beforehand).

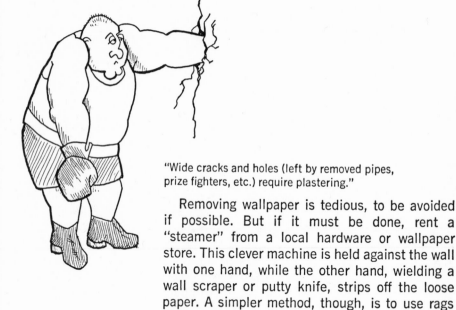

"Wide cracks and holes (left by removed pipes, prize fighters, etc.) require plastering."

Removing wallpaper is tedious, to be avoided if possible. But if it must be done, rent a "steamer" from a local hardware or wallpaper store. This clever machine is held against the wall with one hand, while the other hand, wielding a wall scraper or putty knife, strips off the loose paper. A simpler method, though, is to use rags soaked in hot water.

Order of Painting

Paint your room in the following order:

A. Ceilings: Use a paint roller, attached to an extension, and apply paint with a fairly dry roller.
B. Walls: Always start in one corner near the top and work down, making long vertical strokes from ceiling to floor. Use a roller for large areas and brushes for the corners and trim. Do moldings and woodwork last.

C. Windows: Paint windows in the following manner, after coating the panes with Vaseline or masking tape:
1. Raise bottom half of window.
2. Lower top sash more than halfway down. Paint the wood on this section first.
3. Lower bottom sash nearly to the sill, while raising the top sash almost to the top. Paint the remainder of both sashes, checking for runs.
4. Paint frame and sills.

Use a cardboard shield, in addition to the film of Vaseline, to protect the glass from paint. A shield of this sort is also good for protecting floors when painting baseboards. Wipe the shields frequently.

Painting windows

D. Paint doors in the following order: frame, edges, panels, face. Avoid brush marks by finishing with light, parallel strokes along the length of each piece.
E. Paint baseboards, using a cardboard shield as described above. Wipe the shield periodically to avoid paint accumulation.

A Few Tips 1. Roller: Keep the roller uniformly covered with paint, which should be applied with slow, steady strokes. On walls, make your first roller stroke upward. On ceilings, the first stroke should be away from you, to minimize the amount of paint that drips on you. Wrapping a cloth around the top of the roller handle may keep your hand and arm reasonably clean.

2. Brush: Dip brushes about one-third of their length into the paint; tap off excess. Don't scrub the paint on: be gentle.

3. Try to complete the painting of one wall or ceiling without stopping, and don't allow the edges of a paint swath to dry before applying the next strip of paint. Otherwise, marks will remain when the work is done.

4. Paper plates make good trays for paint cans, rollers, and brushes to rest on.

5. During temporary halts, slip the roller or brush into a plastic bag. This will keep the paint from drying out.

6. Rubbing your hands and face with cold cream before beginning to paint will allow you to wash up more easily later on.

Cleaning Up

Clean up paint spatters while you work, before they dry.

Brushes: Wipe off excess paint by rubbing the brush against newspaper. Wash brush with water (turpentine, if you didn't use latex), cleaning the center of the brush as well as the outside. Shake brush to remove water; several rinses may be necessary. Comb out bristles and store brushes flat, wrapped in newspaper or plastic. This procedure is only for expensive brushes; throw cheap ones away!

Rollers: Roll out excess paint onto newspaper. Remove the cover of the roller and wash it thoroughly. Then wring out the cover, wipe it with a clean rag, and store in plastic.

People: Wash with soap and water or turpentine, or use what is called waterless hand cleaner. This jellylike substance, available where you buy your paint supplies and at hardware stores, can painlessly remove anything from human flesh.

Massage it on and wipe it off with a cloth or paper towel.

Paint Cans: Never slam the cover on while there is paint in the lid channel. Before throwing away the last, nearly empty paint can, put a little paint into a small jar for later touch-ups.

Roller Trays: Discard Styrofoam roller trays, along with cardboard buckets.

The Room: When the paint is dry, remove dropcloths and wipe the film off windows and hardware. Any miscellaneous paint specks can be scraped off glass and metal with a single-edged razor blade.

AND WHAT
ABOUT
FLOORS?

There are four ways to deal with floors:

1. Leave them the way you find them.
2. Clean and wax them: the "natural" finish.
3. Paint them.
4. Cover them with a rug.

NATURAL FINISH: If your floors are unpainted and in half-decent condition, you might consider sanding them with a rented sander; vacuuming and wiping them clean; applying a "penetrating wood sealer"; and then waxing and polishing them. Apply the wax—paste or water-base liquid —in thin layers, using a cheap paintbrush or "wet mop." Allow sufficient drying time between each application. Finally, polish with an "electric buffer," rented from the same hardware store from which you rented the sander.

As you can see, it takes a lot of work to produce a "handsome natural hardwood floor."

PAINTING, on the other hand, is not nearly so difficult. Use latex floor paint, since it dries in less than an hour, is free of smells, and can be applied over a slightly damp surface. (If your floor is covered with old linoleum, rip the stuff off, throw it away, and paint the wood surface beneath.)

1. Wash grease, wax, oils, and other varieties of dirt off the wood floor, using a commercial grease-cutting detergent and a stiff scrub brush. Rinse with clean water.
2. Scrape peeling paint off with a putty knife, and use sandpaper to rough up any "slick spots."
3. Sweep or vacuum thoroughly.
4. Apply the latex paint with a wide brush or roller, starting in the corner farthest from the door. If necessary, a second coat can be applied twenty-four hours later.

   Pretty designs can then be painted on your new floor, in different colors, of course.

Rugs   Most bedroom and living-room floors end up being covered by rugs, the last solution to your floor problems. Rugs can be purchased cheaply or scrounged from friends or relatives. They provide color and texture for your rooms, insulation against interapartmental sounds, pleasure for

"Pretty designs can be painted on your new floor."

bare feet . . . and demand less initial work than either polish or paint. A carpet pad (that brown thing often found under rugs) is useful for added warmth, cushioning, and sound insulation, but is hardly essential. Layers of newspaper can, if desired, be used instead.

Vacuum your rugs weekly, or as often as you can get your hands on a vacuum cleaner. Otherwise, sand particles will chew up rug fibers quickly. A satisfactory alternative is to buy a manual carpet sweeper (available at Sears for seven to fifteen dollars). You may have seen one of these handy devices in Grandma's cellar. They went out of fashion some years ago, but they are nearly as effective now as they were back then . . . that is, nearly as good as vacuum cleaners are, at least on rugs. Clean the carpet sweeper's brush occasionally by detaching the brush, clipping and removing hairs and threads, and then washing the brush in detergent and water.

Rugs can be shampooed with special cleaners and machines rented cheaply by many hardware stores and supermarkets. These machines are easy to use and do a good rug-cleaning job. Remove all furniture from the room, then vacuum the rug. Shampoo in blocks about four or five feet square. Then vacuum up loosened dirt; the suds will disappear on their own. Leave your windows open to speed drying, and replace your furniture when the rug is completely dry.

A less professional shampoo job can be done by dipping a damp, stiff broom into a bucket of water to which a little detergent has been added. Sweep your rug briskly with the barely damp broom. This loosens dirt, which can then be easily vacuumed away.

Dyeing an old or faded rug can give both the rug and the room it's in a brand-new appearance. Vacuum the rug, then hang it on an outdoor clothesline or spread it on the ground. Dissolve a half dozen packages of all-purpose dye in one-half the water suggested on the package. Use a stiff broom or scrub brush to apply the dye, brushing from every direction, so that the rug will be evenly colored despite nap or other texture. Repeat this process once a day until the rug reaches the color intensity you want.

Splice two or more small rugs or pieces of rug together in the following way: Place a long board on your floor. Put the edges of rug to be joined to each other—bottom sides up—on the board. Using a mat knife and a yardstick as a guide, cut the two edges so they are straight (necessary only if the edges were bound, smashed, or frayed). Tack the two edges to the board with shingle nails, placing the nails about two inches away from the rugs' edges. Spread Elmer's Glue along the four-inch swath outlined by the rows of tacks and cover with a strip (two layers thick) of burlap or cheesecloth. Coat with more Elmer's Glue and let dry. Remove nails and board. Turn rug right side up. One friend uses this method to make rugs that

"Splice two or more small rugs or pieces of rug together."

* You might find it easier to purchase a quart of white glue and a cheap paintbrush (for spreading the glue) and stick the assembled rug scraps to a large carpet pad. Even detailed mosaics and "impressionistic paintings" can be done in this way. A third method of rug-splicing that is not quite as sturdy as the other two is to lay the rug pieces upside down, assemble them in the design you've worked out, and then cover the entire back surface of the scraps with long strips of wide masking tape.

are large-scale copies of Mondrian paintings, using rug scraps purchased cheaply from a local carpeter.*

To repair frayed rug edges, cover with gummed carpet binding and press down with a warm iron.

Indentations can be raised by holding a steaming steam iron over the crushed portions of your rug. Watch the levitation act!

Worn spots and holes can be concealed by re arranging your furniture to cover them. Or, dye the backing under the worn spot to match, the dominant color of the rug.

Limp rugs can be made firmer by laying them upside down on a flat surface and brushing the back with a combination of one pound of wallpaper size and four quarts of water (stirred smooth). Use less water if the rug is extremely limp and/or loosely woven.

Holes that go through the backing should be patched by sewing burlap to the underside of the rug. With a crochet hook, yarn of the appropriate color can then be pulled through the burlap. Use gummed carpet binding or a layer of wallpaper size (as above) to further reinforce the back of the burlap. If the rug is really beaten up, cut it into two or more smaller rugs, binding the edges with gummed carpet binding.

Curled corners or edges should be held flat with one hand while the other hand holds a steam iron just above the area. If this doesn't flatten the rug, cut the rug smaller and tack down its edges, or just live with it as is.

THE ART OF CHEEEP FURNISHING

An entire apartment can be furnished—comfortably and stylishly—on a budget of about $150. Starvation-budget furnishing is a fine art, one demanding sharp eyes, a degree of inventiveness, and the willingness to tackle such simple tasks as repairing and repainting the broken limbs of discarded chairs and tables.

What furnishings do you own, and what must you and your roommates somehow obtain? * Necessities include:

Beds
Bookcases
Chairs and Couches
Chests of Drawers
Desks
Lamps
Rugs
Tables
Miscellaneous items, including curtains, pots and pans, brooms and other cleaning supplies, and appliances.

Admittedly, this is quite a bit. So, most Starvation-Budget Furnishers combine the technique of purchasing (used items, of course) with both scrounging and improvising in establishing their homesteads.

* Renting furniture for a two-bedroom apartment will cost at least fifty dollars per month, and this price will not include desks. Forget this alternative!

Purchasing

* See the Yellow Pages under "Social Service and Welfare Organizations."

Cheap furniture of all sorts can always be found. The Salvation Army, St. Vincent DePaul Society, Goodwill Industries, American Rescue Workers, and similar organizations* that take from the rich and all but give to the poor (you and me) are the standard suppliers of Cheeep Furnishings. Frequently, such places maintain a large inventory and will deliver goods for a small charge. Sometimes, excellent "finds" are to be had at Salvation Army and Goodwill stores; more often, however, the demand is greater than the supply—a state that, as would be expected, results in "slim pickins" and higher than rock-bottom prices.

A better bet for cheap furnishings is to look at supermarket, Laundromat, and college bulletin-board for-sale notices and at the classified ads in local newspapers for "Garage Sales" and for the ads of people moving out of town.

A little bit of haggling—"How about letting me give you five bucks for that whole mess of plates,

"Organizations that take from the rich and give to the poor"

pots, and pans?" (kitchen equipment and cleaning supplies bought in this manner will quickly secure you what you need and save you twenty-five dollars or more); or, "I'll cart that rickety table away for free if you want me to!"—more often than not elicits an affirmative response: "Hell, yes!"

Many times, the goods you buy have passed through many hands, selling each time at a lower price. The people who advertise are usually in a hurry to move and will sell cheaply to the first moneyed buyer. And, if you buy a lot of things, a package deal can reduce prices considerably: "You say you want ten dollars for the table and fifteen dollars for the bed? How about nineteen dollars for both?"

Soon you will become an expert bargainer, bulletin-board hunter, and furniture appraiser. You will find it best to buy the most rickety things being offered, for the owner usually values these items very little and regards himself as lucky to be able to sell them at any price, even a buck or two. On the other hand, you and I know that it takes only fifteen minutes to make most furniture sturdy and serviceable, if you're willing to wait, look, and fix.

Cheap furniture for sale may also be found at warehouses and moving companies (see the Yellow Pages). Few people realize this, but those who do are at a great advantage. For just as laundries sell unclaimed linen and clothing, and as radio- and appliance-repair stores do the same with their unclaimed merchandise, so, too, do warehouses and moving companies sell abandoned furniture, pianos, refrigerators—often for no more than the cost of moving them to your apartment. When you consider that much of the expense of a piano or refrigerator is in the moving, it will be clear that warehouses and moving companies should be first on your list of places to

"Wear your most pathetic-but-honest-looking clothing."

Scrounging

check when furnishing an apartment—before you've rented your truck for moving!

If all else fails in terms of furniture purchasing, examine your Yellow Pages under "Used Furniture," and call around. This, however, is the very last resource to tap.

Important Note: Whether you visit social service and welfare organizations, private sellers, warehouses and moving companies, or used-furniture stores, be sure to wear your most pathetic-but-honest-looking clothing, subdue all enthusiasm and self-confidence to a stony-faced whimper, and carry cash—ones and fives only. When examining the furniture, decide what you want and what it's worth to you. Bid a price somewhat lower, and never forget that there are always more Cheeep Furnishings around the corner.

Finally, before buying anything, spend a day looking and calling around, to see and compare what's available.

The most consummate of Cheeep-Furnishing Artists purchase few pieces of furniture. Instead, their search techniques are confined, almost exclusively, to the realm of Scrounging. This respectable and time-tested method of getting something for nothing (or making something from nothing) often yields the most interesting and sturdy—not to mention cheap—furnishings.

Skills needed for this art are:

a. The ability to remember, at all moments of the day, what you need or might need.
b. The talent of constantly keeping your eyes open.
c. The unabashed willingness to ask for what you want.
d. The wherewithal to cart away your scroungings (strength, a friend's car, or cab fare).

Much scrounging is of the personal sort: just make it known that you're on the prowl, telling friends, relatives, etc., what you need. Mentioning the items to them helps them recall what it is they actually own.

The janitor of your apartment building is likely to be a pack rat—a collector of old mattresses, tables, wastebaskets, and pincushions. A mere bottle of wine will often be sufficient currency to purchase such items.

Cellars of large apartment buildings are often treasure-troves, as are abandoned buildings. And, if you can find it, most towns have one dump where everything except gooey garbage is sent. For a Scrounging Artist, one day in such a place is more profitable than winning a jack pot from a Vegas slot machine.

If going to a dump is going a bit too far for you, grab the merchandise slated for that distinguished cemetery before city trucks take it from city streets. In most towns one day each week (or month) is set aside for those people who wish to discard furniture. On that day large trucks rumble through each and every alleyway, collecting gems that would make any Scrounger's heart go pitter-patter. Call your local town hall and, pretending that you have a lot of furniture to discard, inquire as to the appropriate day. Then, at the wheel of a borrowed car, set forth on a sunrise scrounging expedition. Personal experience has indicated that best results are to be had not in wealthy neighborhoods but in those so-called lower-middle-class areas, where people are "on the rise." *

Mattresses are the only ems that are usually bet- r bought than scrounged. ot only are secondhand nes generally in miser- le shape; they also carry ultitudinous diseases d can't be cleaned thout special equipment. ood, cheap sleeping uipment can be had at e Salvation Army and oodwill, army-surplus ores, or factory outlets uy "seconds"). For com- rt, mattresses should be firm as possible. Foam- bber mattresses are st, and can be made om chunks of foam (Use lyurethane: $12–$20 for double-bed size. Two ch thickness will suffice I use it—though you ay prefer the four-inch ickness.) bought at ars or at stores listed der "Rubber" in the ellow Pages. For econ- ny, convenience, and mfort, don't bother with dsprings (or box rings). They are not nec- sary. Simply put your attress or foam mat ou may wish to buy or ake a zippered mattress g for the foam slab.) a piece of one-half- or ree-fourths-inch plywood d mount on either a dframe or on cinder ocks—or, for a space ver, on two chests of awers.

FURNITURE REPAIR

Regardless of where or how you obtain your cheap furnishings, some at least will be in need of repair.

Furniture repair can be divided into two general categories. The first of these is structural repair. Structural repair is work done in order that all parts of any one item of furniture will be stuck firmly together—so that the chair, table, or what-

"At least some of your cheap furnishings will be in need of repair."

have-you does not wobble, creak, or fall apart under use. Structural repair consists of:

1. Gluing cracks and loose joints, etc.
2. Fixing or replacing tired upholstery.

Surface repair, on the other hand, is work done toward aesthetic aims. It is staining, painting, and scratch removing, together with all the miscellaneous surface preparations that must accompany such endeavors.

It is easiest to do all your repair work at one time; most of the work is simple and quick, and doing everything during one morning or afternoon makes equipment- and parts-getting—and clean-up, too—much easier.

Structural Repairs

Tilting chairs, tables, dressers, etc.—which rock, though they have no loose parts—may be cured as follows:

Place the item in question on a flat surface, to determine which leg or side is short. Nail a metal glider (see diagram) under that leg. For tilting or rocking desks and dressers—items that are rarely moved—a folded cardboard "shim" may be used under short legs or sides as a good, temporary measure.

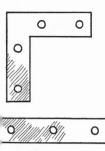

If the furniture has loose joints, however, other tactics are required. Never be dismayed by rickety furniture; in fact, the looser it is, the easier it is to repair, since taking the piece apart for regluing is half the job.

Wobbly legs on a chair, for example, usually indicate not only loose legs but loose underbraces as well. Regluing is a relatively simple job.

Necessary Tools and Supplies

Assemble everything (tools, parts, etc.) before starting the job:

a. Old newspapers and rags, for the floor and for wiping off excess glue from wood.

b. Screw driver, knife, and hammer.

c. Sandpaper (rough).

Hide glue should be used for repairs requiring a lot of strength. White glue (like Elmer's although Sears has a cheaper white glue that is similar) is used for most household repairs of fabric, paper, cork, leather . . . and many wood jobs as well. Buy white glue in large containers, since you're bound to use it a lot, and then transfer it to smaller bottles.

d. Wood screws or threaded nails (plus a bar of soap with which to lubricate them).

e. Flatware braces (see diagram).

f. Glue, either ready-mixed hide glue or white glue.*

g. Small brush (optional) to spread the glue.

h. Clothesline or nylon cord for tourniquet braces.

i. Shirt cardboard and a few pieces of scrap wood to protect the wood being clamped.

Procedure for Regluing Loose Chair Legs and Rungs

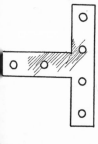

1. Cover work area with newspaper and assemble tools and materials.

2. Disassemble the loose chair parts. Pull the rungs apart and take the legs off the seat (if very loose), unscrewing wood screws where necessary. Don't touch firm joints. This disassembling process takes only a couple of minutes.

3. Scrape and clean all the old glue off ends and out of holes, using a knife and sandpaper. Work until the pieces to be reglued are fairly smooth. Two reminders: Don't wash pieces to be joined—the wetness will prevent the new glue from sticking. Too much whittling results in loose-fitting joints.

4. Using a piece of cloth, a small brush, or even your fingers, coat all contact points with glue. That is, for any given joint, both pieces to be joined

should be coated with glue. On loose underrungs the joint end may now be wrapped with a layer of sewing thread, to provide a tighter fit.

5. When the glue becomes slightly tacky, refit all pieces and wipe off excess glue with a slightly dampened rag.

6. For extra strength, hammer in thin threaded nails or wood screws. A hardened spiral floor nail driven into the mended leg from the top of the seat, will add to the strength of the leg (especially if the leg had been broken off at the seat). Rub all nails and screws on the damp bar of soap, to lubricate them, before driving them into the wood. This helps prevent the wood from splitting.

"When the glue becomes slightly tacky . . . ."

7. Apply to the joint a tourniquet brace made of cord and a stick (see diagram). To protect the wood, slip pieces of cardboard or wood blocks between the cord and the furniture. Do not tighten the tourniquet so much that all the glue is squeezed out of the joint.

8. Let dry forty-eight hours.

The above job, in all of its steps, will take about thirty minutes and will transform a rickety one dollar piece of furniture into something that will last for years. If you make structural repairs on all your furniture at once, you will discover that one morning spent in doing relatively relaxing and easy work will leave you with an apartment filled with serviceable furniture, not to mention a sense of accomplishment and a source of pride.

Loose Seat: If the legs and rungs of your chair are fairly tight, but the seat still wobbles, there are two easy cures:

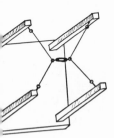

1. Install corner braces (small blocks of wood), gluing and screwing them onto the underside corners of your chair. Or, if the chair already has such braces, reglue them and replace the screws with ones that are slightly larger. Angle irons and nails can also be used.
2. Install screw eyes and heavy wire, and a turnbuckle. This impressive arrangement takes less than ten minutes to set up and costs less than a half buck. Before tightening the turnbuckle, smear glue over corner joints.

Splits in chair legs, backs, rungs, etc., are fixed as follows:

1. Using your screw driver, wedge open the crack.
2. Fill the crack with Elmer's Glue or prepared hide glue.
3. Tie the pieces together with strong string, padding the wood with cardboard or wood scraps. If the luxury can be afforded, a C-clamp (one dollar at hardware stores) is much more convenient than string.

Flat wood joints (if loose, but not falling apart), such as the junctions of arms and backs or seats and legs, can be fixed by a method still simpler than those described above. That is, with metal plates (flat corners, flat tees, mending plates, and corner braces—purchased for pennies at hardware stores), which are screwed to the edges or faces of the pieces to be joined. These plates,

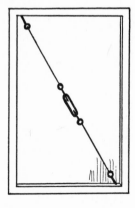

though inferior to glue, reinforce the joint and keep parts from working loose.

The above methods, described in terms of crippled chairs, apply equally well to chests, cabinets, tables, and bookcase sides and backs. Whenever a joint is loose, the procedure is the same. Scrape away the old glue and apply new, high-strength glue to board joints and structural blocks. Replace screws and nails with ones of slightly larger diameter, and apply tourniquet braces for a day or two.

Metal plates and turnbuckle braces can be used on nearly any sort of furniture and provide a quick substitute for a gluing job.

These techniques are so simple, and take such a minimal amount of skill, that you will never be content to live with a rickety piece of furniture again. And, more important, you will never be afraid to buy or scrounge a piece of furniture that is a fantastic bargain, but an item that less knowledgeable people would ignore or even throw out.

Reupholstering

* Clean upholstery by vacuuming, and then use a foam cleaner (made for the purpose) that comes in an aerosol can with a brush on top.

When stuffing is oozing out of chairs and couches, repairs are not difficult.* Since the upholstery is open anyway, check to see whether the padding is intact and whether the springs are sound or in need of retying or replacing.

If everything is pretty much in one piece, shove the padding back into its original position, and hand sew the torn cover (using a patch, if necessary). Functionally speaking, this will suffice, although you may want to cover the entire piece with a store-bought slip cover (or simply with a handsome bedspread) for the sake of appearance.

If, on the other hand, not only the cloth but the stuffing itself is pretty lumpy, holey, and generally miserable, you can try a home reupholstery job. Remove the old upholstery fabric and the muslin underneath. On a pad of paper, note carefully how they were attached to the chair frame.

Smooth out the padding. If it is necessary to add new padding, use thin layers of foam rubber, placing it in sheets with tapered edges. Use the old upholstery fabric as a pattern for cutting out new covers. Then, following the notes you have made, tack and sew the new upholstery in place according to the method of the original. Cotton, muslin, trim, and tacks can be obtained at up-holstery shops (see the Yellow Pages); fabrics can be purchased there or at many other discount/mill-end/wholesale fabric stores (again, see the Yellow Pages). The job of reupholstering a large couch will take two people a full day. Perhaps you'd rather use a slip cover?

Individual CUSHIONS on chairs or sofas, can be slip-covered or easily re-covered with fabric or bedspreads. Or, if the cushions are truly in hope-less condition, replace them with foam rubber (or polyurethane) covered with fabric. Such replace-ment cushions are quite easily made (Sears car-ries foam rubber that can be cut to size; cheaper prices might be available through stores listed under "Foam" or "Rubber" in the Yellow Pages). Of course, Sears, five-and-tens, and many other stores carry cushions (foam, or spring construc-tion, nicely upholstered) of all sizes, although the prices are often more than you might wish to pay. Army-surplus stores can often order army-surplus cushions for you. Look into this: they are cheap.

If your cushions' upholstery is intact, but the chair or sofa has springs and padding that sag, place a thick chunk of foam rubber between the seat of the chair or sofa and its seat cushions. A shim of this sort will serve to prop up the failing seat.

If a straight-backed wooden chair has a PADDED SEAT (or if you have a plain wooden chair whose seat you want to pad), repairs are made in a somewhat different way. First, if the chair has upholstery, strip off the old cloth and padding. Then, from a piece of cardboard, cut out a "template" that is the shape of the seat to be covered. Take this to a store dealing in foam rubber or to an upholstery shop. Let them cut a piece of foam to the exact size you need.

At home, place the foam on the wooden seat. Cover with a piece of fabric, using the old upholstery as a pattern. Draw the fabric down to the base of the seat's rim, fold under the loose edge of the cloth, and anchor with a few staples or upholstery tacks. These fasteners can then be hidden, if you so desire, with fringe, cloth tape or ornamental nails—all of which are available at most fabric and upholstery stores.

If the wooden seat can be easily removed (screws on the underside hold it in place), a neater reupholstery job can be accomplished by removing the seat, wrapping the fabric over the rubber and over and around the edges of the seat, and then tacking the fabric to the bottom of the seat. The entire unit can then be placed back into position on the chair.

Ripped LEATHERETTE should be fixed with a patch cut out of matching material. Apply a thin coat of Devcon Patch Glue to the back of the patch and smooth the scrap over the hole. (Masking tape will clamp the patch to the surface of the chair while the glue is drying.) Let dry for several hours.

About Metal and Bamboo Furniture

METAL FURNITURE is usually sturdy and useful. It is, however, difficult to repair without special tools. So, when purchasing metal furniture, make sure that:

a. No riveted or welded joints are broken, loose, or cracked.
b. No parts are distorted out of shape.
c. No parts have rusted badly.

Also, try to avoid metal furniture with legs that

have sharp or naked ends. Instead, look for rubber tips, or even better, self-leveling glides, on all legs. Otherwise, your rugs and floors will be quickly chewed to rags and sawdust.

Most metal chairs and sofas are fitted with cushions that can be repaired in the same way as the cushions found on wooden furniture. Wobbly metal desks, bookcases, etc., can often be fixed merely by tightening—with a screw driver and adjustable wrench—the nuts and bolts that hold them together. Also, a turnbuckle brace (see diagram) can often add stability to a rocking metal bookcase.

Generally speaking, a good piece of sturdy metal furniture will require, at most, a spray paint job.

BAMBOO FURNITURE. When the windings on bamboo, reed, or fiber furniture begin to loosen up or fall off, the cure is simple. Wrap a hot, wet cloth around the loose strips. When they have softened, carefully unwind the strands. Then, with a little white vinegar, remove the old glue from the base of each strand, and recoat with new Elmer's or hide glue. Rewrap the strands and use a few strips of masking tape as a clamp, wrapping the strips tightly around the bamboo, reed, or fiber strands. Let the piece of furniture dry overnight.

The above discussion of the structural repair of furniture should enable you to tackle any and all furniture problems. Next, we will briefly consider ways in which to make your furniture more pleasing to the eye: painting, refinishing, and surface repair.

But first, the following chart is offered as a summary to the past section on structural repairs.

USED FURNITURE TROUBLE-SHOOTING CHECK LIST *

Chairs and Similar Pieces

PROBLEM	REMEDY
Missing piece of carving	Remove counterpart to balance appearance, or replace with similar pair of carvings.
Upholstery, stuffing, springs	Remove completely, replace webbing, and redo with foam cushioning. Reupholster.
Open dowel joint	Clean away loose glue, recoat with gap-filling glue, and clamp joint until glue sets.
Broken cane seat	Replace with new caning sold in sheet form by cabinetmakers' supply houses. Or cover area with plywood and use a foam cushion.
Short leg break near seat	Fit broken ends together carefully after coating both with gap-filling glue. Drive hardened spiral flooring nail down from the top to reinforce.
Casters missing	Replace all, or front or rear pair only. If holes are too small for new casters, redrill.
Short break in midleg	Drill broken ends about three inches to take a one-fourth- or three-eighths-inch steel-rod reinforcement before gluing ends as for short break (see above). The rod is available at large hardware stores. Do not use polyvinyl glue.
Long split in leg	Glue parts together with polyester, acrylic, or resorcinol glue.
Wide split that will not close	Place cellulose tape firmly under the split and over the end to form a dam. Then fill the split with acrylic glue, like 3-Ton Adhesive (H. A. Callahan Company, Mamaroneck, New York). When glue sets, remove tape.

* Reprinted from *Furniture 1970*, courtesy of Science & Mechanics Publishing Company.

Cabinets

Local veneer "blisters"	If small, cover with a layer of heavy paper, press down with a hot electric iron. Slide a block of wood onto the blister as the iron slides off. Hold until cool. Heat softens hide glue, so that the blister is reglued. On large areas, slit the blister so it can be flattened, then repair as above.
Cracked marble top	Glue parts together with MarFix polyester glue made for this purpose by Vermont Marble Company, Proctor, Vermont. If small pieces are missing, or edges chipped, fill with the glue, matching marble color with mixed-in pigments made by the same company.
Veneer edging separating	Iron back in place, as in blister treatment above. Or remove completely by wet-rag soaking and replace with new edging made for plywood. Buy it at lumberyards.
Missing period hardware	Try matching it at cabinetmakers' supply houses. If it can't be matched, replace with nearest type.
Parts separating due to glue failure	Separate parts completely, clean away old lumpy glue from joints. Reglue with white (polyvinyl) glue on non-load-bearing joints. Use casein, aliphatic resin, or other noncreeping glue on load-bearing joints.
Rot in cabinet feet or base due to damp storage	Drill into rotted part; restore hardness to rotted wood by permeating with Calignum from H. A. Callahan Company. Liquid resin soaks into rotted areas, hardens, and makes wood stronger than new.
Plywood delaminating	If only a small area is involved, run glue into interply spaces, spread with a spatula, and clamp plies tightly to rebond. If area is large, it's best to replace the entire panel.

**General Tips on
Used Furniture**

Fastenings: Screws and dowels are more substantial than nails. Dovetail and "finger" joints are better than simple nail-and-glue types. Joints held by glue only, though separated by dampness in old pieces, can be made waterproof by regluing with modern resin glues, like the acrylics, polyesters, and resorcinols. The strength of the joint will be greater than the original.

Upholstery: Unless you are experienced at upholstery, leave tufted work to professionals. Smooth-surfaced forms are within range of most do-it-yourselfers. Complex spring-and-padding systems are best replaced with foam cushioning. Many upholsterers will cut the foam to your pattern if you buy it from them.

To buy or not to buy: If you can do the work required, or have it done, and still have a bargain, buy the piece you want. Used-furniture savings often run to hundreds of dollars on a single piece.

**Surface Repair
and Refinishing**

There are many ways to make a piece of furniture attractive. This section describes several of them.

Sometimes, a thorough cleaning and polishing of the piece is enough:

1. Wash the furniture with soft, clean rags and mild soap and water.
2. Then, if you find no scratches or gouges, simply apply some furniture polish and wipe off with a soft, dry cloth.
3. Finally, apply a couple of coats of any furniture wax, rubbing the surface well between each coat. For painted surfaces, omit step (2).

This procedure will give a beautiful finish to your furniture, if the surface was in relatively good shape to begin with.

You can make furniture polish yourself from this recipe: mix equal amounts of boiled linseed oil, turpentine, and vinegar; shake well before applying with a soft rag.

If your furniture has scratches, dents, stains—or even acne—you can often cure it of these ills without having to repaint or refinish the entire surface. The following chart lists a few solutions to such cosmetic ailments.

Superficial Scratches and Gouges

A. Use iodine (for dark-mahogany woods), crayon, shoe polish, or commercial "scratch removers" for superficial scratches. Paint these on with a small brush or cloth. Polish and wax. Or,

B. Soften the finish of the surface with the appropriate solvent and "blend in" the scratches, using denatured alcohol for shellac, turpentine for varnish or paint, or lacquer thinner for lacquer.

Brush the proper solvent over the scratches (if you're not sure what kind of surface you're repairing, use the solvents one at a time in an inconspicuous place); let dry for forty-eight hours; rub smooth with very fine emery cloth (from the hardware store) used lightly; polish and wax as described above. Painted surfaces require no polishing. Or,

C. Try applying mayonnaise to light-wood table tops. Apply; leave overnight; rub into wood; wipe off. Or,

D. For painted or enameled surfaces: rub a wax crayon (or a colored "repair stick," obtainable at hardware stores) into the wound; scrape level; wax.

"Try applying mayonnaise to light-wood table tops."

Dents

The following procedure will often eliminate small dents in wood furniture:

1. Place two layers of damp cloth over the dent.
2. Place a bottle cap on top of the cloth and over the spot where the dent is.
3. Place a warm iron on the bottle cap for a minute or two. The combination of heat and water will swell the wood where the dent is, bringing it flush with (be careful not to swell it above) the surface level of the wood.

Deep Gouges and Cigarette Burns

1. Scrape out burned wood and/or other dirt, then sand with fine sandpaper.
2. Fill the hole with plastic wood—almost to the surface.
3. Apply a wax repair stick.

Or, for a more professional job:

1. Surround the scar with masking tape.
2. Heat a spatula on the stove, press this against a shellac stick (available in many colors at hardware stores), and let melting shellac drip into the hole.
3. Level off with the heated spatula or a table knife.
4. Remove the masking tape and do a final leveling job with a single-edged razor blade.
5. Rub with fine sandpaper dampened with water and/or alcohol, then dull with 3/0 steel wool.
6. Polish and wax.

Stains and White Rings from Wet Glasses or Hot Dishes

A. Put a thick blotter on the spot. Apply a warm iron. The heat should evaporate the stain, which will then be absorbed by the blotter. Or,

B. 1. Mix cigar ash or table salt with mineral oil or machine oil.
2. Dip the tip of your index finger into the oil, then into the ash or salt.
3. Rub the spot gently, checking frequently to see if it has disappeared.
4. Wax the area. Or,

C. Hire a magician to do a disappearing act.

Surface Overhauls

* Stripping old paint or other finishes off furniture in order to achieve a "natural" or stained-wood surface is too time-consuming and laborious to be considered here. You shouldn't even think about it! If the idea, however, is still overwhelmingly tempting, seek advice from any furniture-refinishing book available at your local library.

If cleaning, polishing, and surface repairs aren't enough to make your furniture appear halfway decent, or if you want to change the color or overall effect of your furniture, you can either cover it or paint it.*

The first solution is by far the easier. There are many materials that will brighten up or mask defects in furniture. One of the easiest of these (though the most expensive) is Contact Paper.

Available in many colors and patterns in hardware stores and Sears-and-Roebuck-type places (the latter being cheaper), this material is sold by the yard and has an adhesive backing that will stick to any surface. It works like a Band-Aid: cut it to size, peel off the thin backing, and stick it to any clean surface. Used in this way, Contact Paper gives a smooth, attractive, and waterproof surface to desks, counters, table tops, toilet seats, lamp shades, old suitcases, etc.

Cheap fabrics, old bedspreads, decals, posters, and magazine cutouts—all can brighten up unsavory, dreary furniture in imaginative ways. The possibilities for any of these materials, used alone or in combination, are endless, easy, and eye-catching.

Even wallpaper scraps (bought at wallpaper stores) can provide a cheap way to pattern an old piece of furniture. I once saw an old refrigerator to which a huge American flag had been glued. Almost anything can be used! A collage of animal pictures from *Life* magazine brightens up the bureau of one of my friends, and a poster-photo of Sophia Loren serves as a charming, topless coffee-table top. Finally, if the idea doesn't entirely repel you, try using red-plastic electricians' tape to candy-stripe the legs of your kitchen table.

Any of the visual aids mentioned above can be affixed to your furniture by means of Elmer's Glue or rubber cement. Just make sure that the furniture surface is clean. A coat of clear, or if you prefer, "antiquing" (yellow-tinted), lacquer will give any of these adornments a hard, waterproof, and relatively permanent finish. Fabric scraps and old bedspreads, of course, can simply be thrown over whatever needs to be covered . . . although they can also be glued and lacquered for a more aesthetic, and less hasty, effect.

All of these furniture face-lifting methods require less work, and are often cheaper and more effective, than painting or staining. They're also more fun and personally expressive. But if your heart and mind are set on painting, cover your floors with newspapers and get to work.

Furniture Painting

You can usually get away with using only one coat of paint, particularly if you are applying a dark color over a light one. If, however, you're trying to make a black bookcase white, count on using two coats.

Buy a colorful enamel paint (not latex, the colors aren't very interesting or cheery; get semi- or high-gloss enamel), a cheap brush (so what if you can't use it a second time?), and some sandpaper (or "liquid sander"). Metal furniture should be painted with metal lacquer or exterior enamel paint.

1. Remove hardware, such as handles and knobs, and cushions from furniture.
2. Patch cracks—if you feel like it—with plastic wood.
3. If the old painted surface is peeling, sand it with a piece of sandpaper wrapped around a block of wood. (For rounded edges, use the paper without the block, like a shoe rag, or hold it in the palm of your hand.) Try to sand in full-length strokes, to make your work even.

If the surface is shiny, just rough it up a bit with some sandpaper. You aren't trying to remove the old finish. All you want is a fairly smooth, firm surface to which the new paint will adhere.

Instead of sandpaper and elbow grease, you might wish to try one of the "liquid sanders," available at hardware stores. Following the directions on the can will quickly result in a clean and "prepared" surface.

Metal surfaces are prepared in the same manner. Use 4/0 garnet paper to do your sanding, and remove any rust spots with steel wool dipped in kerosene or rust remover. Then let the piece dry before painting.

4. Dust the surface with a dry cloth, then wash with water and detergent. Let dry.

5. Use a cheap brush that can be discarded after the job; dip it no more than one-third of its length into the paint, tap (not wipe) against the side of the can to remove excess, and apply the paint with light, parallel strokes. Finish with crisscross strokes to eliminate brush marks.

6. If a second coat is needed, wait until the first is completely dry; then sand very lightly with fine sandpaper (to roughen the surface a little). Dust, and wipe with a damp cloth. Paint again.

7. Apply a furniture wax, if you like, before replacing the hardware.

SPRAY PAINTING: Metal and reed furniture can frequently be painted more easily with aerosol-can spray paints than with brushes. Use masking tape to cover anything you don't want painted, and do your painting outside if possible (otherwise, use plenty of newspaper). Avoid flames and breezes, and try to work at room temperature.

Two thin coats of spray paint are better than one thick one. Shake the can for one-half minute or longer before using; maintain a constant distance from the surface (about a foot); and clean the spray nozzle after each application by inverting the can and pressing the button intermittently until only gas comes out. Wipe nozzle clean.

THE ART OF IMPROVISATION

Having exhausted the themes of furniture purchasing, scrounging, and repairing, we now turn our attention to the last of the three great furnishing techniques: improvising. This technique consists of using your imagination. So let's begin!

Foot lockers and packing crates become seats and tables when graced with old bedspreads or a bit of paint.

A dinette set can be contrived from discarded nail kegs (topped with cushions) and a large packing barrel (topped with a circular piece of plywood).

That door in your basement, when placed atop a small table or a tiny desk, makes a great study or work surface.* Placed on cinder blocks or six-inch screw-in legs, the door becomes a couch, ready for mat, mattress, or a few cushions.

Wooden cable spools are really coffee tables in disguise, just as old Oriental rugs and bedspreads are often tapestrial art treasures.**

Old bookcases make great kitchen pantry or closet shelves (never, ever reject or pass up an old bookcase!); and wooden (or even heavy cardboard) boxes make superb record or book shelves when anointed with water-color paints or magazine clippings.

A low-cut cardboard or wooden box can be slid under your bed as a shoe, sweater, or underwear drawer.

Chunks of burlap (available cheaply, and in many colors, at fabric stores) make fine screens, curtains, wall hangings, tablecloths, and upholstery. If stretched over a simple frame, they also make great room dividers.

Bricks,*** cinder blocks, and boards are easily stacked into improvised bookshelves and desks. These raw materials are often to be had for free from trash barrels, or cheaply from janitors (an excellent source of boards and doors) or construction sites. Paint (two coats, unless you put a coat of "sealer" on first) or stain the boards; spray paint or leave *au naturel* the cinder blocks.

TO STAIN: Sand your boards smooth. Using a rag or brush, apply a water-base stain, brushing or rubbing the rag in the direction of the grain. Don't overlap strokes. Wipe end grains immediately to avoid overabsorption of the stain.

Let dry for twelve hours, then apply another

* If the door has moldings, cover the entire door with a piece of "masonite," which can be purchased cheaply, cut to size, together with a bag of shingle nails at a lumberyard.

** Attach to a long pole or piece of 1″ x 1″ wood and hang like pictures.

*** When making bookshelves, #10 tin cans may be substituted for bricks. Paint them to avoid rust. Or, cover with Contact Paper. Or, leave them as they are and replace when rusty (in a year or two).

coat of stain, if you're really up to it (two thin coats are better than one thick one). For a professional finish, apply a satin-finish lacquer or flat varnish and wax with a white paste wax when dry. For a nonprofessional (but almost as nice) finish, simply wax the dried stain with paste wax, after smoothing down the board a bit with steel wool.

A fine kitchen or work counter can be made from a stained hollow-core door, a 2" x 4" wood brace, and a pair of discount-store screw-on legs.

Improvise, too, by REARRANGING FURNITURE.

Bookcases and chests can be stacked vertically—or placed side-by-side, according to your needs and space limitations.

Two dressers or file cabinets, topped with a door or boards, make a superb desk, a work area, or even a bed. Even one dresser or file cabinet is a good desk foundation (see diagram) if you support the other end of the desk top with a wall brace (see diagram—brace the end and back of door, anchor the top from beneath).

Finally, remember: a saw can transform one bookcase into two, or a kitchen table into a coffee table (cut the legs, not the table top).

THE LAST LAP

By now, happy reader, your domicile is clean, furnished, and almost habitable. A few finishing touches will complete both your apartment and this chapter, allowing us to wash our hands and get on to other aspects of life. These finishing touches include:

Lights
Curtains
Wall shelves, hooks, and pegboards
Communications center.*

* I leave such sundries as posters, candles, and knickknacks to your own tastes and sensibilities.

A Word on Lights

When the overhead lamp in your room does not shed light on your reading matter, try adding a bulb or putting in one of greater wattage. This may seem like a simple-minded solution, but it usually does the trick! Often, your overhead light is made to hold two bulbs, but contains only one that is alive. Fill up the empty sockets (a bright idea, no?). Remember that bulbs come in a great variety of brightness; so, if your room is dark (and assuming you don't want it that way), get a brighter bulb.*

* If a fluorescent bulb sputters, try replacing the starter (a twist-out, cork-sized aluminum thingie). It's much cheaper than the bulb and is usually the problem source.

Comfort demands that a room be lit more or less evenly. A brilliant desk lamp in a dark room leads to eyestrain.

Supplementary lamps can usually be bought or scrounged along with the rest of your furnishings. If the cord is frayed or the socket broken, your hardware store will carry replacement parts. Hardware stores also carry lamp kits, with which you can transform a wine bottle into a lamp within five minutes. Lamp shades can be cleaned with a damp sponge (if they are cloth, soak them in soapy water) and then—like almost everything else—decorated with cloth, decals, clippings, maps, photographs, stale lettuce, or anything else that might be convenient.

"Procedure for removing overhead light fixture"

Chandeliers: I enjoy hanging a candle chandelier in my bedroom. You can make or buy your own and suspend it from the dismantled ceiling light fixture.** Of course, if you do this your room will need lamps for the less romantic periods of your day.

Procedure for Removing Overhead Light Fixture and Replacing with Chandelier Hook

1. On a sunny afternoon unscrew the fuse that controls the electricity in your room.

2. Stand on a stool and remove the light shade and bulbs.

3. Unscrew the bolts holding the fixture plate to the ceiling. Let the plate and light fixture dangle.

4. Untwist the wire splicings that hold the fixture to the apartment wiring. The fixture will come off.

** Chandeliers with electrical fittings can easily be dewired and set up for use with candles.

5. Using adhesive or electrical tape, cover separately

*Ready-made threaded hooks are sometimes available at hardware stores.

the exposed ends of the apartment wiring. Tuck the wires up into the ceiling.

6. Get off the stool and sit down for a minute, and for a drink of lemonade.

7. Unscrew the light fixture from its mounting plate. Replace it with an "eyebolt" from your hardware store. This will cost about twenty cents. Have the hardware-store man cut (using a boltcutter) a piece from the eyebolt so that you have a hook.*

Use a nut and washer on each side of the mounting plate, so that your fixture will be secure.

8. Replace the mounting plate and hang the chandelier a little above your head. (Or, if you are only four feet eight inches tall, hang it a little higher.)

If you wish to install a hook in your ceiling—either for a chandelier or for a heavy electric lamp —in a place where there is no outlet, go to a hardware store or lamp store and buy a toggle bolt with a hook fitting. Drill a hole into the ceiling, a little larger than the anchor bolt, and slip the bolt—with its wings folded up—into the hole. The wings will spread apart, and the hook fitting can be turned clockwise to tighten the unit in place. Hang your lamp from this hook, and plug into a convenient wall outlet.

Making a Lightweight Hanging Lamp

A lightweight, do-it-yourself hanging lamp can be constructed in approximately twenty minutes, using about six dollars' worth of hardware-store and boutique materials. Such a lamp is cheap, illuminates better than a floor or desk lamp, is more attractive and less obtrusive than most standing lamps, and collapses for easy moving.

Buy the following for each lamp:

A. 1 brass bulb socket, the cheapest and simplest available.

B. 1 electrical-appliance wall plug.

C. 1 small, plastic off-on switch (with circular wheel switch), designed for attaching to lamp cord.

D. 1 small box of hammer-in "insulated staples."

E. 1 paper, hemispherical "Japanese" or "Fake Tiffany" hanging lamp shade.

F. 1 spool of electrical "lamp cord" (a fifty-foot spool makes two or three lamps).

Now:

1. Unwind, without cutting, about twenty feet of lamp cord from the spool.

2. With the aid of knife and screw driver, attach the bulb socket to the free end of the lamp cord— following the verbal directions of your hardware-store dealer.

3. Ask a friend or roommate to hold the socket in the air at the spot where you want it eventually to hang. While he or she is holding the socket, climb onto a chair or table and pull the lamp cord taut to the ceiling. Using a hammer, staple the lamp cord in place on the ceiling. This will hold!*

4. Your helper can now sit down and "supervise."

5. Use a couple more staples to bring the lamp cord to a point on the ceiling directly above the nearest electrical wall outlet. Or, better still, if there is a window close to the nearest outlet, to a point above the side window molding closest to the outlet.

6. Placing staples about one foot apart, bring the lamp cord down along the wall or molding toward the outlet.

7. At a point three or four feet above the floor, insert the plastic switch into the lamp cord, following the directions on the package.

8. Complete the stapling job at a point one or two feet from the outlet. Sever lamp cord from spool, making sure you have plenty of slack cord.

9. Attach plug to end of lamp cord, following directions accompanying the plug or those in Chapter 6.

10. Suspend lamp shade by tying its "string" to a point on the lamp cord a couple of inches above the socket. Use thread or thin copper wire for the tying job.

* If you decide to use a homemade construction of poster board, coffee cans, cloth on wire, etc., instead of a paper, hemispherical lamp shade, substitute a one- or two-inch threaded hook (from a hardware store) for the first insulated staple. Screwed into the ceiling, such a hook will support a great deal of weight.

Aunt Martha's attic

Curtains   Curtains can usually be scrounged, purchased from Goodwill, or located in the attic of your great-aunt Martha.

Otherwise, they can be cheaply made from:

a. Cheap cotton (see the Yellow Pages for "Fabric" listings; wholesalers and stores selling mill ends are mentioned there).

b. Bedspreads or sheets (permanent-press ones with prints, stripes, or solid colors).

c. Burlap.

Measure the height of your windows, and then figure on an extra six or seven inches for hems. Buy your fabric and cut accordingly. In terms of width, curtains should be almost twice the width of the windows—if you can afford it. Anything less than one and one-half times the width looks rather skimpy.

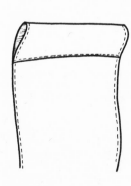

Make a one-inch hem on the sides. (For you nonsewers, fold over one inch of the fabric on each side and sew a pocket, as in diagram A. The stitches don't have to be closer than three-fourths of an inch apart.) Make a three-inch hem at both the bottom and top of curtains. Then, to add a dash of elegance, make a pocket in the top hem for the curtain rod (diagram B).

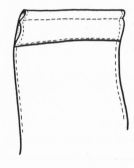

If you dig pleats, don't fuss around with sewing them yourself. Instead, buy "pleating tape" at a fabric store. This tape, which has tiny pockets spaced along its length, is sewn to the top of your curtain. Curtain hooks are then slipped into the pockets. Result: an easy, but impressive set of pleated curtains.

CURTAIN RODS are cheap and come in adjustable lengths. Buy them at the five-and-ten or at discount stores. If the screws or nails holding the end hooks to the window molding are loose, or if you want to install new hooks:

A. Move the hooks to a more solid part of the window frame. Or,

B. Use larger screws or nails than were used previously. Or,

C. Fill in the old holes with plastic wood and let dry before rescrewing.

Sometimes, method (A) is impossible, and (B) splits the wood, so you're left with (C) as the only viable alternative.

Threading curtain on rod: Put the whole curtain

(both halves) on the larger section of the curtain rod, scrunching up the cloth. Insert the smaller section of the rod into the larger. Affix the entire unit to the wall hooks, and it's curtains for you!

Invitation to a Hanging

"There's something that loves a wall," as one American poet observed. No wonder, for they certainly make good surfaces from which to suspend pots, pans, overcoats, pictures, and almost anything else as well.

In a small apartment, space is always at a premium. Wall hooks and pegboards can often make life a bit less of a hassle (though, admittedly, not much less).

Kitchen utensils should always be hung where they can be seen and reached. By hanging them instead of storing them in cabinets, you can also let pots and pans dry on the walls, leaving the drainboard free for cups and dishes.

Use pegboards or simply dime-store hooks. Pegboards are the more efficient, though they cost more. Lumberyards and hardware stores (and Sears) can sell you pieces of pegboard, together with mounting kits (about $1.75 for everything, including the hanging hooks). The mounting kit contains long screws and thick washers. Attach the pegboard to your kitchen wall by putting screws through the board, through the washers, and into the building studs—which are located behind your wallboards, spaced sixteen inches apart, starting at the corner of your room. The pegboard should then be painted with an enamel paint. Hooks of all sizes and shapes are available at discount stores, five-and-tens, Sears, and hardware stores.

There is an easier and cheaper method of hanging kitchen tools and pots. Buy, from a five-and-ten or hardware store, thirty strong screw-type hooks called "cup hooks"; this is a total investment of $1.25. Nail a thin strip of wood across the

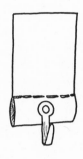

length of one kitchen wall at shoulder height (putting nails at sixteen-inch intervals). Paint the wood, for aesthetic reasons, and screw in twenty of your hooks. Screw the remaining ten hooks to the edges of counters and tables. Then, have yourself a private hanging!

Pictures can be hung with light, cloth hangers that are cemented into place; picture hooks that are held by nails tapped in at an angle; or molding hooks that attach to wall moldings and spare walls some holes from nails. All are available at hardware, five-and-ten-cent, and discount stores for about fifteen cents. Cloth hangers support very little weight, however, since they are only as strong as the paint or wallpaper to which they are glued. Picture hooks, on the other hand, will hold up to twenty pounds of weight. And, if you use *two* of them for each picture or mirror, you might even be able to support a little more weight.

Finally, if it is necessary to support one hell of a lot of weight—for example, a rug tapestry—drive anchor bolts into wall studs and stretch strong wire between them. Such a hanging device will support even a bothersome roommate or two.

Clothing can be hung on wall hooks, or on special hangers (see diagram) that slip over the top of your bedroom or closet door. Both types of hangers are universally available at five-and-tens. The first, a wire-type hook, can be mounted on a small board and nailed onto a wall near the front door, providing a convenient place for overcoats. The back-of-the-door-hanger-type hook will hold a dozen shirts or one-half dozen sports jackets or dresses.

If you are an enterprising type, construct a mini-closet in one corner of your room, using a few pieces of scrap wood and a thick dowel (see diagram). If you're less enterprising, but still in need of more closet space, buy a cardboard wardrobe at a discount or mail-order house and paint or deco-

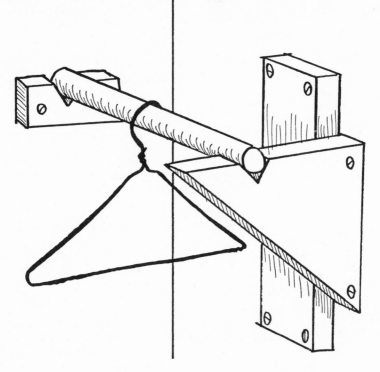

rate it as you wish. For shirts and skirts, turn a foot locker or large trunk on one end, and use a tension rod to support hangers.

Communica-tions Center

In an apartment housing several people, telephone messages can get lost as quickly as they are taken.

Buy a blackboard and some chalk at a five-and-ten-cent or toy store. Hang the board on a wall near your telephone. This will prove more useful than you ever imagined, since shopping lists, doodles, and personal gripes will soon find themselves side-by-side with your phone messages. A damp sponge serves as an eraser.

Incidentally, if you really get addicted to this blackboard idea, you can buy blackboard paint and cover a large section of wall with the stuff. It takes three coats (let dry between coats), but for fun and games—never forget the world of colored chalk!—it can't be beat. You will soon discover why all kids enjoy making crayon murals, much to the chagrin of their parents, who aren't quite so attuned to doing their own thing.*

* On your front door, hang a pad and pencil—or stick a couple of thumbtacks into the door for the convenience of note-leavers.

Celebration

Your journey is finished, the day is done, your domicile is habitable. Why not spend whatever funds are remaining to you in celebration of this blessed event?

I trust that no helpful hints are needed as to the ways and means of joyous celebration.

"You will soon understand why all kids enjoy making crayon murals . . . ."

HEFLING

APPENDIX 3

PERSUADING YOUR LANDLORD TO MAKE REPAIRS *

* Adapted from Boston University Student Union's pamphlet *Boston Housing and You.*

State and city laws set minimal housing standards that landlords are expected to maintain. Therefore, don't spend your own money on repairs that might be your landlord's responsibility. You can find out about legal housing standards by calling your city housing-inspection department or health and/or sanitation department, sometimes called "board of health."

Any of these agencies will be able to inform you of state and city housing regulations. In the Boston area, for example, these are a landlord's obligations according to law **:

** A tenant, on his part, is legally required to pay his rent on time, keep his apartment clean and dispose of trash in the proper containers, allow landlord access to the door to make repairs, and keep the apartment free from conditions that encourage insects and rodents.

A. Condition of building:
1. Provide front and rear entrances with adequate locks on each.
2. Provide workable front doorbells.
3. Provide adequate lighting in front and rear halls.
4. Provide mailboxes with good locks and keys.

B. Building maintenance:
1. Keep the roof and gutters in good repair (no leaks).
2. Protect against gas and water leaks within the building.
3. Protect against electrical and falling accidents. (For example, stair treads and handrails must be secure.)
4. Provide fire escapes or at least two means of egress per apartment.
5. Clean cellars, hallways, steps, and grounds (including snow from sidewalks).
6. Provide sufficient barrels with covers for each apartment, and place barrels of trash on sidewalk and remove them at the proper times.

C. Within individual apartments:
1. Provide lights and at least two electrical outlets in each room.

2. Provide a workable stove, sink, toilet, tub, hand bowl, running hot (minimum of 120° F.) and cold water, and heat (minimum of 70° F.).
3. Provide window screens.
4. Exterminate insects and rodents due to improper maintenance, or where there is infestation in two or more apartments.

A great many landlords, activated by self-interest or a sincere sense of responsibility, make prompt repairs in response to the needs of their tenants and in accordance with state and local statutes.

Other landlords, however, let their buildings fall apart, ignoring the plights and protests of their tenants. These landlords would rather spend their money on a good meal—accompanied by a nice rosé wine—than on a new toilet bowl. Especially when the meal is for them and the toilet for you.

If your landlord is among the latter variety, the following methods might help.

How to Convince Your Landlord to Respond to Requests for Repairs

1. Make it very clear to your landlord exactly what you want. Have your wants written into your lease. Then, if weeks pass without a sign of repairmen, call your landlord on the telephone and make an appointment to see him, and/or write him a letter, keeping a copy and sending the original by certified mail, return receipt requested. If that doesn't work:
2. Try to get a lawyer to call your landlord or write to him. If necessary, groups like the legal aid society might provide you with free legal aid. When available, law students are often a good source of legal advice, and sometimes law professors have time to help. If this doesn't work:
3. Call your local housing-inspection and/or health or sanitation departments, whichever seems most appropriate in your city. They will inform you of your landlord's legal responsibilities and will send an inspector to your apartment. When the in-

spector comes, ask to see his card, write down his name, and note the date of inspection. The inspection department should take steps to see that your landlord complies with state and local housing and sanitation codes.*

* This method of appeal might even net you a new, free paint job. The health department of New Haven, Connecticut, has forced landlords to repaint apartments in which peeling lead paint has been deemed a health hazard to children and pets (eating lead paint results in lead poisoning, which can be fatal).

4. If any tenants in your building are creating problems or health hazards, try to get them to stop. This can make your building more pleasant to live in and will put you in a stronger bargaining position when you speak to your landlord.

Last Resorts

If your landlord does not yield to the above pressures, you may have to organize the tenants or take your landlord to court for violating the sanitary code. Neither of these tactics is difficult or time-consuming, but both should be employed only as last resorts. When they are necessary, seek legal advice and service.

1. Organize the tenants of your building into a tenants' union.

Talk with the other tenants in your building and arrange a meeting of all tenants, inviting, perhaps, residents of other buildings owned by the same landlord.

At the meeting, draw up a contract and negotiate the terms with your landlord. The collective power of several tenants is much greater than that of any individual. A large group can pose a highly effective threat to a negligent landlord's income and public image.

Use your legal right to withhold rent (applicable to many cities, but check first) in order to persuade your landlord to negotiate the contract and comply with it once he has agreed to it.

First, have your legal advisor make sure that state laws protect you from being evicted. Then,

a. Request in writing a special inspection from the housing-inspection department in your city.

b. Get a certified copy of the results. (There may be a small charge.)

c. Have your rent paid up to date and have rent receipts for recent months on hand.

d. Mail a certified letter (return receipt requested), written by a lawyer, to your landlord or his agent informing him that he will receive no more rent until the specified items in the housing report are corrected.

e. Hold the rent in your bank until the housing-inspection department verifies, in your presence, that the items in the report have been repaired. Then pay the back rent to your landlord.

An alternative to Step 1 is to:

2. Ask your city court to name a "receiver" for your rent with the authority to spend it on repairs.

First you check with a lawyer about the feasibility of presenting your case in superior court. Then obtain a certified inspection report as in Step 1 above.

Many states give local judges the power to order landlords to repair all items listed in the housing-inspection report. While repairs are being made, the landlord cannot collect rent, evict tenants, or sell his property. To make sure that the repairs are made, tenants pay their rent to the court-appointed receiver (not the landlord), who will spend the money making repairs on all items listed in the report.

Let's hope that you and your landlord will be friends and that the information contained in this appendix will be of no use to you at all. Friendly words often work better than threats, and should always be tried first.

Perhaps your landlord will be more helpful than you had anticipated. Perhaps you and he can make an agreement by which you'll make repairs in exchange for a month's free rent. There are many amicable solutions to the problem of an apartment in need of repairs. But, when more than friendly hints become necessary, this appendix will serve as a good plan of action.

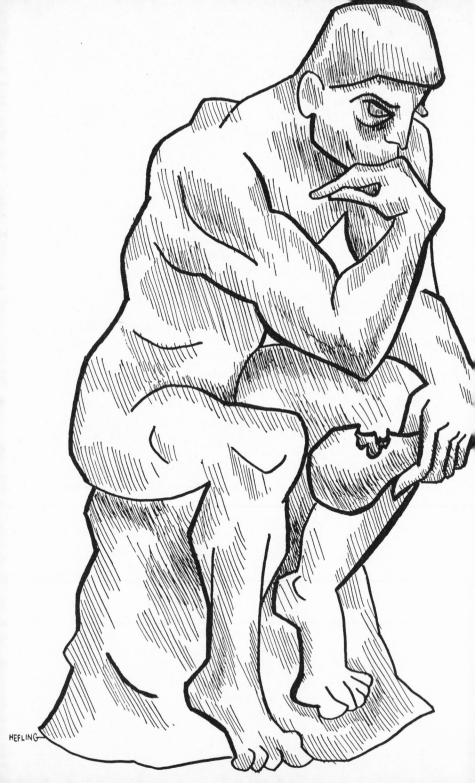

CHAPTER FOUR

THOUGHT FOR FOOD

Staying alive means keeping our bodies fed—no more, no less. Eating is the only unavoidable activity, imposed upon us by dear Mother Nature, that takes both our time and our money. And, as those of meager means well know, food buying and preparation consume a major chunk of both commodities. For these reasons, a thorough knowledge of all processes, short cuts, and economy tricks in the realm of cookery is a prerequisite for those desiring a Good But Cheap Existence.

In the wild West of yesteryear, things were a lot simpler than they are nowadays. When Trapper Joe was hungry, he shot his "vittles," roasted them over an open fire, and then—his bowie knife serving as fork, knife, spoon, and plate—sat down on a log to confront his hearty repast. Cleanup was simple: whatever the dog didn't eat, the campfire would. Today we have supermarkets, electric stoves, frozen onion slices, metal spatulas, and cyclamates. We have so many foods to choose from that our poor minds stagger in confusion. We have garbage disposals, blenders, Danish silverware, and above all—the great culinary invention of modern times—The Recipe.

"In the wild West of yesteryear, things were a lot simpler."

What can we poor mortals do in the face of such specialization, sophistication, and complexity? Where do we start? Are we to consume food, or will it devour us?

Relax, dear reader, "Let flee the fearsome panic that doth grip us." Food getting and preparing can still be as simple and straightforward as in the days of yore if we approach the Realm of Food with knowledge and a healthy attitude. Let's be simple for a moment, yes, almost simple-minded. Forget everything you've ever read, seen, or thought about food and cooking—and we'll start afresh, with a clean slate as it were—or plate, if you prefer. Cooking will be our field of investigation, of scientific inquiry. Our ultimate question: What is the best, most simple, efficient, delicious, creative, and logical way to cook? Or, How to Cook Cheap but Good.

"The kitchen is our laboratory . . . ."

**THE KITCHEN:
WORK AREAS**

The kitchen is our laboratory for the investigation of food and cookery. And, like any scientific lab, it has several well-defined areas. Think of the kitchen as a pentagon in which you must work, moving from apex to apex as the experiment progresses. This Porisian Pentagon, existing not only in concept but in every kitchen as well, consists of:

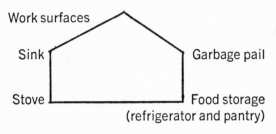

Work surfaces

Sink

Stove

Garbage pail

Food storage
(refrigerator and pantry)

The Porisian Pentagon

*An oven or meat thermometer, available at hardware stores and supermarkets, is indispensable. If you can afford the luxury, buy one of each.

Learn how your STOVE works. Not only do different makes and models vary, but every stove heats at a different rate and to different temperatures. Electric stoves heat more slowly and are less controllable than gas stoves; they therefore demand more care and skill from the chef. The owner of a gas stove, on the other hand, must know how to light ovens and burners and must learn to keep a constant sly eye on the temperature of his oven, which often may not correspond to the dial markings.*

Pots, pans, spatulas, wire whisks, wooden spoons, and other stove equipment should be hung or shelved next to the stove. Pot holders, wooden matches, and a box of baking soda (to smother fires; never use water) will complete the array. Finally, keep your stove clean; a clean stove is your best friend. Without it, your eating fare is confined to tuna fish and sardines.

What can be said about a SINK? Plenty. First of all, water should enter a sink in any desired combination of hot and cold—and should leave quickly when the washing is over. If your sink is old-fashioned, with separate spouts for hot and cold, buy a mixer at a hardware store, so that you can combine hot and cold waters. If faucets drip, spatter, or leak, replacing the proper washers is an easy task (see Chapter 6). All kitchen sinks should be improved by adding a ninety-eight-cent rubber spray attachment, which delivers the water in a fine spray, making dish and vegetable washing much easier. And if your sink doesn't drain quickly, clean it according to the methods discussed in Chapter 6.

So much for the basic mechanics of water flow. What other things should be known about sinks? Keep cleanser (for the sink) and detergent (for dishes) nearby, together with an aluminum or nylon scraping pad (not steel wool or soap pads: they rust), and sponges. A cut-down milk carton should stand in a corner of the sink for food scraps (empty this periodically), and a piece of screen bound with iron-on tape will protect the drain from getting clogged with all sorts of glop. Finally, situate a dish-draining rack, together with a supplementary silverware drainer, on the drainboard adjacent to your sink. A nearby hand towel is a convenience that, if kept dry, will save a thousand paper towels.

WORK SURFACES should be large and near the stove. This is where cutting, mixing, and miscellaneous preparations are done. A sturdy table, built-in shelf (rough boards can be covered with a scrap of heavy linoleum), or the top of an old bureau (store pans, etc., in the drawers) will do perfectly. The larger the area, the happier you'll be. Never count on using the kitchen table as a work area if you can avoid it. If you do use it, you'll be rewarded with Inconvenience Everlasting. Store mixing spoons and bowls, cutting boards, egg beaters, rolling pins, sieves, and knives on, under, or near the work area; store spices on a shelf within reach, and post a spice chart on a convenient wall. Remember, too, to keep a half dozen Band-Aids near the work area, in case you happen to bump into a knife or two.

Buy as large a plastic GARBAGE PAIL as your aesthetic standards will permit. It can never be too big; in fact, a plastic outdoor twenty-gallon barrel is ideal. Line it with paper grocery bags or, far superior, plastic bags made especially for garbage barrels or autumn leaves. To thwart insects and mice, keep the barrel covered. And wash all garbage pails once every month or two.

The fifth and final apex of your Porisian Pentagon is the FOOD-STORAGE AREA, composed of cold storage and pantry, or dry, storage. The fact that this sector exists at all is a miracle, although most of us take it for granted. Until a hundred years ago man had to shop or hunt for food every day of the year, being always at the mercy of seasonal and territorial supply. Not only did food searching and buying occupy much of his time, but it yielded meager results. Today, methods of dry storage (cans, packages), cool storage (refrigerated perishables), and cold storage (frozen foods) permit us to obtain—at infrequent intervals if we wish—better and more varied foods than any king could have demanded until recently.

Thus our storage areas allow us to buy food according to our tastes, whimsy, and convenience —and to buy in quantity, at great savings of money and time.

It takes a while to learn to exploit fully our storage resources. But once a person learns to do so, his food bills drop precipitously. For he will then be taking advantage of sales, leftovers, and large-quantity buying. And he will know exactly how long any food can be kept without spoilage and waste.

For the moment, however, simply concentrate on building yourself as large a storage area as your space and money will allow. Shelves or a large bookcase is essential for dry storage: either can be built into a closet if a pantry is unavailable. Bins, or wooden boxes, make convenient homes for potatoes and onions. Fo. greatest convenience, at least some of your dry-storage area should be located above or below your work surface.

For cleanliness, line shelves with brown wrapping paper (or cut-up paper bags), shelf lining (expensive), or "broken rolls" of wallpaper or linoleum (available cheaply at wallpaper and linoleum stores).

Organize shelves into categories: a shelf for condiments; a shelf for sugar-flour-grains; a shelf for canned vegetables, fruits, and soups. This makes it easier to find what you want when you want it, and also to discover what you don't have when you're writing a shopping list.

Your refrigerator is the "coolest" if not the "neatest" sector of your storage area. Make sure it is in proper working order.

Having two refrigerators wouldn't make life any easier, since half of your refrigerated food would spoil before it could be consumed. So be content with any refrigerator whatsoever, and clean it periodically (see Chapter 3). The size of your freezer space is, however, vitally important. A FREEZER, if big enough, permits you to buy and store large quantities of meats (your biggest food expense) and vegetables when they are on sale. It enables you to prepare and store complete meals in advance (saving hundreds of hours over the course of a year). It enables you to store half loaves of bread, leftover pastries, and so forth for months. And it enables you to chill wines and cold dishes much faster than you can in your refrigerator. In short, your freezer can save you a small fortune, as well as several days of working time per month.

Yet many young people are content to live with a tiny freezer, and they waste even that by filling it with orange juice and ice cream! This sounds preposterous, but it's true. If your freezer is small, buy another. A large investment? Yes, if you buy a new one. But newspapers invariably contain ads placed by moving homeowners who are selling their appliances. And stores and restaurants often —when going out of business—sell their freezers, ice-cream chests, and frozen-food display cabinets for as little as twenty-five dollars. Freezers are available; "seek, and ye shall find," as the Good Book says. And, as we all know, it's as true as gospel. Your investment will be repaid within a few months of food buying (and eventually, of course, you can resell the freezer for about the same price you paid). Between monetary savings and cooking convenience, you'll never have a single regret. A last point: if you "seek and find" before moving into your apartment, you can move your "new" old freezer with the rest of your belongings, thereby saving time and expense.

The pentagon is now complete. Your laboratory is ready. It now needs to be stocked with tools, and then graced with a table at which your culinary productions may be offered for the delight and pleasure of all.

COOKING UTENSILS

Disregard what anyone, including the best of cookbooks and recipes, tells you. The only cooking utensils you really need are:

A. 1 pot, for mixing ingredients, boiling, roasting, frying, etc.
B. 1 sharp knife, for cutting, stirring, and turning.
C. 1 can opener.

With the exception of the last item, that's all most of humanity has ever used for cooking. Everything else you buy is for your own pleasure and convenience—and should be bought only when you feel like it and when you find it at a bargain price. I say this to emphasize that it is a mistake and a waste of money to go to a store and buy a bunch of cooking utensils. Wait a while and keep your eyes open. Relatives will die, friends will move away, junk shops will be visited, and Goodwill/Salvation Army stores will be discovered. Cooking utensils, like everything else, can cost lots of money: why spend $150 when $15 and patience will buy just as much?

"That's all most of humanity has ever used for cooking."

What things should you be "on the lookout" for?

Pots and Pans

A. Skillets, large and small, with covers if possible. Black, cast-iron pans are best for slow, thorough cooking. They provide even heat and can be used on top of the stove as well as in the oven. Cast-iron griddles are great for pancakes! *

* "Season" new cast-iron pots and pans by rubbing them with olive oil. Then, after putting several more tablespoons of oil into them, heat them in the oven for twenty minutes or so. The oil seeps into the iron, thereby protecting it from rust.

B. Pots with covers, any and all sizes. The more the merrier.

C. Dutch oven or metal casserole, with cover, of iron or heavy aluminum.

D. Casseroles—Pyrex or pottery—any and all sizes.

E. Roasting pan—one big one (11" x 16"), with rack. The rack can also be used for cakes.

F. Loaf pans and pie plates (for cooking meat loaf, roasting, warming things up, broiling). Baking sheets and Pyrex baking dishes are also good for some of these activities.

G. Coffeepot and teakettle.

H. Colander for draining salads and spaghetti and for inverting over frying foods.

I. Mixing bowls, all sizes (these can be used as molds).

J. Ring mold, for Jell-O, etc.

Tools for the Kitchen

A. Knives—as many as you can get, of all sizes. All secondhand stores carry them. Try to get at least a big carving knife, a serrated bread knife, a serrated paring knife. A stainless-steel knife is never very sharp. Try to find the old-fashioned steel knives (which get sharper and stay that way), even if they're never quite so nice and shiny as stainless steel. Knives with serrated edges are best for cutting bread and can be used for other

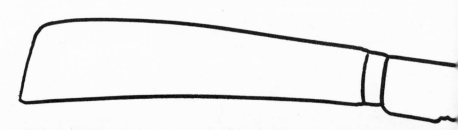

things as well. Never buy cheap knives: they're not worth a damn.

B. Sharpening stone to keep your knives sharp. Buy it at a hardware store: this is almost a necessity.

C. Cutting boards, big and small, though you can get away with using only one big one. Cover new cutting boards with oil, preferably mineral, but vegetable will do. Wipe off excess a day later. Small rubber "legs" with nails sticking out of them can be purchased at a hardware store and stuck on the bottom of cutting boards to minimize "cutting-board skid."

D. Wooden spoon, and also a slotted metal cooking spoon, a long fork, and metal and rubber spatulas.

E. Funnel for transferring liquids and separating eggs.

F. Wooden rolling pin.

G. Basting brush—a paint or shaving brush will do fine.

H. Oven thermometer, and meat thermometer, too.

I. Kitchen timer for eggs, cakes, steaks. Cheap timers can be found at photo-supply stores.

J. Can opener and corkscrew—get the kind of corkscrew with "arms" that move up and down. A jar opener is a handy device, too.

K. Potato-vegetable peeler, one of the most useful of tools.

L. Wire whisk—excellent for scrambling eggs and whipping cream.

M. Manual egg beater.

N. Potato masher.

O. Grater—that is, a metal sheet with holes in it. Eggs, cheese, and vegetables are "grated" through this.

P. Sieve for sifting flour, straining anything.

Q. Measuring cups and spoons.

R. Rubber gloves for washing dishes.

S. Plastic chef's apron.

T. Magnet to hold recipes to your refrigerator door while you cook.

U. Hammer—for tenderizing meat, crushing ice, and straightening bent pans.

V. Phillips screw driver for tightening loose pot and pan handles.

Serving Equipment

A. Pot holders, with magnets attached to them, so they can be stuck to your stove.

B. Hot plates, to rest hot pots and dishes on.

C. Platter(s), for serving.

D. Serving spoons, with and without draining slits in them.

E. Pitcher for serving beverages.

Many items could be added to the above list: butcher's hatchet, double boiler (improvise by putting any pot in a roasting pan half-filled with water; use on top of the stove), cheese slicer, baster, electric blender, omelet pan, wooden mallet, and meat grinder, to name a few. But why buy more than you need? If you have everything in the above lists, your culinary laboratory is more than completely stocked with the necessary tools of the chef's art. And always remember, almost any of the above tools can be omitted, substituted for, or obtained in the distant future.

Disposable Items

There is one last category of tools, not included in the lists above because you can never get them secondhand. This is the category of disposable items, the ephemerae of the cook's laboratory. Every kitchen should contain rolls of:

A. Aluminum foil

B. Handy-Wrap, Saran-Wrap, or Glad-Wrap.
Both types of wrapping are used constantly in cooking and storing foods.
More optional are the following:

C. Wax paper

D. Paper towels.

If you can afford to maintain a supply of all four, in wall dispensers near your work surfaces, your cooking career will be a lot easier. Finally, paper plates and cups, together with foil roasting pans, are guaranteed to make your life a little more pleasant. All these items, however, are inessential luxuries.

Your kitchen is now designed and stocked with tools. We are ready to consider food, the raw materials with which you will experiment and, ultimately, create masterpieces. But first, Four Final Thoughts about Cooking Utensils:

1. When buying used pots, pans, mixing and salad bowls, roasting pans, cutting boards, knives, etc., think big. Small items are always available, but when you see a twenty-quart pot, or an absolutely huge mixing bowl, grab it. They're hard to come by, and once you get them, you'll use them every day. They're easier to work with, and they're essential when cooking for groups. In short, choose a larger utensil over a smaller one. You'll always find plenty of the latter.

2. Interchangeability: "A container is a container is a container." Mixing bowls can be used to serve salad, spaghetti, or anything else. Pots with handles make excellent mixing bowls (unlike mixing bowls, they don't slither around, because you can hold the handles). Soup can be served in cups, and wine in shallow bowls. In other words, remember that Trapper Joe used one pot and one knife for everything, and don't be up tight about improvising.

3. Keep knives sharp, pots and pans unbent, and handles tight.

4. Keep utensils in the work area where they'll be most used. Keep them where they can be seen and gotten at easily. Hang anything that can be hung. Knives, especially, should be hung, not stored in drawers—for your own safety.

"Don't be up tight about improvising."

FOOD: THE RAW INGREDIENTS

It would be presumptuous of me to say which foods one should buy and in what quantities, for tastes and appetites differ enormously. Instead, the following pages will discuss how to buy food, and what to do with the purchases prior to cooking. Or,

1. How to recognize good-quality food.
2. How to save money on food.
3. How to store food.

FOOD: QUALITY

Regardless of what foods you purchase, you want them to be of the best quality available. It takes a few weeks or months of comparing to recognize good quality, especially in meats, but the following hints should serve as a guide.

Read them carefully—not only your health and eating pleasure but also your pocketbook is at stake. Bad food is good for nothing, except, perhaps, for lining your new garbage pail.

Meats, Poultry, Fish, Dairy

* Girls should smilingly talk to butchers, who like them as much as little old ladies like guys.

This group of products is the most difficult to evaluate. In fact, you will be, for a very long time, almost entirely at the mercy of the butcher or supermarket. So try to find a reputable one.

When you're at the meat counter, try to strike up conversations with the shrewd, knowledgeable little old ladies who are always hovering around doing their shopping.* They will generally be flattered to have their opinions asked, and they'll be able to point out to you differences in quality that a dozen pages here could never describe. When they tell you, "This, my son, is a good piece of meat," more often than not they're right. Try to get them to explain how they evaluated that particular piece of meat, and why they rejected others. You will find that they choose meat of a certain indescribable but very recognizable color, meat with a certain firm texture, and meat with fat that is more white than yellow. Steaks should be fairly "together," that is, not broken up by chunks of bone and fat. Obviously, the less fat

"Disreputable butchers hide the color of meat."

and bone on the piece of meat you buy, the more usable meat you'll be getting for your money.

Frequently, disreputable butchers hide the color of meat that is turning bad and green by placing it in display cabinets with special lights— or by dyeing the meat—which will make any rotting carcass look fit for the Prince of Gourmets. Before buying meat that you're unsure about, ask to see it, outside the case, before it is wrapped.

My final suggestion to you about meats is to send for the booklet entitled *101 Meat Cuts*, available for fifty cents by writing to The National Live Stock and Meat Board, 36 South Wabash Avenue, Chicago, Illinois 60603. This little booklet contains excellent color photographs and descriptions of meats and is the best guide that I know of for the beginning meat shopper.

Chicken

Chicken can be bought whole, cut in half, or cut up into pieces. Although a whole chicken is usually cheaper by the pound (because you must chop it up yourself), buying parts is the most economical, since much of the back is useless. Good chicken is plump and has firm, yellow skin.

Chickens are labeled Broilers, Fryers, or Roasters. A broiler is young and tender (one to two and a half pounds), and is meant to be broiled or fried.* A fryer is somewhat older and bigger than the broiler (two to three and a half pounds); it is therefore a little less tender, but can still be used for broiling, frying, or roasting. A roaster is an old bird, three and a half pounds or more. Use it for roasting, casseroles, and boiling.

* If you don't understand all these cooking terms now, you will by the end of this chapter.

Fish

Fish should be used on the same day it is purchased. It spoils overnight. (You can, of course, buy it and freeze it the same day.) Since fish is so temperamental, make sure it's fresh when you buy it. When a fish is cut up, the pieces are called "fillets"; buy these from a reputable, well-known

"Fish should be used on the same day it is purchased."

dealer only. When buying a whole fish, see that its eyes are bright, clear, and bulging, that its gills are reddish pink and not slimy, that its scales are clinging and shiny, and that its flesh is firm and elastic. Fresh fish will never smell "fishy." When buying frozen fish, make sure that it is frozen very, very solid, that is, that it has not begun to thaw in the display case.

Shellfish

If regular old fish spoil easily, shellfish spoil twice as easily. For this reason, all shellfish (except scallops and shrimp), are sold alive. Remember Molly Malone? Her customers were no fools: they, and you too, should accept only shellfish that are "alive, alive-oh!" You can tell a lobster or crab is alive if it moves; a live clam, mussel, or oyster will hold its shell tightly closed when it's alive.

Dairy

Milk, cream, butter, eggs, and cheese must be kept under continuous refrigeration. Don't buy anything that isn't stored and displayed in refrigerated cases. If these items are stored in boxes bearing dates, the dates usually signify the last day on which they can be sold, not the date of delivery.

When buying cheese, it is often worthwhile to buy it unsliced. You can then slice it or grate it (get "grating cheese" for this) yourself very easily, and your cheese will be cheaper and more flavorful. Cheese can also be stored in your freezer if you happen to buy a large quantity of it on sale.

Eggs, sold in cartons, are graded neither by color nor by size, only by weight: extra large, large, medium, small. Fresh eggs look dull and rough, not smooth or shiny. The color of an egg's shell does not affect its quality—neither do specks or blood spots in the egg itself. Eggs are one of the best and most complete foods you can eat, a fact not surprising when you consider the egg's biological function. Egg dishes provide a less expensive protein alternative to meat, so use them often.

Fresh Fruits and Vegetables

The United States Department of Agriculture has a nine-point buying guide for fresh fruits and vegetables. Somewhat paraphrased, it is as follows:

1. Take a good, close look at every piece of fruit or vegetable you buy.
2. Don't buy something just because it's cheap.
3. When trying to figure out which vegetables and fruits to buy, think of local production times and seasons.
4. It's foolish to buy more than you can use and keep before things begin to spoil.
5. Don't buy low-quality produce simply because it's cheap: if you end up throwing half of it away, you've actually paid twice the original price tag.

6. If a fruit or vegetable is big, it isn't necessarily good. In fact, smaller fruits and vegetables are generally tastier.

7. Learn which blemishes can be removed from fruits and vegetables without affecting the taste—and which defects should warn you not to buy that particular produce.

8. Peer under the top layer of fruits and vegetables sold in containers.

9. Handle fruits and vegetables gently: they damage easily.

"Apples should be firm and unbruised."

BUYING FRUITS In all cases, avoid fruits that appear to be either bruised or damaged by insects.

Apples Should be firm and unbruised. If they yield to slight pressure, they're overripe and will have a mealy texture. Brown spots and insect holes are signs of bad apples.

Avocados For immediate use, get one that's a little soft near the stem end; if you want to keep it a day or more, get one that is very firm (it will ripen at room temperature in two to five days). Do not buy avocados that are soft, cut, or bruised.

Bananas Are ripe and most tasty when the skin is deep yellow with brown dots. Bananas that are completely yellow, or yellow with green tips, should be allowed to ripen at room temperature. Do not buy bananas with brown skin, mold, or bruises.

Berries Should be plump, dry, and clean (check for stains or wetness at bottoms and sides of boxes). Look for consistent, strong color in berries.

Cantaloupes Are hard to evaluate. When they are ripe, the stem end is a bit soft. Avoid cantaloupes that are soft, bruised, wet at the stem end, or spotty.

Grapes If many grapes fall off when you gently shake the bunch, the grapes are not fresh. Grapes should be plump and not wrinkled.

Grapefruit Should be firm but slightly yielding to the touch. They should feel heavy, indicating juiciness.

Lemons Should be firm and bright yellow. Heaviness indicates juiciness. Avoid lemons that are shriveled or soft.

Limes See Lemons.

Oranges	Like grapefruit and lemons, oranges should be firm, heavy, and brightly colored. Mold and soft spots indicate decay.
Peaches	Should be quite firm; if they are too firm (but not green), they'll soon ripen at room temperature. Very soft peaches should be eaten at once.
Pears	Should not have brown or green spots, lumps, or mushy areas.
Pineapples	Are ripe if their stems come out easily, the outside has an orangy look, and they smell "ripe."
Plums	Should be pregnant with juice and resilient to light pressure. They should not be hard, soft, or spotted or have broken skins. Check containers for leaks.
Strawberries	Should be dry and bright red. Always look under the top layer in the basket: avoid soft or wet strawberries. Smaller ones are tastier than big, fat ones.
Watermelons	You can't tell from the outside if a watermelon is ripe, so buy watermelons in halves or quarters. The inside should be firm and very red. Avoid watermelons with white seeds, as they may be very young and therefore very dry.
BUYING VEGETABLES	In all cases, avoid vegetables that look dull and wilted.
Asparagus	Should be firm and moist-looking—not dry, tough, or with spread-out buds.
String Beans	Green or yellow. Test freshness by snapping one in half. It should be crisp, not soggy or wilted.

Broccoli	Should be dark green and firm, but not dry or wilted.
Cabbage	Should have firm leaves, none yellowed, and with few wormholes.
Celery	Should be crisp. Avoid celery with wilted leaves or soggy stalks.
Corn	Should be bright yellow or white, depending on the variety. Kernels should be firm and bouncy. Avoid corn with worms, dry husks or kernels, large, hard kernels, or soft, small kernels.
Cucumbers	Should be firm and not at all withered. Buy small cucumbers; big, fat ones taste "woody."
Eggplant	Should be neither wilted nor flabby. Should not have wormholes, dark-brown spots, or bruises.
Garlic	Should be clean, dry, hard, and with its outer skin intact.
Greens	Should look fresh, crisp, and green—not dried or wilted.
Lettuce	See Greens.
Mushrooms	Should be clean and fresh. Color: white or beige, with no spots. Closed caps mean fresh mushrooms.
Onions	Should be hard, dry, and mold-free.
Peppers	Should be firm and fresh-looking. Peppers decay easily, so be very careful to avoid those with any blemishes whatsoever.
Potatoes	Should have smooth skins and be very firm and dry. Avoid potatoes that are sprouting.

Rhubarb   Should be crisp and not wilted. Large stalks taste tough, so get relatively smaller ones. Beware: rhubarb *leaves* can be poisonous.

Squash   Summer: yellow or green squash should be firm and free of bruises. Fall/winter: acorn, butternut, and other varieties should have hard skins with no mold.

Sweet Potatoes   Should be firm and of more or less the same size, so that they'll cook evenly. Avoid sweet potatoes that are soft, wet, shriveled, or spotted.

Tomatoes   Should be fairly firm and uniform in color. Scars can be cut out before serving, but avoid tomatoes that have soft spots.

FROZEN FOODS of all sorts should be "hard as a rock" when purchased. Reach to the bottom of the pile in display cases—avoiding dirty and torn packages—and stop buying frozen foods in stores where you find soft packages.

CANNED GOODS should not be bought if the cans are dented or if they have swollen tops. Both of these problems can be signs of possible food poisoning.

When buying BREADS, remember that the darker breads (e.g., pumpernickel, whole wheat, etc.) are much more nutritious than the various tasteless, vitaminless, preservative-ridden brand-name white breads.

FOOD: ECONOMY   Most of us spend one hell of a lot more money on food than necessary. And why? Because food is the one thing we must buy—so we shut our eyes, clench our teeth, and buy quickly, to make the ordeal less painful. And, in our haste, we squander a depressing amount of money: the food that we devour in turn devours 20 per cent of our annual income. If we're lucky!!

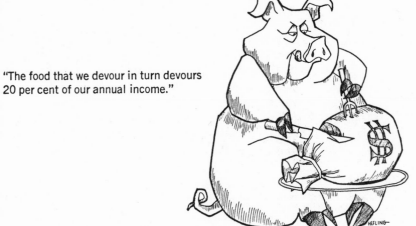

"The food that we devour in turn devours 20 per cent of our annual income."

It doesn't have to be this way. As in every other aspect of life, a little knowledge plus a little thought plus a dash of patience can cut your expenses to a "pale reflection of their former selves." This section will supply you with knowledge; you must provide the thought and patience. And you won't have to sacrifice food quality or quantity.

True, following all of the points I make, you may spend one and a half hours (at least at the beginning) per week in thinking, planning, telephoning, and comparative shopping. A lot of work? Perhaps. But if it saves each person in an apartment of four $150 per year on food (savings of 25 per cent, a conservative estimate), that's a total savings of $600, and your time will have been reimbursed at the rate of $8 per hour. Put another way, that's worth one and a half months of hard-earned pay at a nine-to-five job.

There are eight factors to consider in saving money on food. They are:

1. Quality: Buy food of good quality, to minimize waste.
2. Item: Some foods are inherently cheaper than others. And given any one food, prices vary as to grade and state of preparation. Learn what to buy without sacrificing taste or nutrition. Remember

that price and food value are not always related.

3. Brand: For any one food, brands of comparative quality differ in price and amount of high-quality ingredients per mixture. Learn what to look for when reading labels.

4. Store: Different stores vary widely in price. Do comparative pricing. Also, packers, distributors, and wholesalers can give you reduced food rates.

5. Season: Buy vegetables and fruits when they are in season. Freeze for later use.

6. Day: Food prices vary according to the day of the week. Check newspapers, avoid impulse buying, and shop once weekly. Never shop when hungry!

7. Quantity: It is often cheaper to buy a large quantity of a given item. Group together to buy food. Learn to schedule your shopping and weekly menu with regard to quantity. And know how to store foods properly.

8. High finance: Learn how to divide food costs equitably among roommates.

As you can see, there are many variable factors in the pricing of food. Knowing and exploiting these factors can save you a fortune; you will no longer be a pawn in the hands of advertisers and other "powers that be."

Quality   Study and follow the suggestions given earlier in this chapter on food quality. Also, keep your eyes open. Whenever you pass a market, make a mental note of prices. When shopping, watch what the old ladies are doing and talk to the grocers. In other words, be aware of food.

If you discover wines, or other foods, to be spoiled, sour, stale, or in any way bad—even if you've already brought them home and opened them—take the goods back to the store and demand either new products or your money back. It is your right to do this. And, if it's done with a smile, you won't have any trouble.

Item Meats cost more than Fish cost more than Poultry cost more than Vegetables and Fruits cost more than Starches (bread, cakes, potatoes, spaghetti, noodles, rice).

It would appear that, economically speaking, one should eat only starches. Indeed, most of the world's population live almost exclusively on starches. And they die young. The trouble is, starches have almost no nutritive value, and are fattening besides. They may be cheap, but then again, you're getting nothing for your money. The only starch I ever buy is rice, since it keeps forever, is easy to prepare and versatile, and is less fattening (I like to think) than the others. Regular enriched rice costs less than instant rice or packaged mixes—and is more nutritious. "Whole grain" and "brown" rices are even better, if you can find them.

Remember: Rolls cost more than bread, and cold cereals cost more than hot cereals.

Fruits and Vegetables As for vegetables, fruits, poultry, fish, and meat, they're all good, and what you buy is a matter of individual taste. Vegetables and fruits, if fresh, are a good deal cheaper than protein foods (meats, fish, and poultry). For that reason (among others), Zen and Chinese cookery have had a renaissance among today's youth. I suggest that you give vegetables a try—all vegetables. You say you don't like some of them? When was the last time you tried them? Taste buds change as you get older, so the things you despised as a child might actually taste very good now. It's true! And there are very tasty ways to prepare vegetables and fruits—ways that your mother, who probably

boiled the living daylights out of vegetables, never tried.

Also, if you have access to a bit of land, it is definitely worthwhile to plant a small vegetable garden. About one dollar's worth of seeds can yield a huge supply of vegetables. If you have no land, a small window box is an excellent place to grow herbs. Herbs can be dried for later use.*

* Your local library may have books on growing herbs and herb gardens. If not, ask your hardware-store man for advice. Children's museums are also good sources of such information.

Remember: Strictly speaking, fresh fruits and vegetables cost less than the same foods do when canned or frozen. But generally speaking, frozen vegetables eliminate so much waste and preparation time that they cost the same as or less than fresh vegetables.

Remember: Dark-green, leafy vegetables, like kale and spinach, contain more vitamin A than light-green vegetables, like lettuce.

Poultry

Poultry should be the foundation of every budget-conscious chef's repertoire. It is cheap and easy to prepare in an infinite variety of ways. Poultry—especially turkey and chicken—is frequently on sale; that's the time to stock up on it.

Fish

Fish adds variety to a menu and is usually just a little less expensive than good meats. Buy water-packed tuna during sales: you'll never regret having done so. It's cheap and can be made into hot and cold salads and casseroles. Since a can of solid white meat costs more than the same amount of grated light meat, buy grated for casseroles and sandwiches. Learn from your butcher which fish are in season at the time you are shopping, since fish prices vary enormously over the course of the year.

Meat

Meat is the most expensive food item. For that reason, let's pay close attention to it. When you buy a specific hunk of meat, two aspects of the meat itself help to determine its price:

1. The quality of the animal: how old and well fed was old Bessie?
2. The part of the body ("cut") from which the meat was hewn.

The federal government rates and labels the quality of meats (in descending order): Prime, Choice, Good, Standard, and Commercial. Cuts are

"How old and well fed was old Bessie?"

labeled with descriptive names: sirloin, T-bone, flank, etc. (see the previously mentioned book, *101 Meat Cuts*).

The chief points to remember are two. Though qualities and cuts may vary initially in tastiness and tenderness, meat is meat—it's all equally nutritious. And it can *all* be made tender and very delicious. This means that the cheaper grades and cuts should be bought frequently. Stews and pot roast, and even steaks, can be made from the cheaper cuts: chuck, flank, round, skirt, and Swiss. Stews and pot roasts are cheap and can be made in huge quantities; they store well and improve in flavor when reheated. Later in this chapter, several methods for tenderizing tougher meats are given, and every cookbook has suggestions for making good stews and roasts. Remember, too, that the best grades of lower-priced cuts are cheaper and tastier than the lower grades of higher-priced cuts.

Bacon

Contains so much fat that melts away that it is truly the most expensive of all meats. Buy it as lean as possible to reduce shrinkage waste.

Canadian bacon—I recommend Armour's, which comes in a block that must be sliced before frying—is both tastier and cheaper than the kind you are probably accustomed to eating.

Hamburger

Can be made from any cut or grade of beef. Use chuck for economy's sake, and have the fat trimmed from the meat prior to grinding. Watch the grinding yourself.

Lamb and Veal

Are expensive meats. Instead of buying "chops," buy shoulders of lamb or veal, and have the butcher cut these into chops. Sometimes—once in a long while—lamb will be cheaper than beef. Buy it then, and stock up.

Pork

Pork chops are also expensive. Buy "end-cut pork" or "pork steaks" instead. Or, buy "pork roast" and cut it into chops yourself (or have the butcher do it).

Chuck

"Chuck roast" can similarly be cut into steaks, for large savings in your steak bill. Buy a big chuck roast on sale and have it cut in three ways, to serve three meals: steak, roast, and stew meat.

Finally, remember that boneless cuts of meat often end up costing a good deal less per serving, especially when they are on sale, than the cheaper-priced bone-in cuts. This is a fact not generally known, and most people are deceived by the apparent savings of a bone-in cut.

So we have seen that some classes of food are cheaper than others, and that within each class of food, some are cheaper than others. One could live very cheaply and well on a diet of fruits and vegetables. Or if that wouldn't suit you, on a diet of vegetables and fruits supplemented with lots of poultry and well-prepared inexpensive meats. (Note: Use cheese, bean, and egg dishes now and then to replace meat for your daily protein. These three foods provide inexpensive variety.)

Five Final Points About Economizing on Food Items

1. Margarine and corn oils (Mazola, Crisco, Wesson, etc.) are much cheaper than butter and olive oil. Also, you may want to save fats from cooked foods (e.g., chicken fat and bacon drippings) to use for seasoning and future cooking. Finally, if you do buy butter, you'll find it more expensive when bought in one-fourth-pound bars than if purchased in a one-pound block and cut yourself. The excess can be frozen.
2. A gallon of milk is less expensive than four quarts. Also, evaporated skim milk is much cheaper than whole, liquid milk. Use the former in cooking.
3. "Instant mixes" and other convenience foods are much more expensive than the raw ingredients from which they were made. TV dinners, for example, cost up to three times what it would cost to make the same thing yourself. Don't buy vegetables with sauces or butter when you can melt the butter and add salt and pepper yourself with no trouble at all. In short, don't buy more "convenience" than you need.
4. Things packed in small quantities, such as cheese, cereals, and cold cuts, are much more expensive than larger, or unwrapped, quantities of the same food. Buy "cheese ends" at cheese stores, for about half the price. Or, buy grating cheese in

blocks, and grate it yourself on a grater or in a blender.

5. Frozen vegetables can be bought relatively cheaply in large plastic bags. Dump out only as much as you need for a given meal. Keep the rest frozen until you are ready to use it.

Brand

"Be careful to read and compare the weight and volumes stated on the package."

Many supermarkets package products under their own labels. These products are often just as good and—since no money was spent in promotional campaigns—are always far cheaper than advertised brand-name products.

Given any one product, prices vary somewhat from brand to brand. When you buy the cheaper one, however, be careful to read and compare the weight and volumes stated on the package. The size of a container may be deceptive; boxes or cans of the same size often contain different amounts of food, so that what appears to be a bargain is really a gyp. In order to see whether you are actually getting more for your money, perform the following mental arithmetic:

Divide the price of each item by the number of ounces the package contains. This will give you the price per ounce. Compare these among the brands you are considering.

Example:
A 10-ounce box of Munchies costs 60¢ (60¢ ÷ 10 = 6¢ per ounce)
A 9-ounce box of Crunchies costs 55¢ (55¢ ÷ 9 > 6¢ per ounce)
Moral: Buy Munchies . . . if you like them.

While you're reading the label to determine the weight, remember that ingredients must be listed in the order of descending quantity. That is, if the label of Joe's Beef Stew says that the can contains "potatoes, carrots, beef stock, meat, rice," there are more potatoes than carrots in the can, more carrots than beef stock (liquid), and a little bit of meat.

Finally, take labels seriously: "Orange Drink" is not orange juice. All juices must, by law, be labeled "juice," and anything that is not orange juice cannot be called so.

The above discussion of brands and of possible traps for buyers indicates, once again, that twentieth-century advertisers have made a science of old-fashioned sneakiness. Buyer, beware!

Store   Stores vary widely in price range, food quality, and degree of honesty. Many people buy food at the corner grocery store, which usually charges much more for canned, frozen, packaged, and staple items than a supermarket does. Even supermarkets vary in price range, quality, and honesty. Chain stores, such as A & P, also vary from place to place, according to the neighborhood and the management of a particular store.

Shop around your neighborhood, and get acquainted with the personnel and merchandise at local markets. Then, settle on regular grocers and butchers. You needn't go to the same store for all the different kinds of food you'll need, but settle on a regular group to patronize. Sellers who see you returning week after week are less prone to cheat you and will be more helpful in giving advice and suggestions and in pointing out particularly good bargains. This is true even in large, "impersonal" supermarkets. Trying to get to know the people you buy from is well worth the effort. This is true not only in markets but everywhere else as well. Treat the salesman like a "capitalist salesman," and he'll treat you like one of those "suckers born every minute." Seek his advice, and treat him as another person like yourself who just happens to have something for sale, and (there's a chance that) he'll be more sympathetic to your needs.

"Stores giving trading stamps boost their food prices."

Remember:

A. Stores giving trading stamps boost their food prices.·

B. Small fruit and vegetable stands often have better vegetables, fruits, and prices than supermarkets. And at the waterfront you can often buy cheaper and fresher fish than at supermarkets.

C. Different stores hire different numbers of check-out staff. Find out which markets are better staffed, so that you won't always be forced to kill half an hour waiting at every check-out line you encounter.

D. Avoid those small grocery stores where the turn-over of stock is very slow: you're more likely to end up with stale and spoiled goods. This is true for canned and cartoned, as well as fresh, foods.

Finally, look in your Yellow Pages under "Gro-cers—Wholesale," "Meat Packers," and "Meat—Wholesale." * These people are the middlemen who distribute foods to stores and restaurants. (See the discussion on quantity later in this chap-ter.) Since they sell mostly in quantity, and have a small store front and few personnel, their prices are much cheaper than those of retail markets. Such middlemen will often sell to you, too, if you make the effort to visit them at their business addresses and meet them on a personal basis. (Some things shouldn't be done over the tele-phone!) Frequently, but not always, buying from wholesale grocers or meat packers can save you a lot of money. Always be careful to make sure that you are indeed saving money per ounce, and don't forget to compare the prices of different wholesalers.

* Some cities have market districts, where food can be bought cheaply . . . if you have trained yourself to recognize good quality, f you can haggle, and if you know how to shop comparatively. Call your ocal police department to ask for the location of the nearest farmers' market.

Season

Your grocer will tell you which fruits, vegetables, and fish are in season—and therefore cheapest (even when frozen). Buy these foods, and store them in the freezer you bought several pages ago.

Day

In most supermarkets prices drop toward the end of the week. It is then that competing supermar-kets advertise their "specials." Usually, such sales are mentioned on Thursday in local newspapers. Ten cents spent on that newspaper can save you dollars. Buy it, check ads carefully, cut out the coupons, and plan your next week's menu (and freezer stock) with these specials in mind.

On Saturday most markets try to clear out all their fresh food stock, so that they can start the next week with new food. For that reason, Satur-day afternoon is the time to try haggling for lower prices in all stores, even in large supermarkets.

Another consideration about day is the following: do all your shopping at one time. Keep a running list of "Groceries Needed" on your refrigerator door, next to your list of "Food Money Spent" and to the "Tentative Weekly Menu." Whenever you run out of something, make a note of it, and before you go shopping, make a list of all the foods you'll need for the next week. Then, make sure you have enough staple items (flour, sugar, coffee, cereals, toilet paper, detergent, light bulbs). With a Grand List like this, you can do all your shopping on one day and at one time—saving yourself time, aggravation, and money (since you won't have to run out and get rooked by Friendly Al, your corner grocer, every time you need something).

Time of Day

If possible, shop in the early morning, as soon as the stores open. The stores are then empty, so personnel have time to help you, and you won't have to wait at the check-out line.

As I've said before, never shop for food when you're hungry. If you do, you can easily wind up buying all sorts of strange and unexpectedly expensive and useless items.

Quantity

* Remember that 'economy size" packages are not always cheaper, per ounce, than the smaller sizes. Also, if a sign says "four boxes for $1," don't feel that it's necessary to buy four boxes. Buy two and pay 50¢! Never buy more than you can use before it spoils.

Buying foods in large quantities reduces long-run costs. Quantity-buying permits you to take advantage of special sales, seasonal variations, and large packages, or even wholesale prices.* Also, buying in large quantity gives you haggling power with grocers and butchers.

But to buy in large quantity, it is necessary to have enough people to split the food costs and to eat the food before it spoils, and/or adequate room to store the quantity of food you buy.

For the first of these requirements, as well as for convenience, roommates often share food expenses and cooking responsibilities.** I suggest,

** If you plan to do this, be sure to decide whether each person is going to pay an equal share for all food purchased, or whether some foods will be shared and bought under a general food budget, while others will be paid for by each individual. Food staples (and toilet paper, soap, etc.) should always be purchased and shared communally, but sometimes one man likes yogurt and another doesn't —in which case, other financial arrangements may have to be made. Whatever you decide, definite rules should be set up on the very first shopping day, to preclude possible resentment and hassles. A discussion of food-expense budgeting is found later in this chapter.

however, that you expand this concept and think big: set up a food alliance among several apartments (say, twenty-five or thirty people), so that you can really take advantage of wholesale buying and bargaining. With a food alliance you can always buy fresh food in large quantities and distribute it to enough people so that it will be eaten with no waste from spoilage.

It is not difficult to establish a food alliance (many people do it), although it requires one person who is willing to spend four or five hours the first week, and then one hour each succeeding week, organizing and distributing food. Even if this person gets paid for his work by the others, everyone will save money. And if you promise a butcher or grocer a regular amount of good business (and threaten him with the possibility of going elsewhere), you can often get excellent meat at a low rate. You can also, of course, buy from wholesalers and at market districts. So, by putting notices up on local bulletin boards, and by calling your friends, quickly organize a food alliance.

Storage

If you don't have a food alliance, but still wish to buy food in large quantities, you'll need a good deal of pantry space and a large freezer.

Regardless of the quantity in which you buy your food, it is important to know how, where, and for how long food should be stored—before it spoils or loses its nutritive value. It's absurd to buy good food at good prices and then have to throw it out because it's begun to rot. By knowing where and how long to store food, you can avoid such waste.

Here is a quick reference guide to proper food storage (see Appendix 4B of this chapter for a full list of instructions).

Fresh foods should be used as soon as possible, since they deteriorate a little each day. Fruits and vegetables last about a week, although they deteriorate a little more each day of that week. Rinse celery, lettuce, and other greens, and refrigerate them in a tightly closed plastic bag. Meats and chicken should be kept no more than five days, unless they are cured (bologna, cold cuts, etc.), in which case they will last one to two weeks. The exceptions to these meat rules are hamburger and organs, or variety meats (livers, hearts, etc. —extremely nutritious, cheap, and delicious when prepared correctly), which are good for only a couple of days. Fish lasts one or two days only. Cheese can last for a month or more—if stored in a tightly covered jar.

Foods that come in jars, cans, or boxes—if they were stocked on room-temperature shelves in the store—can be stored in a cabinet, along with potatoes and onions. One year is the maximum time that canned goods should be kept. Once a can or jar is opened, however, its contents should be refrigerated, regardless of what the label says. Moreover, it is best not to store food in an opened can, but rather to transfer leftover contents to a covered jar. Throw out all leftovers, of any sort, after ten days.

When in doubt, refrigerate!

Freezer Tips

1. Using a felt-tip pen, mark packages with both the date on which frozen and the last date usable (see Appendix 4B of this chapter as a guide).
2. Place new packages toward the back or bottom of your freezer, so that the oldest food will be used first.
3. In the event of power failure, keep your freezer closed, try to buy Dry Ice to put in it (from dairies or ice-cream distributors), and—if the worst comes—organize a banquet.

High Finance, or How to Divvy Up Food Costs

Now that we've discussed how to buy food, let's talk about how to pay for it. For congenial roommate relations, it is important that no one feels he is being gypped when paying for groceries. Setting up an organized food-payment plan is therefore as necessary as splitting up the monthly rent.

There are two basic ways to divide your monthly food bill. They are the total-expense method and the meal-by-meal method.

The Total-Expense Method, or Equality Across the Board

In this payment system, each roommate shares equally in grocery costs. (Groceries include items like dish detergent, toilet paper, and light bulbs.) This system is a simple and practical one if all roommates eat roughly the same number of meals and entertain the same number of guests.

Keep an account sheet in an obvious place— on the multipurpose refrigerator door, for example. Each roommate should list every amount he spends on food. At the end of the month, total the amounts spent, then divide the sum by the number of roommates. This will give you each person's share of the expense. Finally, subtract the calculated "share" from the amount each person spent. Or, if "share" is more than "spent, ' ubtract the amount he spent from his share. From the final results, figure out how much who owes whom, so that everyone's total expense for the month is the same.

JULY, 1971

$ SPENT LIST

E	JOAN	JUNE
0	$40	$40

The Meal-by-Meal Method, or Equality on the Table

Though this system is more complicated than the one just described, it is often fairer; that is, though it takes an extra few minutes to make the calculations, it pays for itself in reduced intra-roommate resentment, especially in those cases in which certain roommates either miss a lot of meals or tend to invite large numbers of guests over for dinner.

Keep track of the number of meals each roommate and his guests consume per month. The easiest way to do this is to keep a tally on the refrigerator door, along with the grocery-expense tally. At the end of the month calculate each room-

JULY, 1971

MEALS EATEN

RK FOR GUESTS AS WELL AS YOURSELF

NE	JOAN	JUNE
+++	++++	++++
+++	++++	++++
++	++++	++++
+++	+++	++++
	++++	++++
	++++	++++
		++++
		++++
		++++
		++++

mate's share of the bill in the following way:

1. Tally the total amount spent. Divide this by the total number of meals, i.e., individual portions eaten by roommates and guests. This arithmetic will tell you how much an average meal for one person costs. In the example shown here, $100 was spent on groceries and 100 meals were eaten by Jane, Joan, June, and their various guests. Therefore, each meal that was eaten by a person cost the household $1.

    $100 ÷ 100 meals = $1 per meal.

2. Calculate each roommate's share of the bill by multiplying the number of meals he and his guests ate times the cost per meal.

    Example: Jane and her guests ate a total of 20 meals.

    20 × $1 = $20.

    Therefore, Jane's contribution to the month's grocery expenses should be $20.

3. Calculate the balance for each roommate by either subtracting the amount he paid from his share or subtracting his share from the amount he paid, depending upon which figure is larger.

4. From the balances, calculate who owes what to whom.

    Example: Joan's share is $30, but the records show that she spent $40 for groceries. Clearly, June, who ate relatively more than she paid for, should give Joan $10 before all accounts can be settled for the month.

FOOD: COOKING

Your "lab" is copiously supplied with tools and ingredients. And you're hungry. One last, simple step—COOKING—remains before you can enjoy your carefully purchased goodies.

What is cooking? A fine and mysterious art? A science? No! It is anything you choose to do—anything—to your raw ingredients before consuming them.

To be more explicit. Any ingredient you buy—

meat, poultry, vegetables, fruits—can be eaten raw, with no preparation whatsoever, if your taste buds like it and your teeth can chew it. All vegetables and fruits can be eaten freshly picked: the Japanese and others enjoy raw fish; oysters and clams on the half-shell are raw; and steak tartare is an elegant term for the delicacy of raw steak!

Cooking, then, is superfluous. I stress this point so you'll never ask, "How long should a raw Armpfark be cooked?" The answer is, since it doesn't have to be cooked at all, cook it as long as you damn well please, in any way that happens to agree with you.

Cooking Methods

Most people think of heating when the word cooking is mentioned. Heating does three things:
1. Kills bacteria.
2. Makes ingredients more chewable and digestible.
3. Blends flavors.

Since any kind of heat kills bacteria, never ask, "Should I bake it or fry it or boil it or broil it?" All these methods work! And every method will tenderize and blend flavors. A piece of chicken, for example, can be thrown (with a little butter) into a frying pan and cooked on top of the stove. That same piece of chicken can be tossed into a pot of boiling water and boiled for a while. Or, it can be stuck in the broiler and cooked by direct heat, or popped into the oven and cooked by hot air.

Who cares which method you choose? I certainly don't! Or for how long—so long as you don't burn that unhappy fowl. Each of the four heating methods—frying, boiling, broiling, roasting (or baking)—can be used to cook nearly any fish, fowl, meat, vegetable, or fruit.

So what's the big deal about cooking? All you have to do is to learn a few rules of washing, cutting, heating, and cooling, and you can do whatever you choose with your raw ingredients.

What about recipes? They're nice—but remember, they're simply elaborate ways of heating up ingredients. How is a recipe born? Somebody decides to cut up some raw onions and put them into a pan with some chicken. Why? Because he likes onions and happens to have a few in the pantry. He also likes green peppers, so he throws them into the pan, too. Maybe he has a couple of ounces of wine left over from last night's party—in they go. A little salt, and he's created a "new recipe." Bravo!

As you can see, recipes are neither sacred nor mysterious. They are simply guidelines to the practical and suggestions as to the possible. Nothing more. Always keep in mind how flexible cooking is, and never be afraid to add or subtract ingredients or to vary cooking temperatures, lengths, or methods.

We'll soon talk about selecting and working with recipes. First, however, a discussion of cooking techniques will serve to introduce you to cookery and keep you from starving. The following information will allow you to handle everyday cooking situations more easily. It will also provide information on how to alter those recipes you eventually select, according to your tastes.

Into the Pot   This section discusses the fundamentals of food preparation, including:
1. Heating methods.
2. Tricks in washing, peeling, cutting, sifting, and mixing.
3. Working with the most common ingredients.

Heating Methods   As we have already discovered, we can heat almost any food in many ways. The simplest methods for cooking food are:

On Top of the Stove: Frying and Boiling
Inside the Stove: Broiling and Roasting

Here's how to cook meat (or anything else) by each method.

Frying Cook on top of the stove, in a pan with fat. For all meats and vegetables.

* Brown: To fry briefly, no longer than necessary for the outside of the meat (or vegetable) to turn golden brown.

1. Melt a small amount of fat (e.g., vegetable oil, butter, Crisco) in the pan, and brown* the meat on both sides.
2. Season the meat (for example, shake salt and pepper on it).
3. With the pan uncovered, cook at medium heat until the meat is as done as you like it. Turn meat over occasionally as it cooks. For most meats, it is best to turn only once—half the time on each side—to maintain juiciness.
4. Remove meat from the pan. Serve hot.

Boiling Cook on top of the stove, in a pot with liquid. (If there's very little liquid in the pot, or if the liquid is just below the boiling point, this method might be called "stewing" or "simmering.")

1. If you wish, brown the meat first. If you're boiling eggs, start at Step 3—using cold water. Vegetables, including ears of corn, should be placed in the pot when the water has already begun to boil.
2. Season meat as you want it.
3. For soups, cover the meat with water. For pot roasts or stews, use just a cup or so of water, wine, consommé, stock, etc.
4. Add a teaspoon or two of salt.
5. Let the contents cook just below the boiling point (bubbling lightly) until the meat is tender (test by shoving a fork into it). If you're boiling spaghetti, noodles, or vegetables, let the water boil furiously.
6. If you're cooking a stew, add vegetables and potatoes well after the meat—about one-half hour before serving time.

Broiling Cook quickly by direct heat, from either above or below the food.

1. Set your oven dial for "broil." Start heating the broiler at least fifteen minutes before use, or place a metal oven rack over the stove's top burner, or

make a nice charcoal fire in a hibachi or charcoal grill, which should be used outdoors *only,* since charcoal releases lethal carbon monoxide when it burns.

2. Place meat three to five inches from the heat: thinner meat closer to heat, thicker meat farther from heat.

3. Broil until the side facing the flame is brown.

4. Season as desired.

5. Turn the meat and cook until the inside reaches the right degree of "doneness" for your taste. Juices coming from the top of the meat can be a sign that you should turn it. To make certain, cut into the center of the meat and look or taste.

6. If you are grilling vegetables, fruits, or other foods with the meat, place them on the cooking rack when you turn the meat over.

7. Season and serve the meat and trimmings while they're hot.

Note: Some foods, like chicken and liver, tend to dry out when they're cooked by direct flame. Brush these foods frequently with butter or pan drippings as they broil, and broil them relatively far from the heat (five to seven inches).

CLEANUP TIPS: By rubbing your broiling pan with a bit of fat from the food you are about to cook, you will help prevent the food from sticking to the pan. If you use a broiling pan with a rack that fits into it, either line the pan itself with foil, or fill it with about one-half to one inch of water. Both techniques make cleaning up much easier, though the second technique sometimes prevents the meat from browning well.

Roasting

This method uses a lot of hot air to good advantage. It is also called "baking" when applied to certain foods.

1. Season your meat as you like it

2. Put the meat in an open roasting pan, fat side up. The melting fat will help tenderize the meat. If the meat is very lean, rub all over with oil or put strips of bacon on top of it.

3. Insert a meat thermometer. The sharp tip of the thermometer should touch the center of the meat; leave the dial where you can see it easily when you open the oven door.

4. Leave the pan uncovered. Add no liquid.

5. "Roast" in a 300° to 350° oven.

6. Let the meat cook until it is as done as you like it. *Watch Your Thermometer!* For rare roast beef, figure about fifteen to eighteen minutes per pound. But to play it safe, see the chart of cooking times in the appendix to this chapter.

7. Vegetables and potatoes added to the pan in the last stages of roasting will cook in the meat's juices. When cooking vegetables and potatoes, it might be necessary to add a little water.

Note: Certain foods—notably turkey and chicken—tend to dry out as they roast. These foods should be basted (brushed) periodically with pan drippings. Alternatively, brush chicken and turkey with fat before putting them in the oven. Cover with a tent of aluminum foil—do not baste. To brown, remove the tent near the end of the cooking period.

"Watch your thermometer."

CLEANUP TIPS: Lining the floor of your oven with foil will make oven scouring much less tedious. When baking casseroles, grease the bowl lightly before you put the food in. This makes washing much easier.

Rules to Beat the Heat

1. Never think that a handle might not be hot. Even if you think that the stove is off, use a pot holder.

2. Fires on the stove are quenched by:
   a. Turning off the heat, and
   b. Covering the pot or pan with a cover.
   c. If that proves insufficient, throw baking soda—

never water—onto the fire.

3. If you get burned, apply neither butter nor ointment. Run over to the sink, turn on the cold water, and hold the burned finger, hand, arm, etc., under the running water for at least twenty minutes. Ice water and cubes in a deep pitcher are just as good.

Tricks in Food Preparation

Every women's magazine offers tips concerning food—peeling, cutting, mixing, etc. Why? Because these activities consume most of the chef's time. But, alas, this work cannot be avoided. Tips are fun to read and easy to forget, while washing remains washing, and cutting is cutting.

For this reason, I'm listing just a few good ideas for food preparation, omitting those that would serve only to clutter page and mind.

Washing

1. Vegetables and fruits can often be washed more thoroughly when you use a vegetable brush.
2. Chopped vegetables and fruits, berries, lettuce, etc., can be dumped into a big colander and rinsed together under the sink faucet.

Peeling

1. Peel over paper towels or newspaper. Afterward roll up the whole mess and discard.
2. Use a sharp vegetable peeler instead of a knife.
3. Tomatoes, peaches, etc., can be peeled by sticking them on a fork and rotating them over a gas flame. When the skin softens, rinse the fruit in cold water and the skin will come off easily. An alternative method is to plunge the fruit into boiling water, remove after a few seconds, and rinse in cold water.
4. Garlic Cloves: Pour hot water over cloves before removing skin.
5. Pineapple: Use a sharp vegetable peeler or a knife. Slice peels downward on chopping board. Alternative method: slice pineapple, then peel the slices.

"Use a cutting board
and a sharp knife."

Cutting and
Slicing

1. Use a cutting board and a sharp knife.
2. Lettuce: Rip apart with hands.
3. Vegetables and Fruits: Always cut several stalks or strips at the same time.
4. Mushrooms: Use both tops and stems, after removing the foot of the stem. If you have an egg slicer, employ it to cut mushrooms.
5. Onions: I hate peeling and cutting onions so much that I invariably buy chopped frozen onions or minced dry onions. For those who prefer to peel and cut their own, the following procedures will enable you to reserve your tears for other occasions:

   a. Always keep a few onions in the refrigerator. Cold onions don't give off as many tear-jerking vapors.

   b. Slice onions under running water, which sends the vapors down the drain, not up to you.

c. Slice onions before peeling them. The outer rings will then slip off easily.

6. Meats: It is easier to cut meats for shish kebab, hamburger patties, veal cutlets, in a semifrozen state.

Sifting

A sieve can be filled with dry ingredients (sugar, flour, etc.) and then shaken back and forth over a piece of wax paper. Why use a bowl? You'll only have to wash it later.

Measuring

1. Do not measure over the pot or bowl into which you're planning to put the ingredient being measured.
2. Always use measuring cups and spoons. If you're using the same cup or spoon to measure both dry and wet ingredients, measure the dry ones first.
3. Pack brown sugar down firmly when measuring it.
4. Sift flour before measuring it.
5. Break up lumps in all dry ingredients before measuring.

Mixing

1. Pour, mix, and handle foods over easily cleaned work surfaces, like wax paper. Not like the stove or floor.
2. Use your hands to mix dry and moist foods and salad. Don't be inhibited: no other tool (unless it's electric) can do as good a job. And besides, it's more fun to use your hands.
3. A deep pot with a handle won't move around as much as a mixing bowl if you hold onto the handle with one hand while mixing the ingredients with the other.
4. An electric blender is a great device to have around. Buy one used, if you can. You can cut up garlic, onions, bread crumbs, nuts, ice, and soft vegetables in them. And, you can make cold drinks and soups, or mix sauces and salad dressings in it.

Seasonings and Sauces

Seasonings and sauces should be added to your meat, fish, and poultry in the pot or pan you'll eventually use for cooking. Why wash two utensils?

Exception: When a recipe asks you to dredge or coat an ingredient such as meat, put flour and seasonings in a paper bag. Add the item to be coated and shake the bag.

Butter or Margarine

To soften sticks of butter or margarine quickly, put them in a sturdy plastic bag, twisting the opening of the bag tightly shut. Then hold the bag under hot running water.

Working with Some of the Most Common Food Ingredients

When you get right down to it, most of our diet is limited to the same old things, day after day. That doesn't mean, however, that we should continue to prepare them in the same old ways! The following suggestions have been compiled to make your everyday meals easier, cheaper, or more interesting to prepare.

Breakfast Foods, A Few Tips

Eggs

Fry eggs in large quantities by breaking a half dozen or so into a buttered roasting pan or baking dish. Add a little water and bake in the oven (350°) on the upper rack.

Boil eggs by putting them into a pot of cold water. Heat to a boil. Start timing: three to twelve minutes, depending on how you like your eggs.

Poach eggs simply by cracking them into a pot of boiling water. A tablespoon of vinegar will keep them from spreading out in the water. Fish them out when they look somewhat firm.

Scramble eggs in more than one frying pan if you have to make a lot. And remember: the more you scramble them as they cook, the better their texture and taste will be. Add a tablespoon or more of cottage cheese and a drop of milk to your scrambled eggs, it adds lots of flavor. Also, a bit of butter, after the eggs are cooked and on your plate, will do wonders.

Toast   Why buy a toaster? First try toasting your bread in the oven (400–450°), in the broiler, or in a frying pan. (Butter the top side of the bread before putting it in the pan.) These methods are nearly as quick as a toaster, enable you to prepare lots of toast at once, and cost less than a toaster! A lot less.

Bacon   Bacon is a fairly expensive breakfast companion. Don't be inhibited about serving other meats—sausage, hot dogs, steak—for breakfast, even though these may not be traditional "breakfast foods."

"Don't be inhibited about serving other meats for breakfast."

When frying bacon, invert a colander over the pan to reduce spatter and spare yourself a collection of grease blisters.

Pancakes
1. Mix the batter in a pitcher, and pour onto your frying pan or griddle.
2. Use several pans at once, so that your pancakes will have more room, and so that you can have them all ready to serve at the same time.
3. Pancakes are ready to be turned when lots of little popping bubbles appear on the top side.
4. Commercial pancake mixes are an unnecessary extravagance, since most cookbooks can tell you how to combine the raw ingredients in less than three minutes. Store-bought pancake mixes cost two to three times the value of the ingredients they contain.
5. Keep cooked pancakes warm by putting them on a plate and covering them with a cloth towel.

French Toast

French toast is a tasty morning dish that will help rid you of your leftover bread supplies. Simply put a couple of eggs, a cup of milk, and a little salt and pepper into a bowl. Mix this concoction well, dip and soak bread slices in it, and then brown the bread—both sides—in a buttered pan. French toast is delicious with maple syrup or powdered sugar.

Soup

Don't laugh. A good cup of soup is a marvelous breakfast, especially on cold winter mornings.

Meats, A Few Tips

Hamburgers
1. Use chuck meat. It's cheap but good.
2. Add liquid (water, wine) or an egg to the meat for juiciness.
3. Add shredded stale bread to inflate quantity (if necessary) and to add texture.
4. Hamburgers cooked slowly (low heat, long time) are tastier than those cooked quickly.

a. If you fry hamburgers on top of the stove, cover the pan and use a low flame.

b. Wrap patties in foil and broil in the broiler. Very tasty.

c. When you're making many, many hamburgers (or hot dogs) for a back-yard or dining-room picnic, use the following procedure: Line a baking pan with aluminum foil. Alternate layers of hamburgers or hot dogs with sheets of foil (maximum of three or four layers). Bake at about 350°: thirty to forty-five minutes for hamburgers, fifteen to twenty for hot dogs.

Steak: Broiling

1. Slice into the sides of the fat surrounding your steak, or else the edges will curl up. Make one slash every two or three inches.

2. Optional: Pierce the steak several times with a fork. Then marinate (soak) the steak for one or two hours in French or Italian salad dressing before broiling. An alternative marinade may be created simply by combining oil and vinegar (or wine).

3. Frozen steaks should be broiled almost twice as long as you would cook unfrozen steaks. Broil frozen steaks at a low temperature (350°), so that the surface doesn't burn before the inside cooks.

4. If your steak is thin (and/or if you want it rare), put it close to the heat source. If your steak is thick (and/or if you want it well done), start it close, then move it away from the heat for slower cooking.

5. Tenderize steaks by pounding them with a hammer wrapped in a towel or rag.

6. Avoid commercial, chemical tenderizers until science has figured out what they do to *our* flesh after they've finished destroying the fibers of the steak!

7. Let steaks stand a few minutes after cooking and before carving: makes for tastier, easier-to-carve meat.

Roast Beef, Pork, Lamb

1. Cheap (i.e., tougher) steaks and chops can be successfully baked in the oven. Line the pan with foil. Add seasonings. Place vegetables alongside. Cover the entire pan with foil. Bake at 300° for a good long while.

2. When cooking roasts (beef, pork, lamb), use a meat thermometer. It will tell you when the inside of the meat is ready. Remember the old saying: "You can't tell a roast by its cover!"

3. To make slicing easier, let roasts rest (covered with foil on your work surface) for fifteen or twenty minutes after cooking.

Chicken

Chicken is by far the cheapest and most versatile of meats.

1. Tenderize by rubbing all surfaces with lemon or lime juice.

2. Unconventionally fried chicken: Throw some bread crumbs into a bag; add salt and pepper, paprika, and anything else that's handy. Dump in one piece of chicken. Shake the bag like mad, remove chicken, and put in a baking pan that has an inch or so of oil in it. Flip the chicken over to cover it with oil. Repeat the procedure for your other pieces of chicken. Stick in the oven (preheated to 350°) for forty-five minutes to one and one-half hours—whatever is convenient. "Butter" with honey after bringing chicken to the table.

3. Boil chicken by dumping it into a pot, adding either nothing, or else some salt, bouillon cubes, peeled and halved onions, chopped carrots and celery, and/or anything else you have in the refrigerator. Cover the collection with water. Add one lid. Boil for an hour or two. You end up with a bunch of boiled chicken and a pot of chicken soup.

4. Broil chicken as is, or anointed with oil, butter, salt, seasonings, or anything else you see handy. Place your chicken pieces in the broiler or over a charcoal fire—farther from the heat than you

"Chicken is by far the cheapest and most versatile of meats."

would put steak. Turn the chicken over when the top side looks goldenesque. Broiled chicken tastes good with honey, too; add this condiment after removing chicken from the broiler.

5. If you're lazy, simply put the unfortunate beast on a pan and stick it in the oven at more or less 350°. A few strips of bacon on top will automatically baste it. Leave the chicken until you're good and ready to take it out.

Moral: Use your imagination when cooking chicken. Or don't bother to use it. Chicken responds beautifully to either condition.

Fish   Like everything else, fish can be cooked in any way: fried, baked, boiled, or broiled. Whatever you do, however, keep it brief! This is the most important rule about cooking fish!

1. Never broil fish more than twelve minutes.

2. When broiling fish, season simply. Melt some butter in a pan. Add salt and garlic. Slop some of this mixture on your fish, using a clean sponge, paintbrush, or official "baster" or "basting brush." Broil your fish five to seven minutes per side. It's by far the best method of cooking a good piece of fish.

3. Fish sauteed in butter is also pretty good. Dip fish in flour and salt and pepper. Have a mess of butter bubbling merrily in a pan on the stove. Put fish in pan, skin side up. Cook until browned on the bottom. Turn only once. Cook very briefly on the other side. This is good for small fish and fish fillets, since neither dries out during cooking, and takes about two or three minutes of cooking time per side.

4. Fish baked in the oven is fine when you're desperately in need of variety. Cover the fish with tomato sauce, onions, mushrooms, green peppers finely chopped, cream of celery or chicken soup, or other things of that ilk.

**Starches, the
Filling Part of
the Meal**

Spaghetti, noodles, rice, potatoes, and bread are cheap and filling. That's why we eat them. Any of them can be served at any meal whatsoever.

Since they are so cheap, always make more than you think you'll need. If you're short of something else, you and your guests can still fill up. Leftover starches (rarely do you have any) can be added to stews or casseroles. Or—since they cost so little—you can throw them out with few if any pangs of guilt. Then again, you can put them in a box on your window sill to feed birds and squirrels—thereby helping to maintain some semblance of ecological sanity.

Spaghetti and
Noodles

1. Add vegetable oil (a couple of teaspoons) to spaghetti or noodle water. Prevents boiling over, and also prevents sticking.
2. Make spaghetti sauce en masse when you make it. Leftover sauce can be frozen. Cook sauce in the oven rather than on top of the stove. When cooked at 250° for several hours, you rarely have to watch the sauce, and large quantities can be managed easily. Cover your baking pans with foil pierced by a fork to prevent your sauce from drying out.
3. When cooking spaghetti for many people, use either one huge pot or several smaller ones. Start your water boiling very early, since water invariably takes longer to boil than you expect.

Rice

1. Use brown rice (available at some supermarkets and all health-food stores) when you can get it, since it's tastier and much more nutritious than white rice. Second best is "long grain" rice.
2. Add two chicken or beef bouillon cubes to the boiling water. The taste is improved so much that you'll never want to be without bouillon.
3. Try chopping and browning an onion in the pot in which you plan to cook your rice. When the onion is golden brown, add the rice, bouillon,

and water. From there on, follow directions on the back of the rice box.

4. More water produces soggier rice. Less water produces drier rice.

5. Lemon juice tastes good on rice.

6. Drain rice and spaghetti in a colander placed in the sink. Tap the colander against the side of the sink to loosen clinging strays.

7. Add anything (tomato slices, green pepper slices, hot peas, pimientos, raisins) to rice, hot or cold, to make an eye-pleasing, tasty salad.

8. Rice is Nice. Serve it with every meal, in any combination of foods you can think of.

Potatoes   1. To fry them: Peel the potatoes and slice them into thin strips. Dump them into a frying pan in which oil is sizzling. Fry until golden. Drain on paper towels.

2. Potatoes take an hour or so to bake. If you rub butter on them first, their skins will be softer and tastier. Punch holes in the potatoes with a fork before tossing them into the oven. Remove them whenever you remember to do so.

3. Mashed potatoes are prepared in the following way: Peel and quarter the potatoes. Throw them into a pot of boiling water to which a little bit of salt has been added. Twenty minutes later, drain the water from the pot. Add a little milk and butter and squoosh the potatoes with a fork or "masher." A little bit of minced onion adds flavor to mashed potatoes.

Bread   1. Many people find that dark breads are tastier than light. Dark breads are definitely more nutritious.

2. Buy bread in a bakery, not in the supermarket, unless the supermarket just happens to carry unpackaged, fresh bread from a local bakery.

3. Biscuits are idiotically simple to make from packaged mixes. So simple, in fact, even I make them.

4. Somewhat stale bread and rolls can be made edible by dampening them slightly with water, then placing them in a brown paper bag and heating them in a warm oven.

Vegetables: Frozen, Canned, and Fresh

As we have already discussed, all vegetables can be eaten raw, and all are quite tasty in that state. The more you cook vegetables, the more soggy and the less nutritious they become. Moral: Cook vegetables briefly, and with as little water as possible.

Frozen Vegetables

Because they contain no waste and are nutritious, frozen vegetables are economical, especially when purchased on sale.

1. Firmly frozen packages are the only ones you should buy.
2. Keep frozen vegetables completely frozen until cooking time.
3. Cooking times differ. Follow directions on the package.
4. Before opening the package, whack it hard on all sides against a table or stove. This activity serves to break up the chunks and make the vegetables cook faster.
5. Sugar, pepper, salt, butter, lemon, onion pieces, and oregano (used alone or in combination) are good seasonings.

Canned Vegetables

Don't boil canned vegetables, just heat them. (They've already been cooked more than enough.)

1. Avoid bent cans or cans with swollen lids.
2. To prepare: Open can, pour off about half the liquid. Dump the remaining liquid, together with vegetable, into a pot. Heat.
3. If you choose to heat canned vegetables in the can:

   a. Open can. Place in a pan on the stove. Put enough water in the pan to reach about halfway up the can. Boil water briefly.

b. Remove label and then remove lid. Place can on bottom of oven while cooking roasts, etc. Heat ten to twenty minutes.

4. Season with anything (butter, lemon, lime, sugar, salt, pepper, onion, mint, thyme).

5. When fresh vegetables are out of season and expensive, add canned vegetables (cold) to salads. Examples: green or yellow beans, asparagus, carrots.

Fresh Vegetables

If eaten within a couple of days of purchase, fresh vegetables are much more nutritious than canned, and are somewhat more so than frozen. It's debatable as to whether they're ultimately cheaper than frozen vegetables, especially when the latter are bought under a store label.

1. Never soak fresh vegetables in water. They lose nutritiousness.

2. Don't boil fresh vegetables! Steam them. That is, put the vegetables in your pot and add about an inch of water. Cover tightly and heat fifteen to twenty minutes. Be sure to use low heat or the vegetables will burn. This method keeps them tasty, crisp, and nutritious.

3. Broil such vegetables as peppers, eggplant, and tomatoes, especially if you're broiling meat for the same meal.

4. Bake potatoes, squash, tomatoes, and eggplant if you're roasting meats at the same time.

5. Quick-fry vegetables for variety. Put vegetables in hot oil. Stir constantly for a couple of minutes. Try adding hard fruit slices (apples, pears, etc.) to a combination of vegetables (e.g., cucumber, carrots, cabbage) when quick-frying.

6. If quick-frying doesn't make the vegetables soft enough for you, drain the oil after a couple of minutes. Add a small amount of water and steam the vegetables. The oil will have sealed in the flavors of the fruits and vegetables; the steam will soften them.

Sandwich Suggestions

Sandwiches can be made, wrapped, and frozen well in advance. Since they take about three hours to thaw, you can take them out at 9 A.M. and have them for lunch at noon. Don't freeze sandwiches with mayonnaise, and don't store sandwiches longer than two or three weeks.

Drinking Tips

1. Get used to drinking water with meals. Tasty, nonfattening, thirst-quenching, and cheap.
2. Experiment with different kinds of tea, many of which come in loose (unbagged) form. Place loose tea in one of the special metal containers available at hardware stores. These containers are perforated, and serve as reusable "tea bags."
3. Soda and wine can be chilled most quickly in the freezer part of your refrigerator. But don't forget you put them there!
4. Ice:
   a. Collect and store ice cubes in plastic bags in the freezer.
   b. Crush ice by wrapping a few cubes in a towel, twisting up the end of the towel. Place this package on a hard surface and hit it with a mallet, pot, shoe, or other handy weapon.

Soups

1. Serve soup in cups for easy drinking.
2. Don't be afraid to add things to canned soup: milk or wine; canned mushrooms; cooked and chopped-up hamburger or hot dogs; leftover rice or vegetables.
3. Try mixing different kinds of soup, such as one can of pea soup and one can of vegetable soup.

Desserts

This is a delicate topic, since everyone has his own idea of what constitutes a dessert. Some people eat *no* dessert. Some like only fruit, cheese, or nuts (items that other people eat only as before-dinner appetizers).

Let me commend, to those who choose to live cheap and good: Fruit, Puddings, Gelatins.

I omit pastries, since they are relatively expensive to buy and a pain in the neck to make. (I've been told, however, that ready-mixed cakes are fairly easy and can be doctored up with little effort.)

1. Fruits can be served hot or cold, sliced or whole, topped with liqueur, cream, nuts, etc.

   a. All fruits can be baked—most with good results. Add brown sugar and lemon (or lime) juice before baking.

   b. Fruits can be frozen. Send twenty cents to: Superintendent of Documents, U.S. Government Printing Office, Washington, D.C., 20402, for the booklet entitled "Freezing of Fruits and Vegetables."

2. Puddings and gelatins are easy to make. Follow directions on the package.

   a. For faster cooling: Divide in two the amount of liquid called for. Heat one half and dissolve pudding or gelatin in it. Add this mixture to the remainder of the liquid (which is still cold). Your pudding or gelatin will chill faster. If recommended on the package, ice cubes can also be used to speed chilling.

   b. Gelatins and puddings can also be chilled, quite quickly, in the freezer part of your refrigerator. Be careful not to freeze them.

   c. Add chopped nuts or fruit to puddings and gelatin while they are still in the liquid state. When the puddings and gelatins chill, they can be cloaked with cream or chocolate sauce if you choose; otherwise, they can be left standing naked.

MEAL PLANNING—I

Thus far, we've considered buying foods and basic preparation techniques. Now, how do we wed food and knowledge and wind up with a meal?

Recipes

Many cooks are slaves to recipes: if they didn't have one, chances are that they'd starve. A meal, they think, requires secret formulas that only authors of official recipes can devise. We've seen and will see, however, that recipes are fairly arbitrary and that it takes only a little creativity to "create" a tasty dish.

Still, for the beginning cook, recipes provide good guidelines and should be followed carefully. So, I suggest you make yourself a collection of recipes with which to start off your culinary career. But Don't Go Out and Buy Any Expensive Cookbooks! Cheap and good recipes can be gotten by the thousands from:

1. Public and school libraries, which invariably have a good selection of cookbooks. Borrow them! (Nobody else does.)
2. *Women's Day, Good Housekeeping,* and *Family Circle* magazines—available at most grocery stores—contain each month enough recipes to keep you much more than busy. Men: Don't be hung up about buying such "feminine" reading fare. Whisper to the cashier to hide them amid your groceries, and when you get home, you'll find them fascinating.
3. Newspapers usually carry recipes.
4. Your local gas, electric, and oil companies will often have giveaway cookbooks and pamphlets.
5. Good recipes are sometimes printed on the backs of food packages.
6. One of the best sources of recipes is mothers.
7. The U.S. Government Printing Office (Superintendent of Documents, U.S. Government Printing Office, Washington, D.C., 20402) will send you copies of many great recipe and cookery pamphlets. Considering Uncle Sam's ineptitude in some other departments, it seems amazing that he is such a fine chef. But he is.

The following is a partial listing of available government cookery pamphlets. Allow six to seven weeks for delivery.

"It seems amazing that Uncle Sam is such a fine chef."

Beef and Veal in Family Meals	15¢	Cat. No. A 1.77:118
Dare to Excel in Cooking	25¢	Cat. No. D 201.2:C77
Eggs in Family Meals	15¢	Cat. No. A 1.77:103/2
Family Fare, Food Management, & Recipes	30¢	Cat. No. A 1.77:1/5
Fish for Compliments on a Budget	15¢	Cat. No. I 49.49/2.9
Fruits in Family Meals	15¢	Cat. No. A 1.77:125
Honey, Some Ways to Use It	10¢	ιCat. No. A 1.77:37/2
How to Cook Halibut	20¢	Cat. No. I 49.39:9
How to Cook Tuna	20¢	Cat. No. I 49.39:12
Lamb in Family Meals	15¢	Cat. No. A 1.77:124
Let's Cook Fish, a Complete Guide to Fish Cookery	60¢	Cat. No. I 49.49/2:8
Money Saving Main Dishes	20¢	Cat. No. A 1.77:43/3
Potatoes in Popular Ways	15¢	Cat. No. A 1.77:55/3
Poultry in Family Meals	15¢	Cat. No. A 1.77:110/2
Principles of Cookery	₊5ʹ	Cat. No. A 1.68:692
Tips on Cooking Fish and Shellfish	10¢	Cat. No. I 49.2:F53/8

The pamphlets suggested above are only a few of the thousands that you can write for. If you wish a complete listing of cookery pamphlets, write to the Superintendent of Documents for the free price list entitled "Home Economics: Foods and Cooking—Price List 11."

If you must buy a few cookbooks—again, I repeat, there's absolutely no need to waste the money—avoid large, encyclopedic compilations (which often neglect to select recipes or sift information carefully), and get a cookbook that:

1. Has straightforward names for recipes: "Beef Stew with Carrots," rather than "Aunt Susie's Super Stew."
2. Contains a good index.
3. Is well organized.
4. Stays open flat (not always possible).

For a superb introductory cookbook, buy *The I Never Cooked Before Cook Book,* a paperback by Jo Coudert, Signet No. T 2797. Clear, dependable, and well organized Invest the 75 cents.

For a few laughs, buy: *The I Hate to Cook Book* (paperback), by Peg Bracken, a Fawcett Crest Book.

For a complete and cogent approach to cookery, buy either *The James Beard Cookbook*, Dell, Laurel edition, or *The Fanny Farmer Cookbook* (paperback or hardback).*

For a cheap but good set of recipes—borrow the four cookbooks I've just mentioned from your local library.

* It is my opinion, and the opinion of many cooks I know, that *The Joy of Cooking* is greatly overrated and should serve, if anything, as an addition to, rather than a substitue for, other cookbooks.

Recipe Filing

After a month of cooking, you'll have an unmanageable, disorganized pile of loose notes and clipped-out recipes, unless you start out by buying a 3 x 5 card file (fiber-glass ones are cheaper than metal), and file your recipes in some semblance of order.

On Using Recipes

Analyze your recipes, rather than following them blindly and unquestioningly. Keep asking why am I doing steps 2 and 3 in this order? Why for this length of time? Why in this way? If you keep asking such questions, soon you'll never need a recipe.

For example, ask: "Why does the stew recipe say to put meat in the pot first, green peppers second, potatoes later, and tomatoes last?" Answer: Since you want everything to end up as soft as (and not any softer than) everything else, it is necessary to cook harder, tougher things longer than soft things. If you pay attention to recipes, you'll soon know which foods take how long to cook—and adding ingredients at the proper intervals during cooking will become second nature.

MEAL PLANNING—II

Variety is not only the spice of life, it is also the best seasoning for food. When trying to figure out "What the hell should we have for dinner," think "contrasts."

Designing a Meal

Nutrition	In every meal have some protein (meat, poultry, fish, eggs, cheese, milk); some vegetables (green, yellow, etc); some starch (bread, rice, noodles, potatoes).
Temperature	Serve cold foods together with hot ones. Regardless of the season, this is always a safe bet for a happy meal.
Color	Any brightly colored food adds striking appearance, class, and even taste to meals. Add tomato slices, paprika, parsley sprigs, apple quarters, etc., to plates of almost any kind of food.
Flavor	Use sweet dishes with sour ones; strong flavors with mild ones. And don't use the same food more than once per meal.
Texture	In any given meal, plan to have a group of dishes that contrasts the smooth with the crisp and chewy. It makes a big difference.
Shapes	Juxtapose food that's sliced in round pieces with strips or with mounds. And remember, it takes no more time to arrange different foods attractively on one big platter than it does to put them on separate dishes—and there's less washing up later on.

I'll never forget one meal, prepared for me by a beautiful young maiden. We started off with French bread, still warm from the oven. The main course consisted of buttermilk pancakes and mashed potatoes. Can you believe that I turned down the angel food cake dessert? Admittedly, Janice had never read this book. So I forgive her.

Let's face it—eating is fun, even more fun than cooking. So design your meals well—and eat well!

"Plan the week's menu before doing the weekly shopping."

MEAL PLANNING—III

Thinking Ahead

1. Plan the week's menu before doing the weekly shopping. Consider main dishes that can be eaten twice; which is another way of saying, plan on using Monday night's leftovers on Thursday night —or at least for a lunchtime snack on Tuesday.

   For example, if you're making fried chicken anyway, make yourself an extra half-dozen pieces. During the next few days, you can eat them cold, warmed-over, or in sandwiches.

2. Make your cooking a "One-Shot Deal." Fifty per cent of the time you spend cooking consists of waiting for something to happen: the stove to heat up, this or that to get done. To best utilize that potentially wasted time, prepare tomorrow night's meal, too, and refrigerate or freeze it. Many cooks prepare a whole week's worth of food on one mammoth Sunday afternoon cooking spree!

3. If you're not ambitious or well-organized enough

to follow the above suggestion, the least you can do is to make double batches of whatever you are cooking for dinner. It takes very little extra time to make four quarts of a stew, for example, instead of two quarts. If you refrigerate the extra stew, it'll last several days. Frozen, four to six months.

a. Double your recipe, thereby cooking twice as much food.

b. Do your cooking in two pots or casseroles (at the same time).

c. Line one of these cooking vessels with aluminum foil before cooking.

d. Undercook by about one-third the food in this pot. That is, if the casserole, for example, is supposed to cook for two hours, cook the one to be frozen only an hour and twenty minutes to an hour and a half.

e. While you're eating the finished casserole, let the food to be frozen cool.

f. Put the whole thing, pot and all, into the freezer.

g. Next day, lift the frozen food out of the pot, wrap it up tightly in the foil, and leave it in the freezer.

h. When you eventually reheat the frozen casserole, do it in the pot in which it was originally prepared.

This is a great method for stews, casseroles, spaghetti sauces, and soups.

COOKING THE MEAL: TIMING

The most difficult thing about cooking a meal is making sure that everything ends up ready to eat at the same moment. But just three minutes of planning the night before will guarantee a well-timed supper the next day.

First, decide on the menu. (Let's say it's steak, rice, frozen peas, bread, pudding.) Then decide on the serving time (6:30 P.M.). Then, with a pencil and paper, work out the timetable you will have to follow. Remember that:

1. In the late morning you'll have to defrost the steak

and put the pudding in the refrigerator so it will have time to jell.

2. Since rice takes about twenty-five minutes to cook, you'll have to put it on at 6:05.
3. Since the steak takes twelve minutes to broil, you'll want to put it on at about 6:15. But since the broiler must be preheated, you'll have to turn it on at 6:00.

"The most difficult thing about cooking a meal is making sure that everything ends up ready to eat at the same moment."

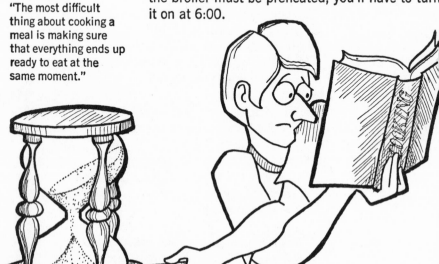

4. The frozen peas take ten minutes to bring to a boil and five minutes to simmer. You should start them at 6:15.

On a scrap of paper, then, you will have jotted down the following timetable:

A.M. Defrost steak.
A.M. Put pudding in frig.
6:00 P.M. Broiler on.
6:05 Rice—boil.
6:10 Rice—simmer.
6:15 Steak and peas on.
6:25 Simmer peas and flip steak.
6:30 Serve dinner.

Regardless of how simple or how complicated

your meal, three minutes of such written-out fore-thought—together with a trusty watch or kitchen timer—will make you a chef admired for your "sense of timing." Nothing will ever burn and nothing will be forgotten. Your mind can be at rest as long as your timetable is by your side (this means that you can chat and not worry about for-getting things). Furthermore, cold things will be served cold, hot things hot. And no one will have to wait for hours while you figure out what the hell you're doing. Eventually, this kind of planning will become second nature.

Timing Tips: Temperature Considerations

1. Defrost things in time, so that you can cook foods from room temperature. Cooked "icicles" don't taste very good.

   a. If you think ahead, move frozen meats, poultry, or leftovers from freezer to refrigerator the night before using them. (This is the best way to thaw frozen foods.)

   b. Otherwise, take things out early in the morning and leave them on a work surface.

   c. If you're really caught short, you can defrost things by heating them in a pot of hot (not boiling) water.

2. Always preheat your oven or broiler for fifteen or more minutes before you put food into them.

3. Never keep spoilable foods ("perishables") at room temperature for more than three hours.

4. It always takes much longer than you anticipate to boil water. So, put on a pot or two of water before you begin cooking. Once it's boiling, it takes little heat to keep it that way! And, whether you've planned on using it or not, it always comes in handy—for rice, noodles, coffee, vegetables, etc.

5. Put wine, soda, puddings, salads, into the re-frigerator early. There's nothing worse than some-thing being warm when it should be cool and refreshing.

178

Standard Recipe
Errors

A. Cooking Time: When a recipe says a food item should cook for a given length of time, that's only an approximation. Every oven, stove, and palate is different; watch and taste frequently whatever you're cooking.

B. Number of Portions: There is a convention among recipe writers: always tell your readers that your recipe serves a lot more people than it does. When a recipe says "serves eight," it means it serves five to six. When it says "serves six," it means it serves four. And when it says "serves two," it means that it is an appetizer. Moral: Make about one-third more portions than your recipe says is necessary.

A Semblance
of Order

1. Line up all your ingredients and utensils before starting to cook. Put them far away to one side as soon as you use them. This avoids:
   a. "Where the hell is the sugar?!?"
   b. "Oh God, did I already put the sugar in or not?"
2. Save jars and their covers for food storage.
3. While you're cooking, put wet stirring spoons and spatulas on a saucer next to, or on top of, the stove.

Tasting: The Key
to Good Cookery

Remember our original postulate: cooking is superfluous, so cook as long as you want and put in whatever you want?

Well, when you cook, every stage that a dish goes through is potentially a finished product. So taste it. Good cooks sniff and taste continuously. How else can you know whether you've prepared something you'd like to eat? Don't look at the cookbook; it won't tell you whether you like what's in the pot. See if it's as hot, or moist, or salty, or thick, or well done as you like it.

How do you know if those hamburgers are raw inside? Break one open and look! Cut that steak open; taste that spaghetti sauce. Stick a fork into that vegetable, and see if it's still too crunchy for you. In short, from the moment you start cooking a dish, taste and continue to ask yourself, "Do I want to eat this now?" And if not, why not?

The Minutes Between

While you cook, there are always a few spare minutes. And cleaning up as you go prevents headaches and future work. All I ask is that the moment you finish with a pot or pan, you put it in the sink and fill it with hot water and detergent. For this one little suggestion, you will continue to thank me for as long as you cook.

Furthermore, rinsing out pots and bowls during "the minutes between" allows you to reuse them while cooking.

Good idea, eh?

DINNERTIME

The Dinner Table

O.K. Your meal's been cooked, the guests—and you—are hungry. Where will you eat? For many people, the answer is: on the kitchen table.

But some of us don't have big enough kitchens for tables, and others of us don't enjoy eating within smelling distances of stoves and eyeshot of dirty dishes. And most of us are blessed with neither dining room nor "kitchen nook."

So get a "hollow-core door." If it's damaged on one side (which won't bother you or your diners), it won't cost more than six or seven bucks at a lumberyard.

This door, when stained, will make an elegant banquet table. Simply get a couple of wooden (milk) boxes, or some cinder blocks or stools, for supports, and you can set up your groaning board in the living room in less than one minute. Such a table is cheap, can serve eight people (seated on the floor or on cushions) with ease, and can be hidden behind the couch or against a wall when not in use. Painted or decorated, those two boxes can be used for storing things, or as stools or end tables.

The Tablecloth

By far, the cheapest and easiest-to-clean table-cloth is one of plastic or lightweight vinyl. Available at hardware stores, discount houses, and fabric shops, these can either be draped over the table when needed, or wrapped over the table top and thumbtacked to the underside.

Such a cloth never needs machine washing. Sponges off clean! (Use ammonia on the sponge.)

Serving Dinner

1. Serving is usually easier if you cook food and serve it in the same utensil.
2. Remember that foods can be kept warm (without being overdone) if left in a closed oven, at lowest heat, or even after the oven's been turned off.

FACING THE MESS-HALL MESS

All facets of life can be made easier by thinking ahead now and then. Dredging out and cleaning up a postmess mess is no exception.

It's already been noted that the simple act of filling all pots with detergent and water immediately after use (and before eating) can save many painful hours of scrubbing. Still—amazingly enough—few people bother to do it.

The principle is simple. While food remnants are soft and mushy, they can be dissolved and rinsed away painlessly. Once hardened into a mass of bubble-gum or cementlike consistency, burned and leftover foods are a challenge even to a coal miner.

Moral: Water your pot.

"The postmess mess"

Along similar lines:

1. Spills and spatters are harder to remove when dry. Wipe things up quick with paper towels.

   Note: Bath towels sop up floods faster than mops can—and they're usually easier to find in times of crisis!

2. Dishes: Right after dinner, fill the sink with water and detergent. Scrape large scraps from dishes and dump all tableware into the sink to soak. You may not get to the dishes until the next morning. But whenever you do, you'll be glad you spent one minute putting them in the sink to soak.

3. Broilers are easier to clean if you drain the grease from them right after use and then sprinkle some cleanser and water on them. This, too, is a way of saving fifteen minutes of work with ten seconds of foresight.

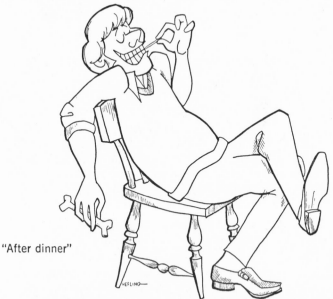

"After dinner"

After Dinner

1. Leftovers should be put in glass or plastic containers (e.g., old ice-cream boxes). Not in aluminum. Cover with Saran-Wrap or Handy-Wrap or Glad-Wrap. Refrigerated, leftovers will keep a

few days; frozen, four to six months. Warning: Things expand when they freeze. Don't fill containers to the top or they'll explode.

2. Dishwashing

a. Soap pads are a rusty, unnecessary expense. Instead, buy nylon scraping pads at the grocery or hardware store.

b. Rubber gloves protects hands. Even men's hands.

c. Do not soak wooden bowls, spoons, or cutting boards or any utensils with wooden handles. The wood will split sooner or later, and it'll probably be sooner. Clean cutting boards and wooden bowls with a combination of salt and lemon juice, or simply wipe with a damp sponge.

d. Iron pans should be washed infrequently. Never scrape them when washing. In fact, iron pans are best cleaned by wiping them with paper towels.

When you do wash them, they must be dried immediately and very thoroughly; otherwise, rust spots will develop. If you have rust problems, rub a bit of oil into the pan and then heat the pan on the stove.

e. Dish Drying: After they've soaked a while, dishes can be rinsed off and placed on the draining rack. Let them air dry! Wiping dishes is a superfluous neurosis. In fact, towels are breeding grounds for bacteria, so it's safer to let dishes dry by themselves.

Note: If you have more dishes than will fit in the drainer, do your dishwashing in batches, fifteen minutes apart.

f. Coffeepots, metal or glass, can be well cleaned once every month or so in the following way:

1. Dump a couple of tablespoons of cream of tartar into the coffeepot. Fill with hot water.

2. One-half hour or an hour later, rinse the coffeepot thoroughly, or boil for a few minutes and then rinse immediately.

g. Food Stuck in Pots: If the food is really stuck

or burned on, don't try to clean it out immediately. The experience is far too frustrating.

Fill the pot with hot water and detergent, or better yet, with hot water and lots of ammonia. Let soak overnight. The next day, you'll be able to chisel out the food more easily.

h. Stove Tops, if wiped with a little cleaner after every meal, will never require a major cleaning.

If you line the pan under each burner with aluminum foil, you can periodically renew the liner and never have to scour up sticky, burned globs of food.

Broilers are a pain in the neck to clean. Instead, line the entire bottom of the pan with aluminum foil. After a meal or two, this can be gathered up and thrown out. Then, all you need clean is the broiler rack: put it in the sink to soak with the rest of your pots and pans.

i. Sinks: Rinse clean and never pour coffee grounds down the drain—or you'll eventually end up with a backed-up drain.

WEEKLY KITCHEN MAINTENANCE

The trick to keeping a well-maintained kitchen is to start by telling yourself no lies. Let's face it. Unless you're a member of the older generation, your kitchen will never be immaculate, or even very clean. After the first week or two of apartment living, it's very easy to be oblivious to all kinds of dirt.

Only a supreme effort will keep your kitchen in decent shape. That means a full twenty minutes per week of work! Sure, that's a lot of work; but if you set up a specific hour for it, say Sunday evening (when most roommates are home), it'll get done. More or less.

1. Stove: Wipe off stove and work areas, using a sponge (not the dish sponge), powdered cleanser (like Ajax), and elbow grease. When needed, ammonia will clean anything off of anywhere!

2. Refrigerator:

a. Throw out unused leftovers, overripe fruits and vegetables, and moldy foods of all sorts. "Good" leftovers can be used. Remember the old saying: "Old vegetables never die, they just become stews and casseroles"? Well it's true!

b. Defrost your refrigerator as needed (see Chapter 3).

3. Sink: Scour the sink bowl and put a couple of tablespoons of regular old baking soda down the drain.

4. Cutting Boards: Clean cutting boards, in the manner mentioned above, using salt and lemon juice. Never soak.

5. Towels: Throw dish towels and pot holders into the weekly (or semiweekly) wash.

6. Pots and Pans: Tighten loose handles with a Phillip's screw driver. If the pot is dented, hold a block of wood over the concave side of the dent. Tap out dent with light hammer blows.

7. Knives: Give dull knives a quick, five-minute sharpening on an "oilstone" or "whetstone" bought at the hardware store. This can be done some evening, after supper, when you're sitting around chatting at the dinner table—or else during TV commercials while others are knitting,

swearing, or snoring. Alternatively, sharpening can be done (although this isn't quite as good for the knife) using a plain metal file, four or five inches long. These, too, are available quite cheaply at hardware stores.

Do not use the small metal sharpeners often attached to walls, counters, and cutting boards. They ruin knives.

8. Sweep the Floor. Wash it when your guests start complaining.

If the above work is faithfully executed, you will be able to rest calmly in the knowledge that even your mother would be proud of you—could she but see the labors you've just performed.

Good Readers:

We've marched a long trail through this chapter. The going may have been hard, but success will shine brightly upon each of you.

Basic training is over. Yet, for you courageous men and women, the battle of teeth vs. food has just begun. I give my word, however, that if you but dedicate yourselves to the values, standards, and principles learned here, in these, the culinary annals of Fort Poriss, you *will* cook well.

Bight Fiercely!

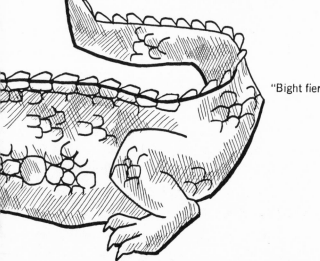

"Bight fiercely."

APPENDIX 4a

SEASONINGS FOR ALL TASTES

A "seasoning" is anything you decide to add to your raw food ingredients in order to change the way they taste. Spices, herbs, bouillon, wine, lemon, lime, jelly, mustard, chili sauce, soy sauce, mayonnaise, etc., all fall in this category, since they're used for taste, rather than for nutrition or substance.

Seasonings have always been used to mask the taste of low-quality ingredients. Nowadays, with better quality food, we still use seasonings to make cheap or uninteresting foods taste good and to make good and interesting foods taste even better. Spice and herb charts indicate how different foods have been traditionally seasoned. But there are no real rules except:

EXPERIMENT AND SEE WHAT SEASONINGS APPEAL TO YOU!

Suggestion I — Don't use so much seasoning that you can taste little else.

Suggestion II — Don't shake a seasoning directly into the food. Measure it with a measuring spoon. Or at least shake the spice (including salt and pepper) into your hand so you can see the quantity you're using. Then, dump it into the food . . . and stir well!

Suggestion III — If you season meat, poultry, etc., a few hours before cooking it, the seasonings will penetrate all layers of the food.

One Method
1. First mix seasonings together.
2. Then rub all surfaces of the meat or poultry with this mixture.
3. Refrigerate the food until about an hour before cooking time.

A Few Well-Seasoned Suggestions

Butter

Is used for its good taste as much as for its properties as a grease. If you can afford its cost and calories, use it. Melt it on the stove and add spices, wine, or whatever to it. Then coat vegetables or meats that are either cooked or about to be cooked. Margarine can be used in the same way.

Bouillon

Add it to the boiling water when making rice, noodles, or anything else you choose.

Cheese

When melted, makes a good sauce. Instead of using sliced or hard cheese, try using either soft cheese sauce or cheese soup (packaged or canned).

Garlic

Is used by many to season any meat, vegetable, or pasta. Either peel and cut the garlic into tiny pieces and rub the raw food ingredient with the garlic, or use garlic powder (not garlic salt) shaken as is or dissolved in melted butter.

Honey

Use on bread, to coat fried or baked chicken, or instead of sugar in your tea.

Lemon Juice

I use lemon (or lime) juice on everything: squeeze some on meats and fish and poultry before cooking, baked potatoes and vegetables after cooking. Lemon will also cut down the sweetness of fruits. Use bottled lemon juice if you're lazy, like me.

Mushrooms

Frozen, canned, or fresh, are a happy (even if relatively expensive) addition to meats, poultry, fish, and vegetables. In fact, if you like them, mushrooms go well with anything! Raw or cooked. Never cook mushrooms more than a few minutes. Throw sliced mushrooms into a pan of hot, bubbling butter to which salt and pepper (and a little wine and dill if you like) has been added. Let cook until golden brown. (They can then be frozen, with the butter sauce, in a plastic container, if you wish.)

Onions
Like mushrooms, can season almost anything. Onion soup (canned or dehydrated and packaged) makes an excellent sauce.

Salad Dressings
Use bottled dressings as quick marinades for meats.

Sour Cream
A good dressing for salads or potatoes (baked or boiled). Try it.

Spaghetti Sauce
Combined seasonings come in envelope packages. They're good, cheap, and save bother.

Wine
Utilize leftover wine by substituting it for part of the water called for in any standard recipe.

Using different herbs and spices can expand one's taste range. Don't be afraid to experiment!

Classification of Seasonings *

* Information on pages 189–91 reprinted by permission of the Durkee Famous Foods Division of the SCM Corporation.

SPICES come from the bark, roots, leaves, stems, buds, seeds, or fruit of aromatic plants and trees that usually grow only in tropical countries. They are always dried and are available either whole or ground. Pepper, Allspice, Cloves, Nutmeg, Mace, Cinnamon, Ginger, Saffron, and Turmeric are spices.

HERBS are the leaves and stems of soft, succulent plants that usually grow in the Temperate Zone. They may be used fresh or dried; most are available whole or ground and some in crushed form. The most well-known herbs include Oregano, Chervil, Marjoram, Mint, Basil, Parsley, Rosemary, Sage, Savory, Tarragon, Thyme, and Bay Leaf.

BLENDS of spices and herbs include Poultry Seasoning, Curry Powder, Pumpkin Pie Spice, Apple Pie Spice, and Chili Powder. Curry Powder contains fourteen different ingredients.

The SEEDS used in our cooking and baking— Anise, Cardamom, Coriander, Caraway, Mustard, Celery, Dill, Poppy, and Sesame—are imported from such exotic places as Morocco, Iran, India, Holland, and Central America. Caraway Seed is almost a must for rye bread.

FLAVORINGS and EXTRACTS are the bottled essenses of spices, herbs, fruits, nuts, and liqueurs with an alcohol base as a preservative. Pure extracts include Almond, Lemon, Pepper mint, Vanilla, Wintergreen, Orange. Pure flavorings include Brandy, Rum, and Sherry. Examples of imitation extracts and flavorings are Banana, Maple, Black Walnut, and Strawberry, to mention a few.

VEGETABLE SEASONINGS are always dehydrated flakes, chips, or powders of distinctively flavored vegetables, such as Onion, Garlic, Parsley, Sweet Peppers, Chili Peppers, Horseradish.

CONDIMENTS are liquid or semiliquid combinations of seasonings, such as Tabasco and Worcestershire Sauce . . . Catchup and Prepared Mustard.

CHEMICALS like Salt and Monosodium Glutamate are also considered "seasonings" and are almost universally used.

How to Buy Spices	Strength, quality of flavor, and good color are the most important considerations. The economy-size packages are not always recommended. Reasonable quantities are best, with frequent use and periodic replacement.
How to Store Spices	Heat robs ground spices of their flavor and dampness cakes and deteriorates the powders, so it is recommended that all spices be stored in as cool and dry a place as possible. Containers should be tightly closed so the precious, volatile oils will not escape.
Length of Spice Shelf Life	Whole spices retain their fresh flavor and aroma almost indefinitely. Ground spices and herbs should be given the "sniff test" once a year. This is done by quickly passing the opened container under the nose and seeing if the contents can be identified. If not, it should be discarded and replaced.
When to Add Spices in a Recipe	Whole spices are best in long-cooking recipes and should be added at the beginning. It is suggested that they be tied in a cheesecloth bag so they can be removed when the desired flavor is achieved.

Ground spices should be added toward the end of the cooking time, as their flavors are quickly released in hot foods. For uncooked or cold foods

—such as salad dressings or fruit punches—let the spices stand in the liquid for several hours, so that the flavor of the spices can permeate the liquid.

How Much
Spice to
Use

The best advice to give is: follow the recipe, measure the spice, and taste the food for your personal approval.

If there is no recipe to follow, start with about one-fourth teaspoon of the spice for every pound of meat or pint of liquid . . . except when adding Red Pepper or Garlic Powder. With these two spices, use a very small amount at the start. One-eighth teaspoon Garlic Powder equals one clove Garlic.

When using Instant Minced Onion or Parsley Flakes, one part is the equivalent of about four parts of the raw product. And one part of Celery Flakes is equal to about two parts of the raw vegetable.

APPENDIX 4b

ALL ABOUT FOOD STORAGE *

* Reprinted by permission from the October, 1969, issue of *Good Housekeeping* magazine, © 1969 by the Hearst Corporation.

Knowing how to store food properly, and how long you can keep it, brings many benefits: the food will be safe to eat; it will be tops in terms of flavor and texture; a high level of nutrients will be maintained; and you won't waste money on spoiled items.

Safety First

The three types of bacteria responsible for most cases of food poisoning (*Salmonella, Staphylococcus,* and *Streptococcus*) are present around us all the time. Normally, they're not troublemakers, but if given the right (actually wrong) conditions, bacteria can multiply in a matter of hours to dangerous levels. The contributing factors to bacterial growth are temperature (between 50° F. and 125° F.) and time. To thwart growth: don't be casual about handling food; always work with well-scrubbed utensils, cutting boards—and hands; cook or serve food as soon as possible after removing it from storage; refrigerate food immediately after the meal is over; always take precautionary care—it's often not possible to tell by taste or smell if food is contaminated.

Foods that Need Special Care

Give special attention to preparing and storing poultry, fish and seafood, meat, creamed mixtures, mayonnaise, puddings, and stuffings—bacteria find these foods marvelous mediums to grow in. In particular: Don't stuff poultry the night before; the cold stuffing may not heat up to a safe temperature when you cook the bird. Never refrigerate cooked poultry with the stuffing in— store it separately. If you've bought cracked eggs, use them only when they will be thoroughly cooked (baked or hard-boiled); Salmonella, which may be present on shells, could contaminate cracked eggs.

Know-How with Frozen Foods

It's safe to refreeze virtually all partially thawed foods if they still have ice crystals in them and are still firm in the center. However, many foods (ice cream and uncooked baked goods, for example) will not maintain top quality. Meat, fish, and poultry purposely thawed in the refrigerator and kept no more than one day may be refrozen. However, don't refreeze combination dishes—pies, stews, etc.—that have been thawed. With the exception of fruit and juice concentrates, foods thawed accidentally in the freezer over a period of days (because of a power failure, etc.) should not be refrozen, unless, of course, they still have ice crystals. If food is completely thawed (on purpose or by accident), warmed to room temperature, and left for more than two hours, throw it out. The exceptions: fruit and juice concentrates, which ferment when spoiled. Toss out fruit if flavor is "off."

Pantry-Shelf Storage

TEMPERATURE: Store food in coldest cabinets—not over range or by refrigerator's exhaust. Use coolest spots for storing large amounts of potatoes, onions, etc., and for long-term storage of canned foods.

TIME: Though most staples and canned foods will keep indefinitely, buy no more than you expect to use—recommended storage times are given below. While foods will be safe beyond the recommended storage times, flavor will fade and textures wilt. Date foods. Then check cabinets every six months and use up the oldest items.

BUYING: Purchase the freshest-looking packages—messy or shopworn labels indicate old stock. Don't buy cans with swollen ends—food has gone bad. Dented cans may be purchased, provided they haven't been punctured.

HOME CANNING: Use first-quality foods and the best techniques

FOOD	TIME	SPECIAL HANDLING
STAPLES		
Baking powder	18 months	Keep covered and dry.
Bouillon cubes	1 year	Keep covered and dry.
Bread crumbs, dried	6 months	Keep covered and dry.
Cereals, ready-to-eat	4 months	Keep covered and dry.
cooked	6 months	Keep covered and dry.
Chocolate, premelted	1 year	Keep cool.
semisweet	2 years	Keep cool.
unsweetened	18 months	Keep cool.
Coffee, cans (unopened)	1 month	Refrigerate after opening.
Coffee, instant (opened)	2 weeks	Keep lid tightly closed.
(unopened)	6 months	
Coffee lighteners, dry		
(opened)	6 months	Keep lid tightly closed.
Condensed and		
evaporated milk	1 year	Refrigerate after opening.
Flour (all types)	1 year	Put in airtight container.
Gelatin (all types)	18 months	Keep in original packets.
Honey, jams, sirups	1 year	Keep tightly covered.
Nonfat dry milk	6 months	Put in airtight container.
Pasta	2 years+	Keep tightly closed.
Pudding mixes	1 year	Keep in original packets.
Rice, white	2 year+	Keep tightly closed.
Rice mixes	6 months	
Salad dressing (all types)	3 months	Refrigerate after opening.
Salad oils	1–3 months	
Shortening, solid	8 months	Refrigeration not needed.
Sugar, brown	4 months	Put in airtight container.
confectioners'	4 months	Put in airtight container.
granulated, molasses	2 years+	Keep tightly covered.
Tea, bags	18 months	Put in airtight container.
instant	3 years	Keep tightly covered.
loose	2 years	Put in airtight container.
MIXES AND PACKAGED FOODS		
Cakes, prepared	1–2 days	If butter-cream, whipped-cream, or custard frostings or fillings, refrigerate.

Cake mixes	1 year	Keep cool and dry.
Casserole mixes	18 months	Keep cool and dry.
Cookies, homemade	1 week	Put in airtight container.
packaged	4 months	Keep box tightly closed.
Crackers	3 months	Keep box tightly closed.
Frosting, in cans or mixes	8 months	
Hot-roll mix	18 months	If opened, put in airtight container.
Pancake mix	6 months	Put in airtight container.
Piecrust mix	8 months	
Pies and pastries	2–3 days	Refrigerate whipped-cream, custard, or chiffon fillings.
Potatoes, instant	18 months	Keep in original package.
Toaster pop-ups	3 months	Keep in airtight packet.

CANNED AND DRIED FOODS

Fruits, canned	1 year	Keep in cool spot.
dried	6 months	Put in airtight container.
Gravies, canned	1 year	
Meat, fish, poultry	1 year	
Pickles, olives	1 year	Refrigerate after opening.
Soups, canned, dried	1 year	Keep cool.
Vegetables, canned, dried	1 year	Keep cool.

HERBS, SPICES, AND CONDIMENTS

Catchup (opened)	1 month	
Herbs and spices		Transfer from cartons to airtight containers. Keep away
whole spices	1 year	from sunlight. At times listed,
ground spices	6 months	check aroma; when it fades,
herbs	6 months	replace.
Tabasco, Worcestershire	2 years+	

OTHERS

Coconut	1 year	Refrigerate after opening.
Metered-calorie products,		Keep in cans, closed jars, or original packets.
instant breakfasts	6 months	

Nuts	9 months	Refrigerate after opening.
Onions, potatoes, sweet potatoes	2 weeks at room temperature	For longer storage, keep below 50° F., but not refrigerated. Keep dry, out of sun. Plan short storage in spring when sprouting is a serious problem.
Parmesan cheese	2 months	Keep lid tightly closed.
Peanut butter (opened)	2 months	
(unopened)	9 months	Refrigeration not needed.
Soft drinks	3 months	
Whipped-topping mix	1 year	

Refrigerator Storage

TEMPERATURE: From 34° F. to 40° F. is best. Above 40° F., foods spoil rapidly. Check temperature with a refrigerator thermometer or an outdoor thermometer.

TIME: Use foods quickly—don't depend on maximum storage time.

WRAPS: Use foil, plastic wrap or bags, airtight containers. When meat, poultry, or fish is bought in a plastic wrapped package, loosen ends of package to dry surface moisture—bacteria grow faster on moist surfaces.

GENERAL CARE: Clean refrigerator regularly to cut down food odors. Remove spoiled foods immediately so that odor can't be passed on to other foods.

FOOD	TIME	SPECIAL HANDLING

DAIRY PRODUCTS

FOOD	TIME	SPECIAL HANDLING
Butter, margarine	1–2 weeks	Keep tightly wrapped or covered. Hold only 2-day supply in butter keeper.
Buttermilk, sour cream, or yogurt	5 days to 2 weeks	Keep tightly covered. Turn unopened yogurt and sour-cream containers upside down to prevent surface drying. Once opened, store right side up.

Cheese

FOOD	TIME	SPECIAL HANDLING
cottage, ricotta	5 days	Keep all cheese tightly packaged in moisture-resistant wrap. If outside of hard cheese gets moldy, just cut away mold—it won't affect flavor For longer storage, see freezer storage.
cream, Neufchâtel	2 weeks	
hard and wax-coated cheeses—Cheddar, Edam, Gouda, Swiss, etc.		
large pieces (unopened)	3–6 months	
(opened)	3–4 weeks	
sliced	2 weeks	
Parmesan, Romano (grated)		See pantry-shelf chart. Does not need refrigeration.
processed (opened)	3–4 weeks	Unopened processed cheese need not be refrigerated.
Cream—light, heavy, half-and-half	3 days	Keep tightly covered. Don't return unused cream to original container. This would spread any bacteria present in leftover cream.
Coffee lightener (liquid)	3 weeks	Don't return unused lightener to original container.
Dips—sour-cream, etc.		
commercial	2 weeks	Keep tightly covered.
homemade	2 days	Keep tightly covered.

Eggs		Keep small end of egg down,
in shell	3 weeks	to center yolks.
whites	3 days	Store in covered container.
yolks	3 days	Cover yolks with water; cover
		container.
Milk		
evaporated (opened)	4–5 days	
filled, imitation	3–4 days	
pasteurized,		Keep containers tightly closed.
reliquefied nonfat		Do not return unused milk to
dry, skimmed	3–4 days	original container.
sweetened condensed	4–5 days	Remove entire lid of can to
		make pouring easier. Keep
		covered.
Whipped topping		
in aerosol can	3 months	
prepared from mix	3 days	Keep covered.

FRUITS AND VEGETABLES—FRESH

Fruits		
apples	1 week	Sort fruit; discard bruised or
berries, cherries	1–2 days	decayed fruit. Do not wash
citrus fruits	1 week	before storing—moisture en-
citrus juices		courages spoilage. Store in
bottled, recon-		crisper or moisture-resistant
stituted		bags or wrap. Keep fruit
frozen, canned	6 days	juices tightly covered. It is
melons	1 week	not necessary to remove
other fruit	3–5 days	canned fruit from can. Wrap
		uncut cantaloupe, honeydew,
		etc., to prevent odor spreading
		to other refrigerated foods.
Vegetables		
beets, carrots,		Remove leafy tops; keep in
radishes	2 weeks	crisper.
mushrooms	1–2 days	Do not wash before storing.
onions, potatoes,		Refrigeration not needed. See
sweet potatoes		pantry-shelf chart.
shredded salad		Keep in moisture-resistant
greens, cabbage	1–2 days	wrap or bags.

unshelled peas,		Keep in crisper or moisture-resistant wrap or bags.
limas, corn in husks	3–5 days	
other vegetables	3–5 days	Keep in crisper or moisture-resistant wrap or bags.

MEAT, FISH, AND POULTRY—FRESH, UNCOOKED

Meats—beef, lamb, pork, and veal

chops	3–4 days	Store fresh meats loosely
ground meat	1–2 days	wrapped. Partial drying of
roasts	5–6 days	surface increases keeping
steaks	3–5 days	quality. If meat comes pack-
stew meat	1–2 days	aged in plastic wrap, loosen
variety meats (liver,		ends. Store in coldest part of
heart, etc.)	1–2 days	refrigerator or in meat keeper.

Fish and shellfish

fresh, cleaned fish,		Store loosely wrapped. Keep
including steaks		in coldest part of refrigerator
and fillets	1 day	or in meat keeper.
clams, crab, lobster		
in shell	2 days	Cook only live shellfish.
seafood (shucked		
clams, oysters,		
scallops, shrimp)	1 day	

Poultry

ready-to-cook		Store loosely wrapped. Keep
chicken, duck, or		fresh poultry in coldest part
turkey	2 days	of refrigerator or in meat keeper.

CURED AND SMOKED MEATS

Bacon	5–7 days	Keep wrapped. Store in cold-
Bologna	4–6 days	est part of refrigerator or in
Corned beef	5–7 days	meat keeper. Times are for
Dried beef	10–12 days	opened packages of sliced meats. Unopened vacuum packs keep about 2 weeks.
Dry and semidry		
sausage (salami, etc.)	2–3 weeks	

Frankfurters	4–5 days
Hams (whole, halves)	1 week
Hams, canned (unopened)	6 months
Liver sausage	4–5 days
Luncheon meat	3 days
Sausage, fresh	2–3 days
Sausage, smoked	2–3 days

CANNED FOOD AFTER OPENING

Baby food	2–3 days	Store baby food covered. Don't feed baby from jar; saliva may liquefy food.
Fish and seafood	1 day	Store all canned foods tightly covered. It is not necessary to remove food from can.
Fruit	1 week	
Gravy, broths	2 days	
Meats	2 days	
Pickles, olives	1 month	
Poultry	1 day	
Sauce, tomato-based	5 days	
Vegetables	3 days	

OTHER FOODS

Ketchup		See pantry-shelf chart.
Coffee, regular	2 weeks	Keep tightly covered after opening.
Honey		Refrigeration not needed, but storage life is lengthened if refrigerated.
Jams, jellies		See Honey.
Nuts	2 weeks	Refrigerate nuts after opening cans or packages. For longer storage, freeze.
Peanut butter		Refrigeration not needed, but it keeps longer if refrigerated. See pantry-shelf chart.
Refrigerated biscuits, rolls, pastries	expiration date on label	Products keep better if stored in back of refrigerator where it is colder.

Refrigerated cooky dough		See Refrigerated biscuits. For longer storage, freeze.
Salad dressings, all types (opened)	3 months	Keep covered.
Salad oil		See pantry-shelf chart.
Shortening, solid		See pantry-shelf chart.
Sirups		See Honey.
Soft drinks	6 months	
Wines, table	2–3 days	Keep tightly closed.
cooking	2–3 months	Keep tightly closed.

Freezer Storage

TEMPERATURE: 0° F. or below is best. Maximum temperature should be 5° F. Check temperature with freezer thermometer or outdoor thermometer, or use this rule of thumb: if the freezer can't keep ice cream brick solid, temperature is above the recommended level. If this is the case, don't plan to store food more than a week or two.

TIME: Date foods with an "expiration date" according to maximum storage time recommended below. Longer storage is not dangerous, but flavors and textures begin to deteriorate.

WRAPS: Use foil, plastic bags and wraps, freezer wrap, or freezer containers.

COMMERCIALLY FROZEN FOODS: Don't buy them if they're battered, a sign that they may have been partially thawed. If foods have been partially thawed, then refrozen, use them within a few days.

HOME-FROZEN FOODS: Use good-quality foods and proper techniques. Freeze foods quickly in coldest part of freezer (on coils, floor), then store in another freezer area.

FOOD	TIME	SPECIAL HANDLING

MEAT, FISH, AND POULTRY

Meat—home-frozen

bacon	1 month	If meat is purchased fresh on
corned beef	2 weeks	trays and in plastic wrap,
frankfurters	1 month	check for holes. If none,
ground beef, lamb,		freeze in this wrap for up to 1
and veal	4 months	month. For longer storage,
ground pork	3 months	overwrap with foil, plastic
ham slices	1 month	wrap, or freezer wrap. Other
ham, whole	2 months	meats should be wrapped as
luncheon meats	1 month	above; make package as air-
roasts		tight as possible. Keep frank-
beef	1 year	furters, bacon, etc., in vacuum
lamb	9 months	packages to freeze. Put two
pork	6 months	layers of waxed paper between
veal	9 months	individual hamburger patties,
		chops, etc.
sausage, dry, smoked	1 month	Keep meat purchased frozen
sausage, fresh	2 months	in original package. Thaw and
		cook according to label in-
		structions.
steaks		
beef	1 year	
lamb, veal	9 months	
pork	6 months	

Fish—home-frozen and purchased frozen

fillets and steaks from		To home-freeze fish, wrap in
"lean" fish—		foil, plastic wrap, or freezer
cod, flounder,		wrap. Make packages as air-
haddock, sole	6 months	tight as possible. Freeze in
"fatty" fish—		coldest part of freezer. For
bluefish, mackerel,		best results, prepare fish as
perch, salmon	3 months	directed in authoritative
breaded fish	3 months	freezing guide.
clams	3 months	Keep fish purchased frozen in
cooked fish or		original wrapping. Thaw and
seafood	3 months	cook according to label direc-
king crab	10 months	tions.

lobster tails	3 months
oysters	4 months
scallops	3 months
shrimp, unbreaded	1 year
shrimp, breaded	4 months

Poultry—home-frozen
or purchased frozen

chicken, whole or cut-up parts	1 year
chicken livers	3 months
cooked poultry	3 months
duck, turkey	6 months

For home freezing, prepare as directed for fish and seafood. Thaw commercially frozen poultry according to label directions. Cook all thawed poultry within 1 day.

FRUITS AND VEGETABLES

Fruit—home-frozen or purchased frozen

berries, cherries, peaches, pears, pineapple, etc.	1 year
citrus fruit and juice—frozen at home	6 months
fruit juice concentrates	1 year

To home-freeze fruits and vegetables, prepare according to authoritative freezing guide.

Vegetables—home-frozen or purchased frozen

home-frozen	10 months
purchased frozen— cartons, plastic bags, or boil-in-bags	8 months

Cabbage, celery, salad greens, tomatoes, do not freeze successfully.

COMMERCIALLY FROZEN FOODS

Also see: Meat, Fish, and Poultry; Fruits and Vegetables; Dairy Products

Baked goods

breads, baked	3 months
breads, unbaked	2 months
cakes	
cheesecake	3 months
chocolate	4 months

Pick up frozen foods immediately before going to check-out counter. Place in home freezer as soon as possible. Purchase only food frozen solid. Cook or

fruitcake	1 year	thaw according to label in-
spongecake	2 months	structions.
yellow or pound	6 months	
pies		
cream, custard	8 months	
fruit	8 months	
Main dishes		
meat, fish, and	3 months	
poultry pies		
meat, fish, and		
poultry casseroles	3 months	
TV dinners	6 months	

HOME-FROZEN FOODS

Also see: Meat, Fish, and Poultry; Fruits and Vegetables; Dairy Products

Breads	3 months	Package foods tightly in foil,
Cakes	3 months	plastic wrap, freezer wrap, or
Casserole dishes:		watertight freezer containers.
meat, fish, poultry	3 months	For casseroles, allow head-
Cookies, dough, baked	3 months	room for expansion. Freeze in
Nuts	3 months	coldest part of freezer.
Pies, unbaked	8 months	

DAIRY PRODUCTS

Butter, margarine	9 months	Store in airtight freezer con-
		tainer or wrapped in freezer
		wrap.
Buttermilk, sour		
cream, or yogurt		Do not freeze.
Cheese		
Camembert	3 months	Thaw in refrigerator.
cottage, farmers'		Thaw in refrigerator. Don't
cheese (dry curd		freeze creamed cottage
only)	3 months	cheese—it gets mushy.
cream cheese,		
Neufchâtel	1 month	Thaw in refrigerator.
hard cheeses—		Cut and wrap cheese in small
Cheddar, Edam,		pieces for freezer storage.
Gouda, Swiss,		When frozen, may show
brick, etc.	3 months	mottled color due to surface

		moisture. Thaw in refrigerator.
processed	3 months	
Roquefort, blue	3 months	Becomes crumbly after thawing. Still fine for salads and melting.
Cream—light, heavy, half-and-half	2 months	Heavy cream may not whip after thawing. Use cream for cooking. Thaw in refrigerator.
Cream, whipped	1 month	Make dollops of whipped cream; freeze firm. Place in plastic bag or carton; seal; store in freezer. Place on top of dessert to thaw.
Eggs		
in shells		Do not freeze.
whites	1 year	Store in covered container. Freeze in amounts for favorite recipes.
yolks	1 year	For sweet dishes: Mix each cup of yolks with 1 tablespoon corn sirup or sugar. For other cooking: substitute ½ teaspoon salt for sugar.
Ice cream, ice milk, sherbet	1 month	Cover surface with plastic wrap or foil after each use to keep from drying out.
Milk	3 months	Freezing affects flavor and appearance. Use in cooking and baking. Allow room for expansion in freezer container. Thaw in refrigerator.

APPENDIX 4c

SUBSTITUTES AND EQUIVALENTS *

Abbreviations
Often Used in
Written Recipes

* Material in Appendixes 4C and 4D reprinted by permission of the Robertshaw Controls Company, from the pamphlet "Better Cooking and Baking," published in 1960.

Teaspoon—tsp. or t.
Tablespoon—tbsp. or T.
Cup—C.
Pint—pt.
Quart—qt.
Ounce—oz.
Pound—lb. or #
Package—pkg.
Hour—hr.
Minute—min.
Degree—°
Degree Fahrenheit—° F.

Equivalents
Helpful in
Recipe Use

1 tablespoon = 3 teaspoons
4 tablespoons = ¼ cup
8 tablespoons = ½ cup
16 tablespoons = 1 cup
8 ounces (*liquid*) = 1 cup
1 cup = ½ pint
2 pints = 1 quart
4 quarts = 1 gallon
1 tablespoon = ½ ounce
2 tablespoons = 1 ounce
¼ cup = 2 ounces
½ cup = 4 ounces
1 cup = 8 ounces
2 cups = 16 ounces
1 pint = 16 ounces

**Substitutions
One Ingredient
for Another**

1 tablespoon flour = ½ tablespoon cornstarch as thickening agent

¾ tablespoon quick-cook tapioca = 1 tablespoon flour for thickening

1 cup cake flour = ⅞ cup all-purpose flour (*1 cup minus 2 tablespoons*)

1 cup honey = 1 to 1¼ cups sugar plus ¼ cup liquid

1 ounce chocolate = 3 tablespoons cocoa plus 1 tablespoon fat

1 cup butter = 1 cup margarine = ⅞ (*1 cup minus 2 tablespoons*) cup hydrogenated fat plus ½ teaspoon salt = ⅞ (*1 cup minus 2 tablespoons*) cup lard plus ½ teaspoon salt = ⅞ (*1 cup minus 2 tablespoons*) cup rendered fat plus ½ teaspoon salt

1 teaspoon baking powder = ¼ teaspoon baking soda plus ½ cup fully soured milk or soured buttermilk = ¼ teaspoon baking soda plus ½ tablespoon vinegar = ¼ teaspoon baking soda plus ¼ to ½ cup molasses

1 tablespoon double-acting baking powder = 2 teaspoons cream of tartar baking powder

1 tablespoon double-acting baking powder = 1½ teaspoons phosphate baking powder

APPENDIX 4d

ONE-STEP METHOD: The following vegetables are best cooked with a minimum amount of salted water (¼ inch water in heavy aluminum pans, up to 1 inch in lightweight pans) in a tightly covered pan. Cook until just tender at 212° to 225°. (If you do not have temperature controls for the burners on top of your stove, use a low flame or heat for 150° to 225°, medium for 225° to 275°, medium-high for 275° to 350°, and a high flame or heat for over 350°.

FOOD	Amount to Serve 4	Approximate Cooking Time in Minutes
Artichokes, French	4	20–45 minutes (until leaf can easily be pulled from stalk)
Asparagus	2 lbs.	Whole—15–20 minutes Tips—12–15 minutes
Beans, green or wax	1 lb.	15–30 minutes
Green Lima Beans	3 lbs. or 1 pt. shelled	20–30 minutes
Beets	2 lbs.	Whole—30–40 minutes Cut—10–20 minutes
Carrots	1 lb.	Whole—20–30 minutes Cut—10–15 minutes
Celery	1 bunch (cut in serving pieces)	15–20 minutes
Eggplant, pared and cut in cubes	1	10–15 minutes
Parsnips	1½ lbs.	7–15 minutes
Peas	2 lbs. (unshelled)	8–15 minutes
Potatoes, white, pared	2 lbs.	Whole—30–35 minutes Cut—20–25 minutes
Tomatoes	1 lb.	10 minutes
Sweet Potatoes	1½ to 2 lbs.	30–35 minutes

TWO-STEP METHOD: For more pleasing flavor, cook the following vegetables uncovered in salted water. It is best to bring water (enough to cover vegetables) to a boil first before adding vegetables, temperature setting 250° to 275° F.

FOOD	Amount To Serve 4	Approximate Cooking Time in Minutes
Broccoli	2½ lbs.	15–20 minutes
Brussels Sprouts	1 lb.	10–20 minutes
Cabbage	1–2 lbs.	8–12 minutes for 2″ wedges 5–8 minutes for shredded
Chinese Cabbage	1–2 lbs.	4–5 minutes
Cauliflower	2½ lbs.	Flowerets—8–10 minutes
Corn on Cob	8 medium ears	6–12 minutes
Kohlrabi	6	Sliced—20–35 minutes
Onions	1½ lbs.	Small, whole, 10–20 minutes
Rutabagas	2 lbs.	2″ pieces, 25–35 minutes
Turnips	2 lbs.	1″ pieces, 15–20 minutes

Meat, Poultry, Fish

METHOD: Preheat skillet about two minutes at dial setting recommended. Add small amount of fat—just enough to keep food from sticking—and add foods to be cooked.

FOOD	Dial Temperature	Approx. Cooking Time (varies with thickness)
Bacon (do not preheat pan)	325°	4 minutes per side
Chicken, cut up	350°	15–20 minutes per side
Chops and Cutlets, pork, lamb, or veal	350°	10–15 minutes per side
Fish, small pieces	375°	until thoroughly cooked
whole fish or large pieces	325°	
Hamburger Patties	325°	3–6 minutes per side
Ham Slice	300°	6 minutes per side
Liver	275°	4–6 minutes per side
Pot Roasts, Chicken, thicker Chops, less tender	350°	to brown on all sides, then 212°, cover and cook until tender. (30 minutes to ˙ ½

Steaks, and Stew Meat		hours)
Sausage, patties or links	275°	until thoroughly cooked
Steaks, minute or cube	375°	2–3 minutes per side
Steaks, rib, club, porterhouse, T-bone, sirloin, round	350°	3–7 minutes per side depending on doneness desired

Other Foods

FOOD	*Dial Setting*
Applesauce	212°
Beef Stew	325° to brown meat; 225° to simmer, covered
Chili	325° to brown meat; 225° to simmer, covered
Cocoa	200°
Coffee—percolator	212° to 250° (depends on pot design)
vacuum	200° to 212°
Cream Pie Filling and Puddings	200°
Eggs—fried (uncovered)	200°
(covered)	225°
poached	200°
scrambled	200°
soft-cooked	212°
hard-cooked	212°
English Muffins	325°
French Toast, preheat griddle	350°
Fudge	250°
Gravy	200° to 225°
Grilled Sandwiches	350°

Hollandaise Sauce	Low
Pancakes	375°
Peanut Brittle	325°
Popcorn	375°
Potatoes, fried	325°
Potatoes, pan-baked (no water) in covered saucepan about 60 minutes	375°
Rhubarb Sauce	200° to 212°
Rice	212°
Seven-Minute Icing	175°
Steamed Pudding	212° to 225°
White Sauce	200°

Temperatures Below 200°—Keep Foods Warm and Ready to Serve

Chocolate, Melted	Low to 175°
Cocoa	Low
Coffee	175°
Gravy	175°
Milk	Low
Rolls *	200°
Shortening, Melted	175°
Soup	200°

* Place baked rolls in dry, covered saucepan (not glass) to warm perfectly for serving—takes 5 to 10 minutes.

Timetable for Baking Fish and Shellfish

	Approximate Thickness Pounds	Time Minutes	Oven Temperature Degrees F.
Fish	1½–1	25–35	350°
Clams		15	450°
Lobster	¾–1	15–20	400°
Oysters		15	450°
Scallops		25–30	350°
Shrimp		20–25	350°
Lobster Tails	4 oz.	20–25	450°

Broiling Timetable

Kind and Cut	Approximate Thickness Inches	Rare	Medium	Well-Done
BEEF				
Steaks (club, tenderloin, rib,	1	10	14	18
T-bone, porterhouse,	1½	16	20	26
sirloin	2	24	32	40
Ground-beef patties	¾	8	12	14
LAMB				
Chops (rib, loin shoulder)	1		12	14
	1½		20	26
HAM				
Slice, uncooked	1			20
Cooked	1			10
BACON				4–5
LIVER				
Calf, young beef, lamb (brushed with butter)	½			12
CHICKEN, halved	2½ lbs. or less			30–40
FISH AND SHELLFISH				
Fish	½–1			10–15

Approximate Total Cooking Time Minutes

Clams			5–8
Lobster	¾–1		10–12
Oysters			5
Scallops			8–10
Shrimp			8–10
Lobster Tails	4 oz.		8–10

Oven Roasting Timetable

Kind and Cut	Approximate Weight Pounds	Internal Temperature Degrees F.	Approximate Cooking Time at 325° (Hours)
BEEF			
Standing Ribs	4	140° (rare)	1¾
		160° (medium)	2
		170° (well-done)	2½
	6	140° (rare)	2
		160° (medium)	2½
		170° (well-done)	3½
	8	140° (rare)	2½
		160° (medium)	3
		170° (well-done)	4½
Rolled Ribs	4	140° (rare)	2
		160° (medium)	2½
		170° (well-done)	3
	6	140° (rare)	3
		160° (medium)	3¼
		170° (well-done)	4
Rolled Rump	5	140° (rare)	2½
		160° (medium)	3
		170° (well-done)	3½
Sirloin Tip	3	140° (rare)	1½
		160° (medium)	2
		170° (well-done)	2¼
LAMB			
Leg	6	175° (medium)	3
		180° (well-done)	3½
	8	175° (medium)	4
		180° (well-done)	4⅔
Cushion Tip	5	180° (well-done)	3

Rolled Shoulder	3	180° (well-done)	2½
	5	180° (well-done)	3
VEAL			
Leg	5	170° (well-done)	2⅓–3
	8	170° (well-done)	3½
Loin	5	170° (well-done)	3
Shoulder	6	170° (well-done)	3½
Rolled Shoulder	3	170° (well-done)	3
	5	170° (well-done)	3½
PORK			
Leg (Fresh Ham)	6	185° (well-done)	4
	14	185° (well-done)	6
Loin	5	185° (well-done)	3
Cushion Shoulder	5	185° (well-done)	3½
Shoulder Butt	5	185° (well-done)	3½
PORK			
Cured, Ham, whole	12	160° (well-done)	3½
	16	160° (well-done)	4¼
Ham, piece	6	160° (well-done)	2½
Picnic Shoulder	6	170° (well-done)	3½
POULTRY			
(Ready to Cook)			
Chicken	1½–2½	(190° to 195°)	1¼ to 2
	2½–3½	(Stuffing 165°)	2–3
	3½–4½	(Stuffing 165°)	3–3½
Duck	3–4	(Stuffing 165°)	2½–2¾
	4–5	(Stuffing 165°)	2¾–3
Goose	8–10	(Stuffing 165°)	3½–4
	10–12	(Stuffing 165°)	4–4½
Turkey, whole bird	4–8	(Stuffing 165°)	3–4½
	8–12	(Stuffing 165°)	4–5
	12–16	(Stuffing 165°)	5–6
	16–20	(Stuffing 165°)	6–7½
	20–25	(Stuffing 165°)	7½–9
Halves and	3½–5	(Stuffing 165°)	3–3½
Quarters	5–8	(Stuffing 165°)	3½–4
	8–12	(Stuffing 165°)	4–5

Baking Chart

Food	Oven Temperature Degrees F.	Baking Time Minutes
BREADS		
Biscuits	425° to 450°	10–15
Corn Bread	400° to 425°	20–35
Cream Puffs	375°	60
Muffins	400° to 425°	20–25
Popovers	375° to 400°	45–60
Quick Loaf Breads	350° to 375°	60–75
Yeast Bread	375° to 400°	45–60
Yeast Rolls, plain	400°	15–20
Yeast Rolls, sweet	350° to 375°	20–30
CAKES WITH FAT		
Cup	350° to 375°	15–25
Layer	375°	20–30
Loaf	350°	45–60
CAKES WITHOUT FAT		
Angel Food and Sponge	350° to 375°	30–45
COOKIES		
Drop	350° to 400°	8–15
Rolled	375°	8–10
PASTRY		
One-crust pie (custard type), unbaked shell	400° to 425°	30–40
Meringue on cooked filling in prebaked shell	425°	4–4½
Shell only	450°	10–12
Two-crust pies with uncooked filling	400° to 425°	45–55
Two-crust pies with cooked filling	425° to 450°	30–45

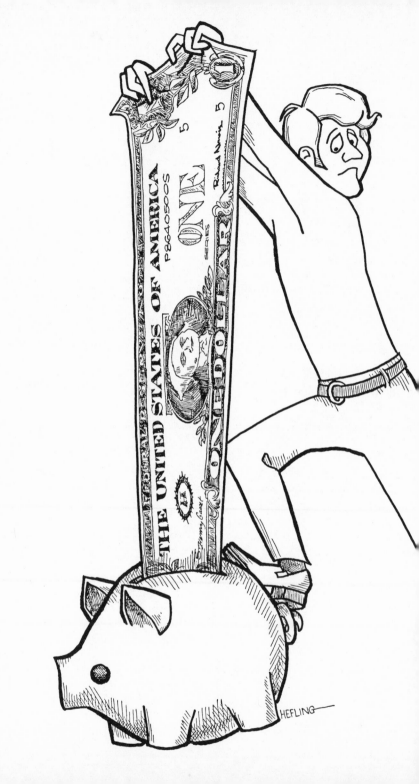

CHAPTER FIVE

GETTING YOUR MONEY'S WORTH

OR

SAVING ON THE MISCELLANEOUS

Folks:

Are you tired of seeing your money go out faster than it comes in? Are you depressed by salesmen who have gypped you, or ads that have tricked you? Does being in the red make you blue?

Then be the first in your block to: Get Your Money's Worth!

In preceding chapters, we've discussed ways to save money on the most obvious expenses of apartment living. We've seen that saving money simply means knowing how to avoid unnecessary expenses and how to elude the guiles of profiteers.

Knowledge and patience permit us to take the fixed sum of money we have available to us and use it to our best advantage. Let's make one thing clear: I'm not recommending that you or I abstain from buying the services, objects, foods, and pleasures we want. Rather, I'm suggesting that we can get more of all of them for our money if we think before we spend, know exactly what, where, and from whom we're buying, and have the patience to avoid falling prey to the advertiser's attempt to make us buy on impulse. Let's make the most of what little money we have.

"The wealthy are generally the most conscious of getting good bargains."

Wise management of personal finances can be a way of life. But it rarely is. In fact, America's entire consumer economy often seems based on the fact that Americans can be manipulated into buying poor-quality items, outrageously-priced repair services, and unattractive styles—all at the whim of Madison Avenue.

It's interesting that the wealthy, whom one might expect to spend most carelessly, are generally the most conscious of getting good bargains on high-quality merchandise and services at fair prices.

But you don't have to be rich to get a lot for your money. This chapter is for those who wish to live cheap but good by saving money on the following:

1. Apartment Utilities: heat, water, electricity, telephone
2. Auto and Appliance Repairs
3. Books and Writing Materials
4. Clothing
5. Health Care
6. Miscellaneous Merchandise.

APARTMENT UTILITIES

Unless your landlord pays utility bills and jacks up the rent for this bit of generosity, you are probably faced with heat, electricity, and phone payments every month or two. These seemingly inevitable bills can take a hearty bite out of anyone's wallet. Here's how to make that bite more of a nibble.

Beat the Heat Bill

In the northern United States, heating bills can cost an apartment dweller up to fifty dollars per month. Decrease your heating bill by reducing the amount of cold air entering your apartment.

1. Place weather stripping around the frames of all doors (especially the bottoms) and windows. This takes only an hour or so, depending on how many doors and windows you have, and will save you a good deal of money, especially in older apartments.

Your hardware store carries a selection of weather stripping at different prices. The cheapest consists of dense wool felt and comes with or without flexible metal (or adhesive) backing.

Nail or press weather stripping into place according to package instructions. Windows and doors should be closed while the material is being installed; afterward, they can be opened easily.

2. Never open windows wider than necessary for air circulation—which is not wide at all—during the winter months. In fact, one gas-company official told me that enough air circulates through walls to make it unnecessary ever to open windows in winter.

3. Lock windows for tighter closing.

4. Window shades and heavy drapes block cold-air leaks around windows.

5. Rugs also help keep out the cold.

6. Keep your fireplace damper closed tightly when the fireplace is not in use.

7. Keep your thermostat set no higher than 72° F. Actually, you can easily get accustomed to living in a 65° or 68° apartment and wearing slightly warmer clothing. The difference in your heating bill will be significant.

8. Lower the thermostat setting (or turn off the radiator) before going to bed, especially if you intend to leave the bedroom windows open.

9. Keep all doors closed, including closet doors.

10. Replace broken windows or cover the hole with cardboard and masking tape.

As you can see, beating the heating bill consists mostly of trying to escape the draft. But there are other things, too, that will help lower your heating bill.

1. Leaky hot-water faucets waste hot water. This waste is reflected in your heating bill. Spend the fifteen minutes it takes to stop the leak.

2. Pilot lights on your stove should always be lit. Otherwise, gas will be wasted. If necessary, call in the gas company to relight pilots.

3. Radiators should always be kept in top working condition. Also, if your radiators are painted with

enamel or metallic paint, repainting them with a dull-finish oil-base paint (common interior house paint will do) can make your room warmer. You needn't remove the metallic paint first; simply paint over it.*

4. Finally, remember that what we call "heat" is really hot air. Keep hot air moving (it generally collects near the ceiling) by planting a small electric fan near the radiator. By aiming it at the ceiling and using it at low speed, the fan will help circulate the air being warmed by the radiator.

Electricity Felicity

" 'The next best thing to being there' is also the next most expensive thing to traveling there."

Reducing your electricity bill consists, basically, of learning to turn off all lights in a room when you leave it.

Besides this seemingly obvious—though rarely observed—maxim, I have only one more bit of advice: Realize that those appliances that convert electric current into heat consume more electricity than all of your lights and other appliances put together. Portable electric heaters, electric irons, toaster-ovens, stoves, and such should be used as little as possible.

Most Important: When you're through with these appliances, make certain they're turned off—perhaps even pull out the plug! An electric iron left on, a toaster-oven with a faulty off-on switch, or a heater that runs all night can contribute greatly to the profits of your electric company.

Phone

"The next best thing to being there" is also the next most expensive thing to traveling there.

As we all know, it's a lot easier and less painful to use a credit card than to pay cash. AT&T knows this, too, and has arranged life so that we don't even need a charge card to buy its product on credit. All you have to do to spend money is to wiggle your finger a few times. No wonder phone bills mount up so quickly!!

1. Get the longest phone cord available. Hang excess on a brass coat hook affixed to nearest wall.
2. After a year of phone (or other utilities) service, ask for your deposit back. You've proven your reliability, and they owe you the money.
3. Extension cords and phones purchased through firms like Radio Shack for $7–$10 can save you a bundle. Though their legality is still being disputed, they are advertised widely and over one million of them are sold annually. If you are slow and nonmechanical, installation may take you ten minutes. Salesmen will explain the installation procedure.
4. Get the cheapest, most limited form of telephone service. After the first month, carefully examine your phone bill for message unit charges. See if a costlier basic monthly rate would save you money over your present basic charge plus unit charges.
5. There's a monthly charge if you want to have your phone unpublished and unlisted. To avoid the charge, which can amount to $8–$12 annually, list your phone under your dog's name. So long as you pay your bills (put bill stub and check into the same envelope, they'll be greedily accepted) and no fraud is intended, aliases are perfectly legal.

To reduce unanticipated costs and hassles between roommates:*

1. Register the phone in the name of the roommate who will be making the most long-distance calls. If you're not sure who that will be, place the phone in the name of the one whose girl (boy) friend and/or parents live farthest away.

2. Keep a small notebook next to the telephone. After making a long-distance call, you and your roommates should mark down the date, your name, and the place called. This will eliminate questions and bickering when the bill arrives. It will also remind you of how much money you've spent each month.

3. If you have problems with one person making calls and never paying his share, or with visitors making long-distance calls at your expense, invest a buck in a telephone lock. It may be ugly and inhospitable, but it might also save you a small fortune. If the problem persists, call your telephone company and ask them to install a pay phone in your apartment.

4. Finally, mail letters—they're cheaper. The written note records your thoughts and will be remembered longer. Furthermore, people pay more attention to something in writing.

For the cost of two seventy-five-cent long-distance phone calls, you can send twenty-five letters.

For speed, remember that a letter sent special delivery takes only a day to arrive anywhere and costs less than the average long-distance call. It also makes a far greater impact on its receiver than a phone call does.

REPAIRS   State consumer-fraud departments (as well as *Consumer Reports* magazine) are constantly bringing predamaged watches, automobiles, TV's, and electrical appliances to randomly selected service shops for repair. Their conclusion: the average consumer can usually expect to pay for many more parts and repairs than he or his appliances actually need. How can you make sure that you pay no more than necessary?

Do It Yourself

Well, the best way is by doing the work yourself. As Chapter 6 will show, even the most complicated of home repairs are idiotically simple. Yet the average American would rather call a plumber or electrician at a cost of fifteen dollars or more than spend twenty minutes or half an hour doing the job himself.

The same thing is true in the case of appliance repairs. Most troubles are due to loose electrical connections or bent parts, which you with a little knowledge could repair in fifteen minutes. But you don't think you're "handy"?!? That's an American myth turned hang-up. If you can read and twist a screw driver, you can save yourself many dollars on repairs.

When you have an appliance or auto problem, first look at the instruction manual to see if your specific problem is mentioned. If not, go to your local library and take out books entitled *Repairing Electrical Appliances* or *TV Repair* or *Repairing Home Appliances.** If you don't know where to find them, the librarian will! Such books assume no prior knowledge on the part of the reader. They contain charts that describe problems in layman's terms and tell you which page deals with each of them. Very easy.

Get one of these books even before one of your appliances or cars or gadgets goes on the blink. Read about the general principles of repair. It costs no more than a walk to the library. Any reading that you do will quickly eliminate or reduce feelings of mechanical incompetence. In a little while, you may even become the neighborhood handy man, and add to your income by doing repairs for others.

* Many small appliance-repair manuals can be purchased cheaply in paperback.

Every car has a manual with easily followed instructions. Sometimes these can't be found in your library. When this happens, write to the customer-service department of the company that manufactured your car. They'll usually send you one of these "shop manuals" for a price somewhere between seven and ten dollars.

"Get diagnoses of the problem."

If You Have Someone Else Do It

If you unswervingly insist that you must spend money on a repairman, it still helps to look at a repair book, so that you understand the problem and won't be charged more than is fair.

Then:

1. Get diagnoses of the problem and estimates of the repair from more than one repairman. See if the estimates are similar. If not, think for yourself.

2. When looking for repairmen or mechanics, get references from friends or neighbors. If you know no one in the neighborhood, strike up a conversation with your postman, corner cop, or druggist and ask them whom they go to with a problem of your kind.

   If available, use a manufacturer's service center, even if it means driving a few miles. This does not mean a "factory-authorized shop." The first is owned by the factory, the second is owner-occupied.

If you're still in doubt about where to go, call your local Better Business Bureau and ask for reports on those repairmen you're considering.

3. Ask to see a written estimate for the repair, before any work is done. Have the service-repair manager of the shop write on the estimate: "No work to be done beyond this estimate without contacting owner."

4. If the repairman comes to your home, watch him. He might work more efficiently, and you might learn what to do if the same problem comes up again. Keep track of the time—look at the clock when he comes and goes.

   If a shop did the repair job, ask to be shown (by the man who actually did the job) what the problem was and how it was fixed. Make sure you fully understand the explanation. Look at the old parts and understand why they needed replacement. How else can you learn? These things are usually simple if you just insist on being taught.

5. If you can, get a written guarantee on the repair that was made, and have the date noted on the guarantee. If the problem that was "fixed" recurs within a short period of time, ask the repairman to fix it and refuse to pay extra for the service. If he won't fix it free of charge and you feel he should, call (or write, if you're patient)

   a. The Better Business Bureau, or

   b. Your state consumer-protection division,*

   or

   c. Your local newspaper for advice.

* Also called consumer-fraud division or consumer council or consumer complaints. This is a division of every state's attorney general's office.

BOOKS AND WRITING MATERIALS

This section is addressed to everyone who likes to read, and especially to students for whom reading is, at least in theory, one of life's main activities.

Many students feel they must first buy all of their textbooks, and then lug them around wherever they go. "Books are my friends," they say. Cartons in my attic attest to the fact that I, too, once felt that way.

During my freshman and sophomore years, I simply couldn't study in the library—or so I thought. Instead, I would buy the principal books for all my courses, take them to my room, and arrange them decoratively on my bookshelf. Where they'd sit. And sit.

Some of these books I read quickly, some not at all. When June came, I'd either carton them, or sell them for peanuts.

But then, in my junior year, I woke up. I asked myself, were books really my friends? They were stealing my money ($100 to $150 every year), cluttering my room, breaking my back whenever I moved from one dorm room or apartment to another, and showing their true value to be twenty-five cents a pound when I finally had to wave them good-bye.

It was obvious to me that this habit of book buying and hoarding, which profited no one but the school bookstore, had to be broken. I tried an experiment that worked so well it soon became a way of life—academic life, that is.

1. Whenever I needed a textbook, I'd go to one of the school libraries and sign it out or read it there. I discovered that if I wanted to take the book out, I'd have to get to the library within a couple of hours of the time it was mentioned in class, because other people used this money-saving tactic. Those books that were "On Reserve" and therefore couldn't be taken out, I read and took notes on in the library. Surprise! I learned that it was easier than attempting to study in my room.

2. If course books weren't in the library, or if someone had gotten there first and had taken them out, I'd wait a week or two, and then borrow the necessary books—one at a time—from classmates who, like me in my younger and more naive days, had bought all books immediately and after a few days had put them aside until just before exam-and-paper time.

3. Finally, at the end of the term, if I felt there were some books I'd read that I really wanted as friends, I'd buy them secondhand (yet in perfect condition) from classmates at considerable reductions. I would watch the bulletin boards for "Books for Sale" ads, or put up my own "Books Wanted" ads on the same bulletin boards; ask students whom I knew had had no interest in the course if I could buy their books; or tape a card to the lecture-hall door on the last day of class (or on the final-exam-hall door), reading: "I want to buy a good copy of *The American Heritage Dictionary* cheaply. Please call me tonight if you have one for sale."

In this way, I cut down my textbook expenses by 80 per cent, and now own a collection of those few books—and only those books—that I would have wanted to keep of the many I might have bought.

To conclude:

1. Whenever possible, borrow the books you need—from libraries or friends.
2. When buying a book, try to buy it secondhand—from secondhand bookstores (check the Yellow Pages), or from classmates, or from students who took the course the year before.

About Stationery

Though a pad of paper may seem cheap enough, in the course of a year the costs of stationery add up to a lot of money.

Avoid going to college bookstores and corner drugstores for these items, since inexpensive paper, pads, envelopes, and pens can be found:

A. In five-and-ten-cent stores
B. In chain-store supermarkets
C. In discount stores
D. At Sears and Roebuck.

Also, a visit to a print shop can net you pads that the shop makes up from leftover reams of job printing. These pads can often be had for the asking.

SAVING MONEY ON CLOTHES, OR FROM RAGS (ALMOST) TO BRITCHES

In our fashion-conscious society, advertisers work tirelessly to convince us that clothes do in fact make the man. Clothing stores expand this motto in an effort to convince us that the more we pay for our clothes, the more Man—or Woman—we'll become.

For people on a limited budget the cost of new clothes has become so high that it's almost prohibitive. But since nudity is not yet the fashion, buy we must.

Following are some suggestions for buying new and used clothing at reasonable prices and caring for them so that they'll last longer and continue to dress you well.

Remember: The key to a good dish is often in the dressing!

Planning Your Looks

A bit of planning and imagination can help you co-ordinate an interesting and versatile wardrobe. As with most things in life, the lasting impression is made not by the price but by the thought.

In buying clothing, know what you're getting for your money. If you do, you'll always be getting your money's worth!

This Garment Inspected By . . .

You!! No matter who else might have inspected it, or how fabulous the salesgirl tells you it is, *you* must inspect it carefully.

To be a "plain-clothes" detective:
1. Read labels with care.
2. Scrutinize the garment's cloth and construction.
3. Make sure the garment fits well. Don't buy undersized clothing.

Reading Labels

All new clothes should, and used clothing may, have labels or tags attached to them. These should tell you:
1. Fabric content: This information can indicate the type of service you should expect from the garment and the type of care you will have to give it.

"Has the fabric been treated?"

Some labels have specific laundering instructions: it's a good idea to file labels in a small box for easy reference.

2. Has the fabric been treated?

A "Sanforized" garment will shrink only about 2 per cent when first washed, which means it will still fit well after washing. A "preshrunk" garment may shrink 5 per cent—which means a considerable shrinkage.

"Colorfast" fabrics will fade little, if at all, if properly washed and dried.*

* Always—regardless of the fabric—be careful of automatic dryers, which have a tendency to cook and shrink your clothes.

Garment Construction or "All Togetherness"

If a piece of clothing has good fabric, a great line, and a lot of class—but is made so poorly that it hardly holds itself together when you're having it fit—it's not much of an investment. Unless you're willing to resew it yourself.

Scrutinize the clothing you're thinking of buying—inside *and* outside. Follow these guidelines:

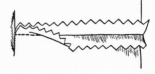

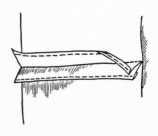

BUTTONS should be sewn on securely. If they are ornate or of a special type, ask for an extra in case you lose one.

HEMS on skirts or dresses, and cuffs on pants, should be securely sewn; also, they should be wide enough to accommodate fashion changes.

HOLES AND TEARS: Examine all parts of the garment for small holes and tears, which may be the result of defective cloth or of careless handling by the manufacturer, the retailer, or those who have worn or tried on the item. The store may be willing to make repairs. If not, and if you want neither to repair it yourself nor wear it as is, pass this garment up.

LININGS should be of good quality and should be preshrunk. Otherwise, they may shrink when the garment is washed, leaving you with something that's uncomfortable if not unwearable.

SEAMS: One-half inch is the minimum seam allowance. Seams should be "pinked" or "bound" to prevent unraveling (see diagram).

ZIPPERS should be sewn in securely, so that they lie flat. Make sure they are not defective; clip threads that may catch on zippers.

Trying It On

If your prospective purchase has survived the above examination, there still remains the most critical of all tests: trying it on!

The salesperson may tell you that this shirt or coat or whatever looks "stunning" or "groovy" on everyone. But "everyone" doesn't necessarily mean you.

So, try it on!

And when you do, make sure the garment hangs properly. Is there enough room where you need it? Is it tapered in the right places for you? Check the fit by walking and sitting. It should be comfortable whenever you move. Don't always trust the salesman's opinion of the way it looks or fits. Instead, make sure *you* like it. If you're still unsure, ask a friend to go shopping with you—chances are that he will express an honest opinion.

The Salvation Army, the Stage, and the Cleaners *

* Army/navy surplus stores sometimes carry good new and used clothing, too.

Unlikely comrades? Not when you consider that each is a potential source of clean, used clothing, which is frequently in very good condition.

Salvation Army clothing stores (as well as other stores of the same ilk: Goodwill, St. Vincent De-Paul, etc.) are located in most major cities. Everything you see on sale has been carefully cleaned, and necessary repairs have often been made. When you buy a garment in one of these shops:

1. You can get real bargains.
2. The money you pay is used to buy food, etc., for the needy.
3. By patronizing the shop, you're helping to employ the needy who work there.

Result: A lot of people are made happier—including you—by your "new" clothes!

The Stage

Although stage costumes are generally of high quality—and hence expensive—actors have little use for them once the show has ended. Theatrical clothing shops are fun to browse in and can be a fine source of stylish, and often very dramatic, clothing.

The Cleaners

A final clothing source is your neighborhood dry-cleaning shop. Sometimes people drop things off to be cleaned, and never pick them up! Strange but true. Perhaps they change neighborhoods. Maybe they decide they don't want the clothes after all. Or maybe they simply forget.

Since dry cleaners often have limited storage space, they hold unclaimed clothes for only a short time, and then are happy to sell them—cheaply. Usually for the price of the cleaning.

So ask your friendly dry cleaner to show you his private stock. You'll be doing each other a favor.

"Very dramatic clothing"

**Thrifty May
Mean Nifty**

With a scrutinizing eye and a bit of luck, you can find excellent clothes and great bargains in thrift shops. These stores may carry either new or used clothes, often at incredibly low prices.

If a thrift shop features new clothing, make sure that the fabric of the garment you're considering is of reasonably good quality and, again, Sanforized or preshrunk. It's especially important to be sure that your prospective merchandise is put together well enough so that it won't fall apart after a few wearings or a single washing!

**You Too Can Be
a Man of the
Cloth**

Religious organizations often collect used clothing and sell it to raise money for various projects. The rummage sale at your neighborhood church, or a clothing sale run by an organization like Hadassah, might be the perfect place to revitalize your wardrobe cheaply.

At this type of sale I've found very fine clothes that have been donated simply because someone didn't feel like wearing them any longer. What I found was both in fashion and in good condition.

House Cleaning

Almost every clothing store holds a clearance sale once or twice a year. To make room for incoming merchandise, they sell what they have in stock at very low prices.

Buying clearance-sale items sometimes involves risks, however. Clothes may be soiled or shopworn. On the other hand, they may be in perfect condition. Be discriminating: six dollars plus the price of a dry cleaning may be a real bargain for a pair of pants or a dress. Then again, it may be no bargain at all.

Remember, too, that some not-quite-so-honest stores stay in business by holding a continuous "close-out sale." At least that's what the window posters advertise. In these cases, the slogan is usually a trap; you will probably find few true bargains. Beware of these operators.

Clothing Care, or How to Treat your Hang-ups	Bv handling your clothes carefully, you give them a life-insurance policy. You also ease both mind and pocketbook, for your clothes will last longer and look better too.

Here are a few practical suggestions for clothing care and storage.

Daily Care for Hang-ups

1. Air your clothes after you undress and before putting them away at night.
2. Your hanging should—if possible—be done in a cool, dry place. Air the closet itself once in a while.
3. Use wooden hangers for heavy clothes: jackets, coats, etc. These help keep the garment in good form.
4. Wet clothes should be dried before being hung in the closet. Otherwise, they may sag and/or stretch on the hanger and may soak other garments.
5. Button buttons and zip zippers after a garment is hung up. This prevents the clothing from slipping (to the floor, for instance), and helps the clothing hold its shape.
6. Brush dirt and lint from your clothes occasionally, using a small whisk broom. Masking tape can also be used to remove dirt and lint. Simply take a piece of tape and press it onto the areas needing to be cleaned. Remove the tape and the dirt comes away with it. Lint and dirt may attract insects and can mean more frequent cleanings.

"Lint and dirt may attract insects."

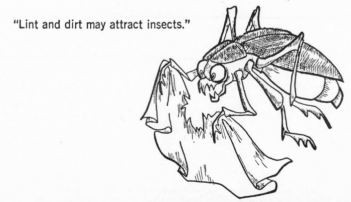

Daily Care for Fold-ups

Many of the principles for care of hang-ups apply also to fold-ups.

1. Air them before putting them away.
2. Dry them if they're wet.
3. Button buttons and zip zippers.
4. Brush them occasionally.

Some additional considerations:

1. Line your drawers with tissue or heavy-duty paper before you fill them with clothes. Otherwise, fabrics may catch on rough wood edges.
2. Fold garments neatly. This will minimize wrinkles and ironing time and will increase their life.
3. Tissue paper laid over the back of a garment before folding works wonders to scare away wrinkles.

Seasonal Clothes

When storing clothes for the long, hot summer, or the long, cold winter:

1. Clean them before putting them away. There's no sense in letting dirt soak in for several months, and your clothes will be clean when you are ready to wear them.
2. Moth protection is crucial for woolens in summer storage or in a relatively warm winter climate. Many products are available to ward off moths and other flying insects.

Looking After Your Soles

Having talked about clothing for bodies let's talk about soles—of your shoes, that is.

1. Air your shoes when you take them off, to give perspiration a chance to evaporate.
2. Alternate between at least two pairs of shoes for maximum life-span. This gives each pair a chance to air for at least one day between wearings.
3. If shoes get wet, stuff them with old towels or newspaper. Let them dry at their own pace. Direct heat, from fireplace or radiator, hardens and cracks leather.
4. Polish shoes frequently to protect them. Coat leather boots with army-surplus "dubbing" in winter. This waterproofs and protects the leather.

Cleanliness is Next to . . . You!

"Some people wear shirts into the shower, and soap and rinse them as they go along."

Or will be, when you launder or clean your clothes properly and as often as necessary.

Different fabrics require different types of cleaning. Follow the instructions that come with each item of clothing. As a general rule, however:

Whenever You Can, Wash It Yourself, being careful to use the appropriate soap. Since underwear and socks are worn daily and need frequent washing, buy several sets to minimize frequency of laundering. This saves time and prevents wear.

One of the modern washday miracles is fabric that has been chemically treated so that, after washing, it dripdries wrinkle-free. Such "permanent press" garments sometimes cost a bit more than others, but the convenience is well worth the price. With items like men's shirts, you'll find that permanent press or drip-dry not only saves you laundry bills but gives you wilt-free performance all day. Some people find that they can wash their permanent-press shirts each night, by wearing them into the shower and soaping and rinsing them as they go along. Others wash their shirts in the sink basin and then hang them up on a hanger on the shower rod.

Be Your Own Professional

If a garment requires dry cleaning, but is not especially delicate—wool sweaters, shirts, and slacks for examples—you might want to take them to a self-service dry-cleaning store. For about $2.50 you can clean eight to nine pounds of clothing (including blankets and sleeping bags)—a great saving over professional treatment.

When using self-service dry-cleaning machines, remember to clean dark and light clothes separately. Should spots fail to come out, seek a professional cleaner.

Seeking Professional Help

For delicate or very high quality dry-cleanables, you need professional services. Don't be fooled into thinking that any dry cleaner is a good dry cleaner. There are good, mediocre, and lousy professionals. And the best charge little or no more than the worst do! A bad cleaner will often severely damage your clothing.

The best way to zero in on a good dry cleaner is to ask someone who's lived in your neighborhood for a while to recommend one.

If a garment is stained, be sure to point out the stain to the dry cleaner and tell him its cause —if you can remember. This will help make his job easier, and your clothes cleaner. In fact, marking the stain with a safety pin and a note stating the source of the stain is not a bad idea. In fact, it's a must for blood, coffee, and grease stains.

Out, Out, Damned Spot!

It is generally best to let a professional dry cleaner tackle all but the mildest stains. However, you can help him and your clothing by using immediate first aid to prevent a stain from setting.

First Aid Immediately After the Accident: *

1. If a stain is not greasy and the cloth is washable, rinse with cold water. Lots of it.
2. If a stain is greasy (like butter), use a little carbon tetrachloride. Since this chemical has fumes that can be lethal, do this in a well-ventilated place.
3. For "organic stains," such as foods or blood, try an "enzyme-active" detergent.

If you decide to try chemical stain or spot removers, be sure to test the effects of any of them on the fabric by dabbing a bit of the liquid onto an unobtrusive part of the garment (e.g., inside the hem or seam). If the stain remover ends up adding stains or circles, the damage won't be too obvious. Use as little stain-removing solvent as possible: it's better to use several applications of small amounts than one big dose. Immediately after application, rinse the solvents out of the cloth.

Final Note: For greasy work clothes, a cup of kerosene added to soapy laundry water works wonders.

Send for: "Stain Removal from Fabrics— Home Methods" (cost, ten cents) from the Superintendent of Documents, Government Printing Office, Washington, D.C., 0402.

HEALTH CARE

On a daily basis, health doesn't seem to cost much. That is, until things start to go wrong and a major overhaul is necessary. Then Good Health becomes an expensive commodity.

Think of your body as a super-automobile. If you don't drive it too fast for too long, and if you feed it the right fuel, give it periodic checkups, and maybe wash it occasionally, you'll prevent major rumblings or at least treat them before they climax in a Transmission, or other organ, Transplant. Take the same car, drive it hard, feed it poorly, and wait until the engine drops dead before you take it to a medic, and you'll soon be spending a lot of money (in bills and inconvenience) for sick bay.

Your body, too, needs good fuel, moderate exercise, and an occasional tuning.

The best way to keep health-care expenses low is to prevent expensive problems from occurring.

Eat Well, Sleep Well, and Exercise Well

In order to discover whether you're eating well, sit down and think about what you've swallowed during the past forty-eight hours. If the list contains a lot of candy, cookies, pastries, soda, pizza, TV dinners, cheap hamburgers, and sandwiches bearing little but bread—chances are you're not eating very well. Change your diet, and move up to a better octane.

SLEEP is something that many people learn to live without. I spent most of two years living on four to five hours of sleep per night. Not only will such a schedule keep you from thinking clearly, it will also put undue strain on your body. Sleep (or at least go to bed) often. Invest eighty to a hundred dollars in a firm mattress (I find a thick foam-rubber one best) and a bedframe. (A box spring is totally unnecessary.) The one third of your life you spend in bed will thank you for it. So will the other two thirds.

EXERCISE: Bones that aren't moved often start

to creak. Hearts that don't get hearty exercise soon lose the ability to handle emergencies. Exercise not only strengthens your muscles but also circulates blood to your brain, lubricates the Excretion Division, dekinks bones, and makes skin rosy and resilient. In brief, a few minutes of daily exercise goes far in maintaining not only happy, healthy bodies but wide-awake brains as well.

A businessman I know began, two years ago at the age of forty-two, to run a mile and do a few calisthenics before breakfast. He hadn't exercised in twenty years. At first, he had headaches. His doctor told him this was caused by blood vessels in the brain that, from lack of blood circulation due to a sedentary life, had almost gone out of commission. The headaches soon disappeared, and he now feels that the twelve minutes a day he devotes to exercise make him feel better and help him to be more productive at work during the day. He certainly looks better!

In elementary and junior and high schools, I consistently skipped gym and played no sports. My time was spent in the library, at the piano, and in coffeehouses. In college, however, I began exercising twenty minutes a day. I was so surprised at how much better I looked and felt after two weeks that I've never stopped this exercise program.

If you don't like running or calisthenics (of course you don't really know until you've tried them for a week), try tennis, Yoga, weight training, hiking, bicycling, or swimming. But whatever you choose, do it Every Day!

Medical Insurance: Cheap and a Little Less So

Good food, sleep, and daily exercise are forms of cheap health insurance. Four other forms are:

1. The swallowing of one vitamin pill per day. Vitamins can be bought at reasonable prices, often at discount stores. They fill in for the foods you don't get around to eating, and supplement what you do

eat. When you're traveling, especially in foreign countries, a steady diet of vitamins will protect you from some of the foreign micro-beasties. So try taking vitamins for six months, a cheap but good experiment, and see if the colds, flus, and "bugs" you have don't grow smaller and fewer.

2. Lying down when you're tired. Instead of moping around or sitting on your tail when you're beat, try taking off your shoes and flopping onto a bed. Fifteen minutes of this, after lunch or supper, will make one hell of a difference—and speed up digestion.

3. Have a complete annual checkup, preferably by the same doctor each time. By going to only one doctor, good records will be kept, advice and treatment can be given with a better perspective, and you will know someone (who knows your medical history) to telephone for medical advice or in emergencies.*

4. Local health departments often provide free immunization programs, chest X rays, and medical tests of various sorts. Call your town hall, and find out what services are available. Shots, chest X rays, and other tests can be expensive when done by a private physician. Community medical services are not charity. They have been established in the hopes of improving community-wide health conditions.

* In a medical emergency, calling the police is the slowest way to get help. Instead, call a private ambulance service. Or, if you're not in abysmal condition, phone for a cab: faster and much cheaper. Tell the dispatcher who answers the phone that there's a $2 tip for the first cab at your door. It works. Finally, hospital emergency wards will give medical advice over the phone.

Less Cheap Health Insurance

Blue Cross and Blue Shield health-insurance plans provide fairly comprehensive coverage at a reasonable cost. Check with your local health department to find out what other insurance policies your state or insurance companies within your state have to offer.

Medical Supplies: A Little Cheaper

One of the things that hurts most when you're sick and in pain is the cost of medicine and other medical supplies.

1. Drug discount-houses and cut-rate drugstores can

save you money on standard-brand drugs, bandages, toilet articles, etc. Ask your doctor to recommend a nearby store of this sort.

2. When your doctor prescribes drugs for you, ask if he will write the prescription for "generics," rather than for brand-name drugs. This can save you a good deal of money.

3. Mail-order houses can send you both prescription and nonprescription drugs at two-thirds or even one-half the retail price. One reputable firm that will eagerly send you a catalogue is Direct Drug Services, 823 Upshur Street, N.W., Washington, D.C., 20011.

To Maintain a Toothy Grin

Teeth tend to be painful and expensive little monsters when they're mistreated. And false teeth are neither as good-looking, nor as comfortable, nor as romantic, nor nearly as efficient, as the real thing.

As with the rest of your body, it's better to prevent dental problems than to try catching your teeth as they begin to tumble out. Remember: If you won't be true to your teeth, they'll be false to you.

There are three things you can do to maintain good teeth cheaply:

1. DIET: Eat as many hard-to-chew foods as possible, particularly raw fruits and vegetables. These foods stimulate, exercise, and clean both teeth and gums. Most people—and especially those eating college or institutional foods—do not get very chewy foods. Everything is ground up (like hamburger), precooked, overcooked, or soft (like American white breads). This is a rather modern, basically American, food habit. A diet of mushy foods will do a lot of damage to both teeth and gums by lack of stimulation. Such damage can cost you hundreds of dollars in repair bills before you reach the age of thirty.

If you are prone to tooth decay, besides eating chewier foods, you should reduce or eliminate

"The swallowing of one vitamin pill per day. . . ."

your sugar intake (e.g., hard candies and gum, sugar on cereals and in hot drinks). The average set of American teeth is confronted annually by three times the amount of sugar that it can handle easily.

2. BRUSH your teeth within fifteen minutes after eating. That is when the strongest enamel-eroding acids are formed. Use an extra-firm, flat-surfaced toothbrush for maximum cleaning and gum stimulation.

When brushing, concentrate your energies on the line where gums and teeth meet. That's where bacteria congregate and engage in violent demonstrations. Be sure to scrub the inside surfaces of the teeth and behind the back teeth—all at the tooth-gum line. Time spent brushing these areas is worthwhile, whereas time spent brushing the tops of your teeth is almost wasted, since saliva can clean them easily.

The areas of the gum line and between teeth are so critical that some dentists say not to bother brushing your teeth, unless it makes your mouth taste better. Instead, for maximum cleansing of important areas, use dental floss between each pair of teeth. Be careful, however, not to remove fillings when doing so.

Whether you brush, use floss, or do both, the time spent will save you a good deal of pain and money.

3. PROFESSIONAL CHECKUPS and cleaning should be done twice a year, never more than a year apart, or your small, cheap problems may wax costly. If you avoid dentists because of possible pain, remember, a little pain early saves a hellish amount later on. Also, a great deal of pain in the dentist's office is due to nervousness. Take a couple of aspirin before going.

Saving Money: Many dental schools will service your teeth as part of their student-training program. The students are carefully supervised. The cost is low. Inquire at local colleges about such programs. Hurry, there's usually a waiting list! *

Remember: A good life cannot be had if your health is poor. Take care of yourself, no one else will. Soon. Eat, sleep, and exercise well. Take vitamins and naps, and care for medical and dental problems before they cut into your cheap but good budget.

* In a similar way, student-training programs at men's barbering schools and women's hairdressing schools should be looked into as potential sources of cheap but good haircuts.

HOW TO BUY

Whether you're buying furniture, cars, appliances, or anything else, you're probably going to be spending money. And you want to get as much as you can for that money. The following ideas may suggest a fairly rational approach to the buying game.

The Merchandise

After deciding what you want and before racing off to shell out your hard-earned cash, THINK. Here are three cardinal rules:

"A little pain early saves
a hellish amount later on."

1. Plan Ahead. Think about what you want and need, and keep your eyes open for bargains, both new and used.
2. Buy good-quality items that won't fall apart, but don't buy "better" (i.e., more expensive) than you need. For example, though I'm a musician by hobby, I don't find the quality of a one-thousand-dollar stereo system much more attractive than that of many portable models. So, why invest more than necessary? Many people are lured into buying stereo quality they cannot even hear, let alone afford!

   Why buy furniture that's more snazzy than the type of apartment you're living in . . . clothes you'll only wear twice . . . cars that go faster than traffic conditions can handle?

   Before buying the brand or make that is reputed to be "the best of its kind," check out the ones that are competing and are "on the way up." They just might be cheaper—because their manufacturers are actively striving for higher quality—and better. This is often true of products like cars, cameras, bicycles, and audio equipment.
3. Don't spend more money than you have. Don't get trapped into installment buying; if you ever happen to fall behind in payments, the seller is usually in a legal position to repossess and resell what you have supposedly "bought" and think you own.

New, Used, and Rented

I invariably prefer to buy items that are slightly used. Whether it be camping equipment, kitchen appliances, textbooks, or anything else, good-quality items can be had cheaply (usually for about 50 per cent of the original cost) once they have been "used." Which really means, once they've been purchased. The attitude of regarding something once-owned and well-cared-for as tainted is a sickness of the American consumer public. But it's a sickness you can happily capitalize on if you use your head wisely.

If you decide, after all, to buy a NEW item, compare brands by looking them up in *Consumer Reports* (a monthly magazine) or in *Consumer Reports Annual Buying Guide*. Both the monthly magazine and the buying guide contain unbiased and extremely reliable information, comparing different brands of all items from mousetraps to tuxedos to sewing machines to cars. Most libraries have monthly issues of this magazine and the annual buying guide.

Once you've checked *Consumer Reports* and other resources * and have decided what brand and model you want, see if you can find a display model (an item that's been on display in the store) or a factory second (one that might bear a scratch before you buy it and start adding scratches of your own) at the store you shop in.

If you decide to buy USED items, check classified ads and bulletin boards. People who are moving will often sell furniture, bikes, tools, appliances, and curtains cheaply—even more cheaply if you are friendly and decide you wish to buy several of the items they're offering for sale.

When I wish to buy used items, I often go to shops that repair them.** Such shops include bicycle, hi-fi, and electrical-appliance repair stores. In these places I try to pick up fully repaired items that were never reclaimed by their owners. In this way, I'm guaranteed that the item needs no repair, and I usually end up paying only the price of the repairs. I've purchased a bicycle, AM-FM radio, tuxedo, and vacuum cleaner this way. When searching for this sort of bargain, it's best to look for out-of-the-way stores that aren't widely known.

Be sure to examine used items carefully. In fact, it might pay to go first to a retail store and ask a salesman to show you a new one so you can see how the item you're thinking of buying ought to work. Ask the salesman to point out its features.

* Ask your friends about the performance of their possessions.

** Visit also army/navy surplus stores and moving-company warehouse clearance sales.

If you buy something that's missing parts or instruction manuals, don't spend time looking in local stores for replacements. Send a note to the manufacturer, whose address is probably written or stamped somewhere on the item. This saves time, trouble, and retailer's markup when trying to obtain parts. Be sure to include the model or serial number in your correspondence.

RENTING: Before buying a specialized tool, sewing machine, musical instrument, bicycle, car, typewriter, etc., ask yourself how long and how often you'll be using it. Renting is often the cheapest way out for items used infrequently. Check the Yellow Pages under "Rental"—and also be sure to call retailers of the item you wish to rent (i.e., typewriter store, hardware store, sewing-machine retailers, etc.). You can often rent through these people, at a fraction of the cost of purchase.

The Buyer

Where I grew up, every family on the street had one-fourth acre of land and fifty feet of sidewalk. Each family also owned a power mower, snow blower, leaf collector, and other expensive items with which to care for its tiny plot. Is this ridiculous?

I'm not sure. But I think so. If explicit written agreements and understandings can be worked out among friends and/or neighbors, joint ownership of many expensive items should be seriously considered. Very clear arrangements should be made before the purchase. These should outline details for:

A. A maintenance fund.
B. Who's responsible for storing and repairing the item.
C. Who will use what and when.
D. What happens if someone moves out of the neighborhood (who sells out to whom at what cost).

If you love, or at least trust, your neighbor—and if you're both fairly considerate types—joint ownership may be a good idea for items ranging from sewing machines to barbecue grills. If each of you needs a particular item, but plans to use it infrequently, joint ownership seems to be a very sensible solution if you'd rather own than rent.

When You as Buyer Ought Not to Buy

Just as Chapter 4 suggests not to shop for food when you're hungry, you should not shop for anything on impulse. When in doubt, think. No matter how good the bargain looks, wait and look around. There's always someone else who wants to sell you the same thing at an even better price.

The Seller

*Such as when cashing personal checks.

It pays to make an effort to get to know local store owners. Establishing friendly business contacts helps you save time, money, and trouble.* When selecting a repairman or similar service from among many, seek advice from long-time residents of the area. Ask several residents, not just one.

When buying anything new, compare the prices of different stores. Call or visit a retail store, a department store, and discount houses. If prices are quite similar, buy from whoever gives you the most at-the-store service. If the product at the discount store is significantly cheaper, make sure it's the same product (with the same warranty or guarantee) before buying it.

Factory outlets often sell seconds cheaply. Look such items over carefully, so that you fully understand why they were labeled seconds.

When a store posts such advertisements as "Drastic Reductions" or "Reduced to 50 per cent," take extra-special care. The same is true for stores that run sales continuously. Compare prices rigorously, and make sure the item being sold is what it's supposed to be!

When answering classified ads, you might occasionally run into a shady dealer using personal ads as a front. This doesn't happen very often, but be aware of the possibility.

If you're at all unsure about the honesty of a store or dealer, check with your local Better Business Bureau or state consumer-protection division. Better still, don't buy from the store in question—look elsewhere.

Don't buy from (or allow goods to be left "on approval" by) door-to-door salesmen. No matter how good the "bargain" sounds. Sometimes the deal is honest, often not. You can easily end up with shoddy goods, mysterious bills, or nonexistent service. Door-to-door salesmen make an art of talking quickly and more glibly than you. That is their forte. If they won't leave quickly, don't try to interrupt them—it's an impossible feat! Patiently wait them out, and wave them good-bye rather than "Good Buy."

The Season

Some merchandise changes seasonally. This is especially true of clothing, linens, and outdoor goods. Other products change models (cars, appliances) in the late fall. Take advantage of these seasonal variations by buying, for example, winter clothes in the spring and summer clothes in the fall, a mower in winter, a snow blower in July.

MONTH: The two best months of the year for clearance sales—times when stores try to unload all their old inventory to make room for new items —are January and August. Buy then.

SALE: Never take the words "Sale," "Clearance Sale," "Close-Out," or "Riddance Sale" at face value. No matter how large or colorful the poster ads, the merchandise may not have any significant price reduction. Investigate before you invest.*

FEATURE ITEMS: On the other hand, most genuine sales (in large discount or department stores particularly) that are well promoted in local newspapers "feature" a few truly marked-down items as customer bait. If you happen to need and want these "feature items" anyway, the sale might be the time to buy.

* When walking through stores, keep an eye open for unadvertised sales, as these can often be bonanzas.

Wheeling and Dealing

Examination

The moment of decision is at hand. Examine the piece of merchandise carefully. Before you take it home, test out the specific item you will eventually own. Insist on plugging it in, turning it on, and testing all aspects. Even the most honest of stores can't predict what's going to be inside any given factory-sealed box. A five-minute test before you leave with your acquisition may save you a long and aggravating trip back to the store two hours or two days later.

If it's clothing you're about to buy, try it on when you're wearing the same sort of clothes you'd eventually wear with it. For example, when buying a man's jacket, wear a shirt and tie. Shoes should be sized with regard for the weight of the sock or stocking to be worn beneath. Winter overcoats should be tried on over the bulkiest of clothing.

Buy good-quality products. They give better service and require less care later on.

"Be wary of anyone who tries to push you into buying quickly."

Take your time

Don't let a salesman fluster you. There are always other brands, makes, and stores. Be wary of anyone who tries to push you into buying quickly because it's such a great buy that you might never find one again. Think it over carefully.

Leave the store with exactly what you came in to buy

Nothing more or less. No other brand or model. No extra gadgets. Disregard sales talk aimed toward adding on extras to raise prices and commissions; don't buy a different brand or model just because the salesman says he's out of what you want, or because he claims that what he has instead is better. He may be pushing items of lower quality for higher commissions. If you did your homework before you entered the store, you know what you want. If the first store doesn't have it, and won't order it for you (get a written guarantee of arrival date for ordered goods), go elsewhere!

Being friendly but firm

Being friendly but firm makes a difference. Don't barge into a store and interrupt the salesman when he's with another customer. First of all, chances are you'll only be told to wait. Secondly, you might learn something about merchandise or about the salesman by listening in on what's going on between him and the other customer. Finally, no salesman will be predisposed to help an inconsiderate person who tries to interrupt him in the middle of a sale.

Speak softly, but be firm. Ask every question that comes to mind. Don't be shy. Don't buy from someone who can't accurately answer your questions about the product. Instead, ask politely, "Has anyone in the store had personal experience with this item? Could I ask him a few questions." A salesman who really knows his product is usually proud to show off his knowledge. Take advantage of this to learn everything you can about what you're buying.

Be sure to ask to see a factory specification-sheet on the product. If there is none, read the labels and instruction pamphlets. Ask questions about whatever is noted on spec sheets, labels, and pamphlets until you understand the meaning of all terms and items noted. This goes for clothes, as well as for furniture, appliances, hand tools, and garden supplies.

Bargaining

List prices or suggested retail prices mean almost nothing. Every store buys item X at the same price, then tacks on whatever profit it chooses. Discount houses usually add on less than retail and small stores do, since discount outfits make up the difference by selling in large quantities.

If you can find out how much the item costs the storekeeper, you can be in a better position to bargain. If you can't wheedle your way into seeing a dealer's price book, figure that the retailer pays 55 to 65 per cent of the list price.

One way to begin bargaining is to look the salesman or store owner knowingly in the eye, and with a slight smile, ask, "Is there any discount if I pay cash?" or "If I also buy a Y, can I have the two of them (X and Y) for only $40 [a sum considerably lower than the combined price of X and Y]?" or "This doesn't happen to be on sale this week, does it?" This last line must be accompanied by a true comradely sparkle or wink of the eye.

You'll soon find out if the dealer is willing to dicker. Some small store-owners expect and enjoy this kind of haggling. But, if wheeling and dealing doesn't happen to be your salesman's game, go elsewhere.

Many a tiny shop-owner will be willing to "special order" you an item for only a small (five or ten dollars instead of fifty dollars) profit. Why shouldn't he? He doesn't have to stock the item, store it, service it, or even give you a sales pitch.

All he has to do is send out a postcard or phone the factory representative, and he's earned himself a few bucks. To try this approach it's best to discreetly find out all details of the item before approaching the small shop-owner. Then tell him: "I would like a Snazzbang, model XYZ. I know you don't regularly stock it, but it'll cost you eighty-four dollars to order it wholesale. I'll give you ninety-five dollars for it—in advance, if you prefer."

Such an arrangement might save you a good deal of money.

Landlord Discounts

Finally, remember that landlords can often get automatic discounts on hardware and lumber products. Ask your landlord to order paints, tools, and wood for you if he is a friendly type of guy.

Concluding the Purchase

Once you've settled on seller, merchandise, and price, the moment of reckoning is nigh. If you must sign a contract or bill of sale:

1. Read and understand every single word—big print and small print—on the page. In fact, start by reading the small print, since it's small for a reason. If permitted, take the contract home to look over and to discuss with friend or lawyer. Sign nothing unless you understand everything.

2. All prices and salesman's promises should be written clearly on the contract. Anything discussed between you and the seller that doesn't appear on the contract should be placed on that paper before you sign it.

   Remember:

   a. Anything you sign—no matter how short or informal—is considered a legal contract.

   b. Always get a carbon copy of any contract or bill of sale that requires your signature. This is very important.

3. Signing. Make sure you're not agreeing to do something or pay for something you don't want or

intend to do or pay for! If you're confused as to what is required of you, don't sign.

If there is a blank space between the end of the printed contract and the line on which you're asked to sign, DO NOT SIGN on the line. Sign immediately under the last provision of the contract. Once you've signed, it's all over. You're legally responsible for everything above your name!!!

The above instructions hold true for your signature on contracts, bills of sale, apartment leases, truck- or equipment-rental forms, credit-card slips, and service (dry cleaner, repair) slips.

Remember: Always sign directly under the last item mentioned.

Paying

If you pay in cash, get an explicit receipt, telling:
1. Precisely what you've paid for.
2. The date.
3. The name and address (printed clearly) of the seller. Even in a department store, have the salesman print his name clearly. You may wish to call or blame him later.

If you use a check, a similar receipt is still necessary. In addition, write on the check (lower left-hand corner) something like: "Full payment for Snazzbang, model XYZ," or "Refundable deposit for Snazzbang, model XYZ." Be explicit. A few extra words on a check can prove to be invaluable protection, especially on deposits that you thought were refundable, but the seller later tries to keep.

Registering Purchases

When you buy electrical appliances, including TV's, stereo equipment, and kitchen items—as well as watches, bikes, jewelry, etc.—register the item with:
1. The manufacturer, who will usually enclose a registration card with the merchandise. Often a guarantee or warranty depends upon your returning this registration card.

2. With your insurance company.
3. In a personal notebook. Note the item, date, price before tax, seller, and manufacturer's code number. An inventory notebook of this sort can include books and recordings. When friends borrow anything, ask them to put their initials and the date next to the item. Such a notebook could be invaluable in the event of theft or fire. Or when you're moving and trying to remember who borrowed what.

Tax Benefits

A notebook like that described in number 3 above might save you a good deal of money on your income tax. Remember, any and all taxes you pay during the year are tax-deductible. This goes for sales taxes (clothing, furniture, appliances), food taxes, property and automobile taxes, customs taxes, and even gasoline taxes and highway tolls! A shoe box full of sales slips and receipts* can save you a load of money when income-tax time rolls around.

* Both gas stations and tollbooth operators have receipts ready to give you if you ask for them. Receipts are also handy to have should you need service on, or decide to return, an item.

PROBLEMS

Who knows what kind of business problems you may have? Maybe the dry cleaner will return your jacket or dress with fewer buttons or more holes. Maybe the food or wine you buy will turn out to be spoiled. Or the merchandise you receive in the mail will not be precisely what you ordered. Or your recently purchased electrical appliance goes on the fritz.

Don't Stand For It. None of the above should be tolerated in martyred silence.**

** Never bother complaining to the salesman. Go directly to his supervisor, or even to the store or company's executive level.

1. Immediately bring the problem to someone's attention. Do not use the ruined dress, spoiled food or wine, unordered merchandise, or diseased appliance. If you do, such use may be regarded as an implied acceptance of the condition or product.

As soon as possible, return the product. But if you cannot get an exchange or payment of damages while there in person, do not leave the prod-

"Who knows what kind of business problems you may have?"

uct with the seller. Take it home again.

2. Call your local Better Business Bureau for advice. At the same time, telephone, write or telegraph high officials in the company. Names and addresses of presidents and other executives can be found in your town library. See *Poor's Register of Corporations, Directors and Executives* or *Moody's Handbook of Common Stocks*.

A letter or telegram to the president—or to the public-relations (or customer-service) department —will often elicit a prompt response. Amazing but true.

I prefer using the phone. Daily. Don't let someone "call you back." They rarely do. Keep calling and asking, "Has my new Snazzbang been sent out yet?" Chances are, they'll send you two new ones pronto. If the call is long distance, call collect, person-to-person, to whomever you choose (after you've first registered your complaint station-to-station). Even if your person-to-person calls aren't accepted (they usually won't be), the person you select will be certain to remember you from day to day. A squeaky wheel gets oil.

3. If things begin to look hopeless (don't wait more than four weeks), go to small-claims court. Each town has one, and for a fee under two dollars, you can have your case heard and judged.*

I have done this several times. The proceedings are informal, and no lawyer is necessary, or even an advantage. You tell your side of the story to a judge, presenting any evidence or witnesses you wish. The defendant (appliance-company representative, dry-cleaner manager, insurance company that didn't pay you, supermarket, person who never repaid an IOU, landlord, or repairman whom you feel did you wrong) presents his side.

The judge will ask a few more questions, and then settle the case on the spot. If you are declared in the right, you'll be paid, or have your merchandise replaced, within thirty days.

* Each court has its own way of handling small-claims cases. Call your town hall for information. It's always made very simple for you. Your case, however, must usually be for an amount under $200 or $250. But call your town hall and find out!

Small-claims court proceedings rarely take more than half an hour, are interesting, and are a good way of settling problems fast. Often, if you tell a company (or landlord, store owner, or other individual) that you're starting small-claims court proceedings, they'll settle with you quickly, because they figure they'll lose and/or it means that they or their representative must lose a half-day's work. If your defendant does not show up in court, you win by default.

FOR WHOM THE PHONE RINGS

It rings for thee. A true friend, it's always at your service.

What a timesaving servant dear Alexander bequeathed to us! Through all our buying, selling, and complaining, Mr. Bell's gift to posterity enables us to prevent many wasted hours if we but wisely take advantage of it.

Before Leaving Home in the Morning

Call to make sure that the store you're planning to visit:

A. Is open.
B. Has presently in stock the item you want.
C. Will "Wrap it for Smith and have the sales slip all written up, to be picked up at ten o'clock."

When you arrive at the store, be it for groceries, pizza, hardware, prescription drugs, or whatever, you'll have no wait at all. For, at his own convenience, the store owner will have put aside whatever you requested. It's to his benefit to do this in slack moments. And to yours, too.

Remember, as a customer, you might have to wait twenty minutes to be helped. A ringing phone, however, demands immediate attention. Your order given, you can pick it up later. The time you spend will be two minutes instead of thirty.

So, plan your day before you leave home. Using the phone for fifteen minutes in the morning will save you hours of running around to the wrong stores and waiting at the right ones.

"Make sure that the store you're planning to visit is open."

How to Be an Expert Phone Pest

In this day of bureaucracy, many people go to work and do nothing. Call and ask any office for something and—even if they tell you the date they'll "do it" or "send it"—you'll soon be lost and forgotten midst paper work and coffee breaks.

When service or merchandise should be, but is not, forthcoming, don't wait at home muttering quiet obscenities. Pick up that phone—that God-sent gift of Bell—and use it. Soon and often! Don't be shy about calling a place two days after you've ordered something just to ask: "Has it been sent out yet? Please check your records to be certain."

Don't hesitate to call a repairman first thing in the morning of the day he's scheduled to arrive and ask, "At what time shall I expect you?" Chances are that he'll have to quickly readjust his schedule to include you. And, then again, he may never arrive.

Being Placed "On Hold"

When an operator asks you to "please hold," pick up a magazine, newspaper, or book. Ten minutes of waiting "on hold" is not so bad when you consider that otherwise you'll end up waiting two to five hours for someone to "call you back right away." Tell that operator, "I'll wait as long as necessary." Then get back to your book. If she asks again, "Will you wait, sir?" reply, "I am reading a good book and I can wait two hours if necessary!" That always brings prompt service, since no one can afford to have a phone line tied up forever. Finally, if you happen to be disconnected, call back, register a complaint with the operator, and start the procedure all over again.

If the person you speak to must hang up to check on something you've inquired about, don't expect him to call you back. Instead, tell him, "Call me if you get a chance. Otherwise, I'll call you back in fifteen minutes," or an hour, whichever seems to be appropriate. This way your salesman won't postpone your order and/or request for information until the next day . . . or the next . . . or the next.

As you can see, Mr. Bell can save you much time and aggravation if he's properly employed.

This chapter has just begun to touch upon the Art of Handling Money. No doubt, experience will teach you other tricks—ones that I might never even dream of.

Between us, despite the day and age, perhaps we can begin to GET OUR MONEY'S WORTH!

"The Art of Handling Money"

CHAPTER SIX

HOME REPAIRS FOR THE POET,

OR

HOW TO KEEP THINGS RUNNING

If you have taken the preceding chapters to heart, you are now undoubtedly in a state of bliss. You have found the perfect apartment, made a successful exodus from your earlier habitat, furnished your rooms cheap but good, found your landlord tractable (or have taken the necessary steps to make him so), and are eating with relish. Indeed, the taste of life is sweet upon your lips. But alas! The toilet won't flush! Or the lights go out! Or the windows are stuck! You return abruptly from a blissful nirvana to the real world and are faced with the question that has plagued mankind since his first broken hoe: "How the hell do I keep things working around here?"

This chapter will not teach you to mend hoes, but it will help you face the more common crises that may arise in your new apartment. This proverbial "Do-It-Yourself" chapter is a first-aid manual for your apartment, a guide to repairs that you can do with little mechanical skill, less interest, and no experience. In other words, this is a Manual of Home Repair for the Poet.

THREE GRAND PRINCIPLES OF HOME REPAIR

Like any aspect of modern life, home repair has laws or underlying principles that must be understood. Like those of thermodynamics, home-repair principles are three in number:

1. Self-confidence
2. Education
3. Planning.

To be more specific:

1. Have Confidence!

You *can* do home repairs. You can! It's really simple, as the rest of this chapter will prove. Don't let mechanical devices terrify you. Most household problems are due to simple malfunctions that anybody, even a poet, can remedy if he has but a little confidence and a little knowledge.

2. Learning can be profitable as well as enjoyable.

Exploit your friendly neighborhood hardware salesman. When you have a home-repair problem that
you have doubts about, or require parts for, this
gentleman is a prime source of information about
both. Ask him questions! Learn everything he
knows!

Your janitor, too, might be a good source of
such information.

3. Plan, Think, Observe, Plan!

Remember, most home repairs require no more
than a dash of common sense.

When disassembling anything, from a plug to a
color television, watch what you're doing! Know
what piece goes where and in what order. It's a
good idea when disassembling to label the parts
with a number (on masking tape) indicating the
order in which they were removed, or to make a
diagram of the assembled unit before you take it
apart and try to arrange all the pieces to look like
the diagram.

Before you begin, plan what tools you'll need
for the operation and have them handy (see the

"Don't let things sit around
disconnected and unassembled."

Handy-Dandy Tool Kit section that follows). Work on newspapers or old towels to minimize the mess, keep things consolidated, and facilitate cleanup.

When repairing something, do it all at once. Don't let things sit around disconnected and unassembled—they have a habit of staying that way.

Your reward for taking these Three Grand Principles to heart will be calm in the face of potential household crises, pride in your ability to do it yourself, and hundreds of dollars that you might have paid to sundry and various repairmen.

THE HANDY-DANDY TOOL KIT

One of the nicest aspects of doing your own repairs is that you get to use some simple and very handy-dandy tools.

It pays to invest in a few of the more basic tools. Here is a list of the items that your tool kit should contain:

A. A small hammer.
B. Screw drivers: either a plastic handle with several types of metal attachments, or one regular screw driver and one Phillips screw driver.
C. Two wrenches: one a monkey wrench, the other an adjustable crescent.
D. Lubricating oil, and maybe a can of "Liquid Wrench" for loosening rusted nuts and bolts.
E. Assorted nails, screws, and picture hooks.
F. Band-Aids.

Your landlord may be more than willing to loan these and other tools to you as the need for them arises—he'll probably be especially generous if you are willing to save him time and money by making the necessary repairs yourself.

Or, if you find that you must purchase tools or parts, ask your landlord if a local hardware store gives him a landlord's discount that you—as a tenant or through him—can take advantage of.

In addition to the basic tool kit suggested

above, it's wise to keep a few extra items around in case specific problems arise.

For Plumbing Repairs
A. A "plumber's helper," or suction cup
B. A wire "snake"
C. A kit of assorted-sized washers (forty-nine cents per kit)
D. Plastic tape, small wooden plug—for leaking pipes
E. Rubber gloves
F. A big bucket or two.

For Electrical Repairs
A. Electrical tape
B. Electrical cord ("lamp cord")
C. Extra fuses
D. Extra plugs
E. Wire stripper (if you can afford the luxury—about one dollar)
F. Flashlight.

For Doors
A. Plastic wood
B. Cardboard.

For Windows
A. A putty knife
B. A candle to use as lubricant.

For Radiators
A. Small wood blocks
B. A pot.

Equipped with the modern-day equivalents of lance, shield, and chain mail, you are now ready to face fearlessly the dragons that threaten household happiness.

Now for the battle . . .

THE FINE ART OF PLUMBING, OR HOW TO DAMN THE FLOOD

Problems with that intricate creation of modern engineering—the plumbing system—are common enough and dramatic enough to add trauma to everyone's life. They are also very costly to repair professionally (some plumbers charge ten dollars an hour; most charge more). And if your

"Let's not get professional help unless it's absolutely essential."

landlord pays for the repairs, you probably won't get speedy action.

So let's not get professional help unless it's absolutely essential—and if it is, ask your kindly landlord to finance the job.

The most common plumbing problems you will face are:

A. Toilet troubles
B. Clogged drains
C. Leaky faucets
D. Leaking pipes.

Each of these problem areas may appear intimidating at first. But, as we'll soon see, your plumbing system consists of a few, very simple elements that are easy to understand. And even easier to keep in top working condition!

First, let's discuss some basics. A plumbing system is simply a system for circulating water: it comes in, then it goes out. That's all. If you have a plumbing problem, it can be due only to:

1. Water coming in.
2. Water going out.
3. Water staying in when it should be going out.
4. Water going out when it should be staying in.

When you move into a new home or an old apartment, take a few moments to locate the water shutoff valve for the whole system (usually in the basement) and the valves for individual fixtures (usually on the wall behind or below fixtures). Label them.

Should a plumbing emergency arise, and the water level in sink, tub, or toilet rise with it:

1. Turn off the water controls for the troubled fixture, or for the whole system, depending on how widespread the problem is.

2. Quickly bail out (even a few bucketsful will suffice) the afflicted fixture(s), so they won't overflow and to reduce the water level to the point where it is low enough to allow you to work at repairing the problem.

3. Now that you have things more or less under control, repair the fixture by choosing and following the appropriate procedure from the ones that follow.

Toilet Troubles, or You Too Can Have Fun in the John

Have you ever wanted to flush your troubles away and been frustrated by an un-co-operative toilet? Well, you need never suffer that frustration again.

Although most of us regard the toilet tank as a semimagical system of complex physics principles, it is, in fact, an extremely simple gadget to understand and repair. A bit of toilet training will dispel the awe too often inspired by this fixture and make repairing it a simple matter.

Toilet-Tank Theory

First things first. There are two parts to a home toilet: the bowl and the tank mounted above and behind it. The tank holds the mechanism that regulates water flow. Two control valves—one to empty the tank and one to refill it—are the crux

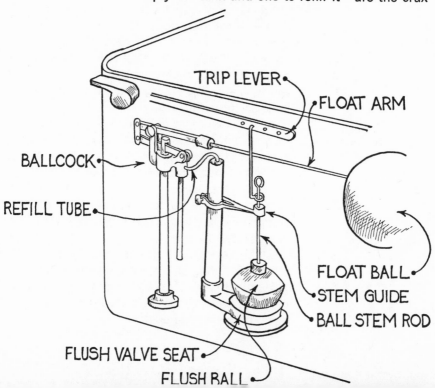

TRIP LEVER

FLOAT ARM

BALLCOCK

REFILL TUBE

FLOAT BALL

STEM GUIDE

BALL STEM ROD

FLUSH VALVE SEAT

FLUSH BALL

of this system. All other parts work to close or open these valves at the right time.

Valve System #1: The flush-valve seat, which is kept closed by the rubber flush ball. When you press the lever that flushes the toilet, all you are doing is raising a trip lever that yanks the flush ball off the flush-valve seat. The water in the tank can then rush out through the flush valve into the toilet bowl, forcing the contents of the bowl out through the bowl drain.

Water pressure is responsible for holding the flush ball tightly over its valve. But when the flush handle triggers the flush ball, the ball will rise to the top of the water, sinking back on the valve seat as the water empties from the tank. Once the flush ball is back on the flush-valve seat, the tank is "plugged" and can be refilled.

Valve System #2: The inlet valve, or ball cock (that's really what they call it!). As the water level in the tank drops through the flush valve, the hollow metal or plastic "float ball" sinks with it, pulling the "float arm" down, too. Inside the ball cock is an inlet valve that is opened by the sinking of the float arm. When the float ball reaches its lowest point, the inlet valve is fully open—and water will flow from the supply line back into the toilet tank via the refill tube.

As the water rises in the tank, it carries the float ball up with it. As the float ball rises, it slowly closes off the inlet valve. When the tank is filled, the flow of incoming water stops because the inlet valve is fully closed.

If, for any reason, the inlet valve does not close completely, a special overflow pipe will drain excess water from the tank.

So there we have it: the toilet tank is either emptying, filling, or enjoying a comfortable equilibrium! However, as you might have guessed, either of these two systems can malfunction. If it does, here's how to doctor it.

"Your toilet will refuse to flush."

For a Clogged Toilet Bowl

Turn to page 273, "The Plunger Prance."

For a Toilet That Cries and Refuses to Flush

If water keeps running from the tank into the bowl, thereby causing the tank never to refill (check this by lifting off the tank cover), your toilet will refuse to flush.

The rubber FLUSH-BALL VALVE is responsible. Since it is rubber, it can in time become spongy, in which case it won't fit tightly into the valve seat and must be replaced.*

To install a new flush ball:

*On many toilets, the older flush-ball apparatus can be replaced very quickly with a recently marketed flapper system that's more easily installed and less troublesome than the old-fashioned flush ball. These flappers are available at hardware stores (Korky is one brand name) or at Sears (Universal Toilet Ball Flapper, which costs about $1.50).

1. Turn off the toilet tank's water supply by tightly closing the water valve on the wall behind, under, or alongside the toilet tank.

   Tie a piece of string to the flush-ball arm. Tie the other end of the string to a high object (like a shower-curtain rod or a shelf above the tank). This assures that the inlet valve is closed and that the tank will not refill when flushed.

2. Flush the toilet to empty the tank.

Note: Steps 1 and 2 should be followed in every repair procedure that necessitates reaching into the tank.

3. Holding the ball stem in one hand, unscrew the flush ball from the ball stem.
4. Rub the exposed valve seat lightly with fine steel wool. This will clean the valve seat.
5. Check the ball stem for bending or corrosion, and replace it if necessary.
6. Screw the new flush ball onto its stem.
7. Turn the water supply on, so that you can check out the flushing operation.

Should you find that the new flush ball does not fit tightly into the flush valve after the tank empties, the problem is either that the BALL-STEM ROD is bent or that the stem guide is not properly aligned. In the case of a bent stem, it is easier to replace it than to try and straighten it.

In the case of a misaligned STEM GUIDE, adjust it as follows:

1. Loosen the control screw that holds the stem guide.
2. Jiggle the guide until the ball drops directly onto the center of the flush-valve seat.
3. Tighten the control screw. This will hold the stem guide and flush ball permanently in the correct position.

Sometimes a tank will refill after flushing, but water will then continue to enter the tank and be forced to drain via the overflow pipe.* (We might call this a "royal flush.") If this happens, the fault lies in either the float mechanism or the inlet valve controlled by the float mechanism.

To locate the culprit, lift the float arm up slightly. If the hissing and flow of water into the tank stop, either the float ball is leaking and needs replacement, or the float arm supporting the ball is in need of adjustment. If this test fails to cut off the inflowing water, the ball cock (inlet valve) needs repair.

* Some old toilets have no overflow pipe. If water continues to run into the tank, be sure to turn off the valve on the wall under the tank.

To test for a defective FLOAT BALL:

1. Unscrew the float ball from the float arm.
2. Shake the ball. If there is water inside, the ball is leaky.
3. Buy a new plastic float ball and screw it on to the float arm.

If, however, you find that the float ball is not leaking, try readjusting the FLOAT ARM:

1. Hold the wire arm in the middle and bend it so that the float ball sinks one-half inch or an inch lower in the tank.
2. Turn on the water and flush the tank. The water should stop flowing before its level reaches that of the overflow pipe.
3. If the water continues to run, bend the float arm a little more and flush, flush again.

Let's assume that, alas, both these simple remedies have failed miserably and that you are still tormented by a hyperactive toilet tank. By process of elimination, if I may be permitted the phrase, we know that the ball cock is to blame. So, undaunted, we tackle this innocent-looking mechanism. Tackling the BALL COCK:

To check for worn-out washers and clogged or rusted plungers within the ball cock:

1. Disassemble the mechanism by first removing the two pins or screws that hold the float mechanism to the ball-cock unit
2. Lift the stem and plunger from the ball cock.
3: Locate the leather washer at the bottom of the plunger, which may be either forced or screwed in place.
4. Replace this washer with a new one.
5. In most mechanisms there is another washer, called an O-ring, that fits around the plunger. Replace this also.

Should you discover that the ball cock is corroded, that parts of it crack or crumble in your hand like a stale cooky, or that the inside seems in poor condition, the wisest move is to install a completely new ball-cock assembly. A few dollars will guarantee carefree operation for years. And, of course, your landlord will most likely be delighted to foot the bill.

Now that we've plumbed the very bowels of your toilet system and have seen how simple it is to repair, let's hope that you'll never be bowled over by another problem toilet.

Clogged Drains

Drains become clogged when people throw crud into them. Kitchen crud includes such delectables as grease, coffee grounds, and chicken fat. Bathroom crud consists mostly of hair, cosmetics, and children's toys. Toilets are stopped up by paper other than toilet paper, sanitary napkins, and a-sordid miscellany.

Remember: If several plumbing fixtures (toilet, tub, sinks) back up simultaneously, the trouble lies in the main line. Notify your landlord at once, if not sooner. Try not to use these fixtures unless it's absolutely critical. Even then, don't use them. Go out to dinner, leaving others to do the dishes; find a public rest room; or simply be patient until your plumbing system is declogged.

Maxim of the Ancient Mariner: Think, but don't use your "head."

Usually, however, drain problems are localized. If you don't want clogged drains, try not to clog them. But if they do become clogged, here's what to do about them.

1. If a fixture is so badly clogged that it is overflowing, first bail out a pot or two of excess water until it stops overflowing. Then you will be able to . . .

2. Follow these simple directions to restore good health to your drainage system:

   For kitchen and bathroom sinks, and for tubs and showers, first try cleaning the top of the drain. Remove and discard all solids—including con-

"Notify your landlord at once."

gealed grease and fat. Use a screw driver, putty knife, or similar instrument to aid you in your labors. If the above procedure doesn't help, two tools may:

1. The plumber's helper, or plunger. This is the first tool to try.
2. A wire snake: either a flexible steel coil, which you buy especially for the occasion, or an unbent wire coat hanger, which you've unbent especially for the occasion.

The Plunger Prance

1. Fill sink, tub, or shower with about three inches of water. Clogged toilets will already be quite full enough. In fact, sinks and tubs might be full, too. But if not, add water before stirring.
2. Fit the rubber suction cup of the plunger over the clogged drain.
3. Press the plunger down and jerk it up quickly about a dozen times. Rest. The suction created should dislodge the barrier, and the system should now drain correctly. If this doesn't work, try:

The Snake Dance

1. Insert the snake into the drain, and push it as far into the pipe as possible, twisting (the snake) as you go.
2. Jiggle the snake to dislodge the obstruction.
3. Push and pull the snake free.

For Sinks Only

Let's assume that both the plunger and the snake techniques fail you and your clogged drain. Escalate to a more high-powered strategy: chemical warfare.

Use liquid drain cleaners only—such as Liquid Drano or other approved products from a hardware or plumbing-supply store. Follow the directions on the bottle.

Do not use powdered drain cleaners: if they happen to stick in your drain, they can magically transform themselves into cement, the removal of which is a costly professional job.*

* Once a week dissolve a few tablespoons of baking soda in a small amount of boiling water. Pour into your kitchen drain last thing before you go to bed. It'll stay in the U all night, dissolving glop. Next day, the first running water will flush out the U.

BEWARE! Drain-cleaning chemicals are powerful. They're designed to eat through biological matter—and that means you!

1. Always wear rubber gloves when you use these chemicals.
2. Be sure the room in which you use them is well ventilated.
3. After the chemicals have worked the amount of time prescribed by the directions, flush out the afflicted drain with plenty of water.

Into the Trap!

If you've strained your muscles by using plungers and snakes, and strained your patience waiting for chemicals to work, and your sink drain still holds water when it shouldn't, either you or your landlord will have to clean out the sink's trap.

The trap is the U of the U-shaped pipe beneath your sink. To clean it:

1. Wear rubber gloves—one never knows what residual chemicals may be lurking in ambush for you.
2. Empty the sink basin of water, by bailing it out with pots and bowls. (Dump water into toilet, unless that, too, is clogged.)
3. Place a bucket beneath the U-shaped pipe.
4. Remove the clean-out plug—which is at the exact bottom of the U—by using a wrench to turn the plug counterclockwise.

If your sink has no plug, remove the entire U-shaped pipe by loosening the nuts that hold it in place. Careful: Don't bend anything—it'll all have to be put back in place later.

A little water, and many other goodies, will drop into the bucket.

5. Wiggle a snake (commercial or coat-hanger variety) from the drain through the pipe that leads into the wall. Jiggle and shake that snake until all the malicious glop dislodges and drops into your bucket. If you've had to remove the entire U, clean it with soap, water, and a long-handled brush.*

* To cure slow-draining bathtubs:
1. Use a screwdriver to pry off or unscrew drain strainer.
2. Unscrew on-off drain lever plate located on front of tub.
3. Pull out lever. A spring or plunger will be dangling from it, plugged up with a huge and billowing "mushroom" of hair.
4. Remove hair from spring or plug and clean out drain opening with an untwisted wire coat hanger.
5. Replace lever. Replace strainer.

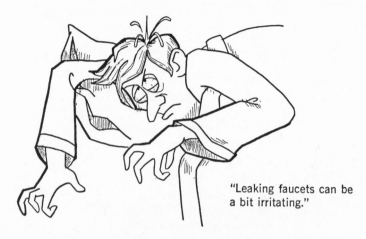

"Leaking faucets can be a bit irritating."

Even a toothbrush will do in a pinch.

By this time, even if your energy's not been drained, your sink will be!!

Leaking Faucets

Drip! Drop! Splat!

Leaking faucets can be a bit irritating—the modern version of the ancient water-torture technique.

Here's how to take a leak gracefully:

Emergency Procedure

In the middle of the night, when you're too groggy to read—much less follow—the instructions for really fixing a leak, simply:

1. Put a long rag around the troublesome faucet or spout in sink, shower, or tub. The water will drip into the rag, thus transforming the loud Splat! into a muffled Plop! A sponge placed where the water hits will perform a similar function.
2. Go to sleep.
3. The next morning, when you're bright, cheery and alert, fix the leak according to the following instructions.

Leak From Faucet Base

If the leak occurs at the base of the knob that turns the water on and off:

1. Tighten the metal cover through which the stem protrudes. (The stem is the piece that connects the faucet handle to the sink basin.)
2. If the leak persists or the faucet handle won't turn, a procedure called "repacking" is in order. Call your landlord for this.

Drip From the Spout

Sometimes water will drip from the spout, even when the faucet is turned off. In this circumstance, there is a faulty washer at the bottom of it all. The washer must be replaced.

1. Shut off the water supply to the individual faucet. (Shut off entire water supply to the apartment if you can't find the fixture's control knob.)
2. Use a crescent wrench to loosen the nut directly beneath the control knob by turning it counter-clockwise. (You may want to wrap a small rag or adhesive tape around the nut first, to prevent wrench scratches.)
3. Turn the faucet handle as if you were turning on the water. With a few twists, the whole faucet unit will come loose. Pull it out.
4. Locate the washer, held in place by a screw, at the base of the unit.
5. Use a screw driver of appropriate size to remove the screw and the old washer.
6. Insert a new washer of the same size, shape, and thickness as the old one. (Bring the old washer to the hardware store when buying your new one, or buy a package of assorted sizes.) Screw the new washer into place, using a new screw if the old one was rusty or corroded.
7. Replace the faucet unit by twisting the faucet handle as if to turn off the water. Twist firmly, but not too tightly. Then retighten the nut that holds the unit in place.
8. Finally, turn the water supply back on and enjoy splashing around in your leak-free shower or tub.

9. But should you find that, despite both your patient efforts and a new washer, you still have a leak (this will happen only very rarely), send an SOS to your beloved landlord, who will have to polish the worn valve seat for you or replace the faucet. One of these solutions will definitely solve the problem.

Leaking Pipes

Leaking pipes can be an even greater disaster than leaky faucets. Pipes are bigger and hold more water, which means they can squirt forth much water when they leak. In brief, a defective pipe can cause a minor flood in your apartment.

As soon as you notice a leaking pipe (or a mysteriously expanding puddle), notify your landlord. He'll probably be happy to repair the pipe before the problem threatens to inundate you and destroy both your property and his.

However, in an emergency—if it's late at night and the landlord is unavailable, or if the leak is either gushing like a geyser or drippingly driving you daffy—here's what to do:

For a Tiny Leak

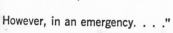

Method I:
1. Shut off the apartment's water supply at the main control valve.
2. Dry the pipe thoroughly.
3. Wind plastic electrician's tape spirally over the leak, so that each turn of the tape overlaps the last. Apply several layers of tape in this way.
4. Turn the water supply on.
5. Notify your landlord of your problem. Don't tell him you tried to fix it, or he may simply forget about it.

Since variety is the spice of life, and you may wish to have a choice among several modes of operation, here are two more approaches.

Method II:
1. Shut off water supply.
2. Dry the pipe.

However, in an emergency. . . ."

3. Taper one end of a small piece of pine wood to a point.
4. Insert the point of this little plug into the hole in the pipe so that it fits snugly. Since wood swells when wet, this is a very dependable plug.
5. Tape the plug into place with plastic electrician's tape.
6. Turn water supply on.
7. Notify your landlord.

Method III: To be employed if the leak is small, and the water pressure not very strong.
1. Shut off water supply and dry the pipe.
2. Fill in the hole with a bit of liquid plastic or liquid cement. Tape.
3. Let dry.
4. Turn water supply on.
5. Notify your landlord.

For a Big Leak

In the emergency event of a large leak in a pipe, try this temporary measure:
1. Run and turn off the water at the main control valve.
2. Press a piece of cloth or rubber (e.g., rubber glove, sponge, tire tube, cut-up bathtub mat) against the hole.
3. Use a C-clamp (see drawing) to secure it tightly until the plumber comes.

Problems with Loose Joints

The key to fixing a water-pipe leak due to a loose joint (that is, the place at which two pipes meet) is to make the joint tighter. To do this:
1. Firmly hold one pipe with a pipe wrench.
2. Use a second wrench to tighten the metal collar, or fitting, that connects the two pipes.
3. If you are able to turn the fitting, this will probably solve the problem. But if the fitting refuses to budge or the leak persists after the fitting is tightened, then—you guessed it—ask your friendly landlord to call on his friendly plumber. Best wishes for Happy and Healthy Plumbing!

ELECTRICAL PROBLEMS, OR CURRENT AFFAIRS

Ever since old Ben Franklin tamed a lightning bolt, men—and women—have been using electricity in creative ways. Modern science has educated those flowing currents so that today electricity toasts our toast, presses our dresses, cleans our carpets, and curls our tresses (female dresses and tresses, that is).

What a fine friend electricity is! But, alas, a sometimes fickle friend. Have you ever reached the final chapter in a great whodunit at four in the morning—and had the bedside lamp blink, yawn, and go to sleep on you? Have you ever been frantically vacuuming your apartment five minutes before your mother is due to arrive—and had the vacuum go on strike? Or been preparing a gourmet dinner, and had the electric stove, the refrigerator, the heat, and the lights suddenly and mysteriously stop working?

Panic not! Fate isn't plotting against you. Such misfortune is quite common and happens to the best of us—often at the worst of moments. And although electricity can be dangerous, many repairs are simple and safe to do. With some care and knowledge, you can make such repairs more quickly and much more cheaply than a professional serviceman can.

Before we get down to the specifics of electrical repair, let's understand what keeps electrically-run gadgets running.

"Modern science has educated those flowing currents."

Electrical Theory Made Very Simple, or Physics for the Poet

Electricity is a lot like plumbing. It is a force —in this case an electrical one—that:

1. Comes into your home.
2. Sheds light on your problems, adds warmth to your life, cooks your meals, etc.
3. And goes away again.

As it does all of this, electricity travels along a defined path. Think of current affairs as water flowing through pipes. If there is a major leak in one of the pipes, the water flow is interrupted and not all the water will be able to travel its full path.

The same thing is true of electricity: if there is any kind of interruption along its path, the electricity stops flowing at the point at which the interruption occurs, and the circuit, or continuous path, is broken, leaving you powerless.

The shocking truth is this: most appliance failures in your home are due to a breaking of the electrical circuit. You can repair them simply by mending the break, so that the electricity can once again flow properly.

When an appliance won't work, check first to see that it's plugged in. Un-pluggedness is a simple and surprisingly common cause of "broken circuits."

If an appliance that is plugged in does not work, follow these three ground rules to prepare for repair.

1. Be sure, be certain, be positive, that you UNPLUG anything electrical before you touch it with the intent to repair.

2. When an appliance—be it a lamp or an electrical heater or anything else—fails, trace the flow of electricity around its path, from wall socket, through plug, cord, and fixture, back to the socket, and try to discover where the break in the circuit is. Most often the problem is in the fuse, cord, plug, or switch.

3. Know where the FUSE BOX (or circuit breaker, whichever applies in your apartment) is located. This will facilitate making repairs in the event of an electrical failure involving several appliances.

There may be labels next to each fuse telling you what area of the building it controls. If your landlord has not supplied such labels, you can easily identify circuits by first making sure that each outlet in your apartment has some type of appliance or lamp working from it, and by then unscrewing fuses one by one to learn which area each of them controls. Finally, add your own labels inside the fuse box.

"Darkness at Noon"

Common Problems	The most common electrical problems with which you will be plagued are:
	1. Frazzled fuses.
	2. Cords that need care.
	3. Perverse plugs.
	4. Switches that need switching.
	The following ways of solving each type of problem can save you hours of inconvenience and frustration, as well as a lot of money.
Blown Fuses, or Darkness at Noon	Once in a while you may find your apartment (or a goodly portion thereof) plunged into sudden darkness. If you're certain that there wasn't an eclipse scheduled for the day, the cause of the calamity may be:
	A. A nuclear attack
	B. A local power failure
	C. A blown fuse or snapped circuit-breaker.
	Unfortunately, there's not much you can do about

(A) or (B). In the event of a blown fuse, however, the following comments may prove enlightening.

Safety First

Fuses and circuit breakers are safety devices. When so much electrical current is flowing through a circuit that there is a chance of an electrical fire, a fuse or circuit breaker will automatically stop the flow of electricity in the "overloaded" circuit.

For example, a fuse or circuit breaker will sometimes "blow" when one appliance too many is plugged into an outlet. When this happens, it is necessary either to replace the blown fuse or to reset your circuit breaker.

Frazzled Fuses

When a section of your home has no electricity due to a frazzled fuse, first locate the cause of the problem by figuring out which outlet was being taxed too heavily. Then unplug one or two of the appliances to eliminate excessive strain on the circuit.

For maximum SAFETY while making a fuse or circuit-breaker repair:

1. If your fuse panel is in a damp basement, stand on a chair or dry platform while replacing the fuse or resetting the circuit breaker.
2. Do all the work with one hand—in order to minimize the chance of completing a circuit and being rudely shocked. Your other hand will be holding a flashlight or candle, so that you can see what the heck you're doing! Now you are ready to do the repair work:

For Fuses:

1. Locate and turn off the main switch of the fuse panel.
2. Use your circuit labels to locate the blown fuse. You can often recognize a blown fuse by its appearance: it will have a dark or clouded window—or at least an inside wire that has been melted by too much current.

3. Unscrew the frazzled fuse.
4. Read its size and ampere rating (on the face) and replace it with a fuse of identical size and power.

Note: Using a penny to temporarily complete a circuit, or repairing a circuit by substituting a larger-sized fuse for the blown one, is an extremely dangerous procedure. Such methods provide no protection against overheating, and therefore invite electrical fires.

Soothing a Circuit Breaker

When a circuit breaker stops the flow of electricity as a warning that the electrical system is being strained, resetting the circuit-breaker system is an easy task.

A circuit-breaker panel looks like a line-up of ordinary light switches. In response to an overloaded circuit, a circuit-breaker switch will snap to an open position.

The first thing to do, once again, is to unplug a couple of appliances from the overloaded circuit. Then reset the circuit breaker in the following way:

1. Locate the circuit breaker that has snapped open. If the open switch isn't easy to see in the dark, you may have to run your finger down the row of switches to find the one that is in a different position.
2. Push the breaker, first to "Reset," then to "On." (It may snap to "On" automatically—if so, don't be alarmed.)

And that's that! Your previously overworked circuit should now behave beautifully.

Cord Care

If an appliance works sporadically or not at all, a faulty cord may be the cause of discord.

With electrical appliances, as with most things, preventing problems is the best way to solve them. The following rules for the use and care of cords will prolong their service and help prevent malfunctions, shocks, and/or fires.

1. Never run cords over or under doors or rugs. The chance of abrasion is great—and of fire, even greater.
2. Never let cords rest on radiators, pipes, or any type of metal that might conduct electricity.
3. Never yank a cord to unplug an appliance. Instead, hold onto the plug itself and gently pull it from the socket.
4. Never try to convert a flexible extension cord into a permanent outlet by tacking or stapling it to wall or floor—the cord's insulation can easily crack and result in short circuits or fires.
5. Finally, repair or replace frayed cords immediately!

Cutting the Cord

A frayed cord can eventually cause a short circuit. And if such a cord is touched or stepped upon, it may inject a good, strong volt-jolt into the unlucky man or beast who happened to do the touching or stepping: something to be a-frayed of indeed!

To fix a faulty cord:

Having made certain that the cord to be cured is UNPLUGGED—

1. Cut the frayed area out of the cord by snipping about one inch above and one inch below the sore spot.
2. Strip about two inches of insulation—the rubber or cloth covering that surrounds the wires—from the newly cut ends.

   If the cord is the rubber-coated double-jointed type—that is, if it looks like a long piece of licorice—use a small knife to separate the two halves; then strip the insulation from each half.
3. Tightly twist each of the four loose end strands of wire.
4. Join the two pieces of cord by twisting together matching end strands.
5. Wrap electrical tape around each spliced wire so that no wires are left exposed.

6. Join the two sets of taped wires by wrapping electrical tape around both sets.

Perverse Plugs

"When a plug plagues you. . . ."

When a faulty cord isn't responsible for an electrical malfunction, a defective plug is often to blame. When a plug plagues you, instead of blowing a fuse, try the following:

1. Bend the plug's metal prongs slightly apart to assure a better grip inside the wall outlet.
2. If this offers no improvement, open the plug (some plugs are a single unit of molded plastic or rubber and can't be opened—in this case, you will have to cut the plug from the cord and replace the old plug with a new one). Once the plug is open, check whether the bared wires are making good contact with the terminal screws. If not, wrap each bared wire securely and clockwise around the appropriate screw.

If it is necessary to replace a bad plug, or to reinsert a cord that has cracked or frayed close to its plug:

1. Snip the cord one or two inches from the plug.
2. Remove two inches of outer insulation from a single-strand (cloth- or rubber-sheathed) cord, or pull apart two inches of the jointed (licorice) type of cord.
3. Strip away one inch of insulation from each of the two wires. Be sure not to cut into the wires themselves. If you accidentally cut more than a few strands of wire, start the process over again from Step 2.
4. Take the cardboard cover off your new plug (or off the old one, if you are simply reattaching a once-frayed wire). Remove any remnants of old wire from the inside of a plug to be reused.
5. Push the cord into the plug.
6. Wrap each cord wire around one prong of the plug (insulation should touch the prong).
7. Then wrap each bare wire clockwise (this is important!) around one of the plug's terminal

screws. Be sure that the wire ends neither touch each other nor stick out from under the screwheads.

8. Replace the cardboard cover.
9. Plug in the plug, and, hopefully, your appliance will now turn on joyfully.

Switching a Wall Switch

If a wall or ceiling light won't light, the problem can probably be attributed to dead or loose light bulbs, or else to a faulty wall switch.

The first thing to do when tackling a "light" problem is to make sure that all light bulbs in troublesome fixtures are live and screwed in securely. Loose bulbs are a fairly common and easy-to-remedy cause of electrical "failure." But if the bulbs seem healthy and there's still no light, a broken switch may be to blame.

To Test a Switch for Defects

1. Remove the fuse (or turn "off" the circuit breaker) that controls the current in the room where the problem is located. This allows you to work safely with the wall switch. Examine the fuse to make sure that it is alive and not responsible for your darkened room.
2. Unscrew and remove the wall plate through which the switch protrudes.
3. Unscrew and pull the switch away from its fitting. Check that all wires are tightly connected. If they are loose, tighten them and see if you've thereby solved your problem. If not—
4. Use a piece of wire to complete the circuit by attaching it to the switch terminals as shown on this page.
5. Reconnect the fuse. If the lights controlled by the switch still don't work, you may have to call in your landlord or an electrician to examine the apartment's wiring.
6. If the lights do work, however, then the source of your problem is indeed a faulty switch. Unscrew the fuse once more, disconnect the test wires, and replace the old switch with a new one.

**To Switch
a Switch**

1. Make sure that the controlling fuse is discon-nected.
2. Unscrew the switch's wall plate.
3. Remove the screws that hold the switch itself to the outlet box.
4. Pull the switch mechanism from the outlet box.
5. Note carefully how the colored wires are attached to the switch.
6. Disconnect these wires and fasten their bared ends onto the new switch. Twist them clockwise around the screw terminals; then tighten the screws.
7. Screw the switch mechanism in place.
8. Replace the wall plate and screw it into place.
9. Reconnect the controlling fuse.
And—*voilà!*—your life and your apartment should be bathed in a divine light.

**To Doctor
Defective
Doorbells**

Follow the procedure for switching a switch. Often, simply tightening the wires inside the push-button mechanism is enough to set a previously silent doorbell chiming with cheer. If not, it may be necessary to replace the push-button assembly. Before replacing it, test the push button by using a piece of wire to complete the bell circuit—the way you tested for a defective wall switch.

What happens if your doorbell cheerfully chimes the arrival of a guest—and the guest is unable to get past your apartment's obstinately sticking front door? Despair not! You won't have to spend the evening alone. Simply read on, courageous reader, to learn how to cope with stubborn doors (and windows, too)!

**DOOR
DISTRESS AND
WINDOW WOE,
OR THE GRATE
ESCAPE**

Doors and windows are vital for communication, ventilation, and getting in and out of places. And as you've probably discovered, doors and win-dows—and even things like window shades—occasionally misbehave, just as toilets and lamps do. But portal problems are quite simple to fix.

To Silence
Squeaking Doors

Once in a while you may open a door and hear something that sounds like a crying mouse or a parakeet in pain. Most likely, it is neither mouse nor parakeet, but simply too talkative a door. To silence the squeak:

1. Hold a cloth beneath the hinge, while dripping oil onto the top of the hinge.
2. When the oil reaches the bottom of the hinge, open and close the door several times to let the oil work in.
3. Wipe off excess oil.
4. Repeat this procedure in a few hours if the squeak continues.
5. Buy earplugs if Step 4 doesn't work.*

* An alternative method is to pull out the hinge pin with a pair of pliers and coat it with Vaseline before replacing. If the pin is a bit stubborn about coming out, hold a screw driver against its head end and tap upwards against the screw driver with a hammer.

Doors That
Stick or Sag

Doors that refuse to open can be so much of an annoyance that you may never want (or in extreme cases, may never be able) to get out of your closet, bedroom, bathroom, or apartment. And guests may, in exasperation, cease to visit. Don't be daunted by defiant doors—instead, let's understand which recalcitrant elements are rebelling and learn how to soothe their grievances.

A door may stick or grate if it is not perfectly centered in its jamb, or frame. If your door sticks when you open or close it:

1. Check the hinge screws. If these are loose, tighten them securely.
2. If the screws don't hold tightly, it probably means that the screw holes have become too big. In this case:

a. Take out the screws.

b. Fill the screw holes with plastic wood, wood putty, steel wool, matchsticks, or toothpicks.

c. Replace screws or use ones of a slightly larger diameter.

If you've tightened the hinge screws, only to find that there's been no decrease in stickiness, a more complete remedy is required:

1. Find out wherein lies the rub! Insert a piece of

paper (a $100 bill will do nicely) into the crack between the closed door and its frame. Move the paper around. When the paper sticks, you've located the problem spot.

2. If the door sticks at the bottom edge along the floor or on the side edge near the top, you will have to tighten the top hinge and/or shim the bottom hinge ("shim" means "insert a piece of cardboard filler under"; see instructions below).

3. If the door sticks at the top near the outside corner or on the side edge close to the floor, tighten the bottom hinge and/or shim the top one.

To Install a Cardboard Shim:

1. Open the door.

2. Put magazines between the bottom of the door and the floor. These will hold the door in place, so that it doesn't fall on you and necessitate a trip to the doctor for skull X rays.

3. Cut a piece of cardboard to a size slightly smaller than the metal hinge leaf that holds the hinge to the doorframe.

4. Unscrew the hinge leaf (frame side only)—either top hinge or bottom, depending on where the door sticks.

5. Insert the shim between hinge leaf and doorframe. Trim shim if necessary for proper fit.

6. Screw the hinge leaf back into place, punching through the cardboard shim with the hinge screws.

7. If a single piece of cardboard does not suffice, add extra thicknesses of cardboard until the sticking is relieved.

If, after all of your efforts, the door still sticks, you may have to shave off a bit of wood at the points on the door's edges where sticking still occurs. For this job, use either a "block plane," a "rasp," or coarse sandpaper wrapped around a block of wood. Your landlord may be able to loan you any of these tools.

But should wood-shaving fail, too—your prob-

"Doors and windows are vital for getting in and out of places."

lem may be that the dear door is warped. In this event, relax and enjoy a well-earned glass of lemonade—and ask your landlord to repair or replace the door. Usually, however, tightening the screws or shimming the hinges is all that any sticking or sagging door requires.

For Sticking Cabinet Doors

Have you ever really been in the mood for a cooky or pretzel and, trembling with anticipation, tiptoed to the pantry—only to find that you had to wage a major battle to get the pantry door open? After which you had completely lost all appetite and desire? There's no need to be plagued by such foul fortune ever again. Simply:

1. Apply a bit of that multipurpose wonder drug—Vaseline—to the latch, and perhaps to the hinges, of the door.
2. Enjoy effortless access to the treasures within.*

Now that we've thoroughly discussed the diagnosis and treatment of doors difficult to open, let's examine the opposite phenomenon: doors that won't close with anything less than a herculean effort.

*If Vaseline doesn't entirely fix the door, see if the door latch needs readjustment or if the door needs to be shaved.

Springing Doors

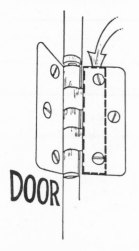

DOOR

A door that is difficult to close unless it is slammed, and tends to spring back at you like an angry kangaroo, can be both a problem and a source of embarrassment.

1. Open and prop the door with magazines as described above.
2. Cut two shims one-half the width of a hinge leaf.
3. Doing one hinge leaf at a time, insert the shim close to the hinge pin (between hinge and doorjamb) and retighten the screws.
4. Test the door to learn if a greater thickness of cardboard is needed.

This procedure tilts the hinges in toward the door opening and thereby allows the door to swing closed more easily and less hostilely. To soothe springing doors, try using a shim in this way.

Locks and Bolts   Locks and bolts are the watchmen of your apartment's security, and no one wants a watchman who falls asleep on the job or who can easily be bribed by an ill-intentioned passer-by.

You can help ensure your safety by keeping locks and bolts happy and healthy. Here's how:

1. If the lock on a door sticks, simply squirt some graphite (a powdered squeeze-tube lubricant that you can buy for fifty cents) into the keyhole. Don't use liquid oil: it will collect dirt, gum up the works, and eventually cause headaches that no amount of aspirin can cure.
2. Sometimes you may find yourself furiously twisting a doorknob—alas, with no results. Either a closed door won't open, or an open door won't close. The trouble may be with:
   a. The doorknob.
   b. The bolt that should hold the door closed or release it to an open position.
   c. The plate in the side of the doorframe into which the bolt fits.

To remedy the problem, use any or all of these steps:

1. Tighten all screws on the doorknob.
2. Lubricate the bolt with a few drops of light oil.
3. Tighten the screws that hold (and adjust) the metal latch plate to the doorjamb.

If none of these methods works alone or in combination, don't rely on Providence for protection! Instead, tell your landlord at once about the defective lock. The bolt mechanism may be broken, and your watchman may be no more active or effective than a sagging scarecrow.

Having a broken lock jeopardizes your privacy and safety, and it's your landlord's legal duty to equip his apartments with doors that lock securely.

Window Woe   Window woe can be at least as disturbing as door distress. But there's no need to fret—or curse—

simply because a window isn't co-operative. A bit of thought, plus a tiny bit of time, can usually bring harmony to homeowners and their windows.

But first, a Word of Window Wisdom: When opening a window, stand as close to it as possible. NEVER reach across anything—desk, sofa, bureau, or bathtub—to open a window that offers the slightest resistance. Doing so is inviting back strain.

Hard-to-Open Windows

Hard-to-open windows can be a super-nuisance. For example, you may not always want your summer sublet to have the temperature and humidity of a Turkish bath. There's no need to sweat and suffer at the mercy of your windows!

Many windows stick because of hardened paint that has formed a seal around the edges of the window. If you have this problem:

1. Insert a putty knife or chisel between the window sash—the movable part of the window—and its frame.
2. Lightly tap the back of a knife with a hammer to break the seal. As you tap, twist the knife slightly.
3. Repeat until the seal is broken at all points.
4. If this doesn't do the trick, the problem may be a seal of hardened paint on the outside of the window. In this case, ask the landlord to take care of the problem. (The procedure is the same for breaking the seal on the outside, but the job is more inaccessible.)
5. When you finally wrench the window open, use sandpaper or a chisel to trim off the excess paint that was causing the problem.
6. Lubricate the sliding parts of the window by rubbing all contact points with hard soap or parafin (a candle). Regardless of the reason that your window sticks, this lubrication is a great idea! *

* Hard-to-reach places can be lubricated by spraying them with a can of silicone spray.

If the above procedure fails to open your window, the window or its frame is warped out of shape. Call your landlord for repair or replacement, citing, if necessary, local laws pertaining to the proper amount of ventilation that a landlord is required to provide.

Windows That Won't Stay Open

Such windows can be as great an annoyance as those that won't open at all. For you, as an apartment dweller, ventilation is important: once your windows are opened, they should stay opened, at least for a while.

If your windows rebelliously slam shut when you try to open them, the problem is that the COUNTERWEIGHT SYSTEM is broken. This means that the weight in the window frame that's supposed to balance the weight of the window sash is no longer doing its thing. The solution:

1. Buy two metal control springs at a hardware store (cost, about fifty cents for the pair).
2. With the window raised, insert a spring on each side—between the sash and the frame (see illustration on the control-spring package). This will hold the window sash open and will also make the window easier to open and close. (Shown here is a side view of a spring.)

Alternative methods are to put a cut-off broom handle under the offender to keep it "upright" or to ask the landlord to repair the misbehaving counterweights. Good luck!

First Aid For Broken Windows

If in the course of apartmental orgies or neighborhood riots, you find a windowpane in pain, here is a temporary remedy:

1. Carefully remove all broken glass.
2. Cut a piece of cardboard and a heavy piece of plastic (e.g., from a plastic bag) to the size of the windowpane.
3. Place the cardboard on the inside of the window, the plastic on the outside (overlap the plastic a bit).
4. Use masking, or black electrician's, tape to secure this quickie "Band-Aid" to the sash.

5. Inform your landlord of the broken window, so that he can replace the missing glass.

Worrisome Window Shades

Well, now you've got all your doors and windows opening when they should open and closing when they should close. But what if a recalcitrant window shade won't behave, letting in either too much or too little light and air? Should this dilemma daunt you—you who have calmed toilets in turmoil and soothed sorry sockets? Hardly! Here's what to do.

When a window shade acts up (or down, as the case may be), the problem is usually due to a lack or excess of tension in the spring located within the hollow wood roller. If your shade won't wind up tightly enough for you:

1. Pull the shade about two-thirds of the way down.
2. Remove the entire shade unit from its wall brackets.
3. Roll the shade up tightly by hand.
4. Keeping it tightly rolled, replace the shade unit in its wall brackets.
5. Test the shade.
6. If the tension is still weak, repeat the process.

If the shade seems to have no tension at all, move from Step 3 above to:

4. Stick the flat metal tip end of the shade between two tines of a fork.
5. Turn the fork around clockwise a couple of dozen times in order to rewind the spring.
6. Before removing the fork, turn it backward (counterclockwise) until you feel it "catch" in place. This must be done very slowly and gently.
7. Replace the shade unit in its wall brackets, being careful not to jar the flat metal tip end; for if you do, the whole spring will unwind.

If both of the above methods prove fruitless, remove the end cap from the spring end and drop a little oil or graphite into the system.

If none of these methods for tightening a shade

"Stick the flat metal tip end of the shade between two tines of a fork."

spring works, your shade has probably sprung a spring. In that case, it's best to chuck the whole window shade. Your landlord may be willing to buy his apartment a new one. If not, curtains are always nice.

If you are a victim of the opposite problem, and too much tension in the spring makes your blind snap up sharply, creating a dramatic ruckus, try the following:

1. Roll the shade up as high as it will go.
2. Remove the shade from its wall brackets.
3. Unroll the shade by hand to about one half of its length.
4. Put the shade back into its brackets.
5. Test it.
6. If there's still too much tension in the spring, repeat steps 1 through 5.

Pin Problems:

If your shade is unsteady of purpose and wobbly, too, the end pin is probably bent. Simply straighten it with a pair of pliers. If the end pin is dirty or rusty, a once-over with sandpaper should clean it and give you greater efficiency.

Shades of Fallout:

Unlike teeth, window shades don't need to be old or decayed to fall out. A few minor adjustments will fix your shades firmly in place. If the shade happens to land in your arms as you pull it, move the wall brackets on which it is mounted closer together by:

1. Putting cardboard shims behind the brackets if they are mounted on the inside of the window frame.
2. Moving one or both brackets closer to the window if they are mounted on the wall or frame above the window.

If your shade sticks, owing to the reverse problem, try your best to move the brackets farther apart. If this necessitates a chiseling job, get your landlord's blessing first.

Blinking Blinds

Venetian blinds seem to be going out of style—which scores at least one point for contemporary designers. But if your apartment happens to have them, and if they blink at you at the wrong times, either:

1. Ask your landlord to repair or replace them (since it's too much of a bother to do it yourself), or
2. Take them down, tuck them away in a closet, and replace with a window shade or cheerful curtain. Incidentally, you can now buy window shades in bright patterns.

RADIATOR REPAIR, OR THE COOL ART OF KEEPING WARM

Since you began this book, you've learned all kinds of tricks for finding a home, eating well, and keeping things running—at very low cost. In fact, if you were stranded on a desert island with nothing but an apartment, running water, electricity, and a grocery store, this book would ensure your survival.

But you probably don't live on a desert island, where plenty of sunshine and friendly natives could keep you warm; instead, you most likely depend—during part of the year—on warmth provided by less romantic but equally effective gadgets called radiators.

Rebellious Radiators

Like toilets, lamps, and window shades, radiators occasionally misbehave and give grief. In these days of civil disobedience, we should hardly be surprised to find ourselves faced with a Radiator Rebellion. Fear not! There is no need to panic, and even less need to call out the National Guard. Simply follow this advice for improving your rapport with rebellious radiators.

When a radiator doesn't function properly, maintain your cool for a few minutes . . . and you'll soon be blessed with a toasty warm room.

Rule for Rambunctious Radiators: Make sure the problem radiator is turned on before you decide to "fix it good!!"

Many people have spent long, cold nights alternately shivering with pain and steaming with rage, when they could simply have turned a knob on their radiator, gotten some heat and some sleep, and saved a good deal of energy.

If your radiator refuses to heat your apartment when it *is* turned on, repair is usually supersimple.

First, figure out whether you are the proud possessor of a steam or of a hot-water radiator.

STEAM RADIATORS have a valve that looks like an oversized Lone Ranger bullet located on one side of the radiator, about one-third or one-half way down from the top. HOT-WATER RADIATORS have a valve located—again on the side—very close to the top of the radiator unit. This valve, which looks like a square peg in a round hole, must be adjusted by using a special key.

Having identified the patient, you can begin the diagnosis and cure.

How to Get a
Steam Radiator
Steaming

Check the air valve for defects. Here's how:

1. Turn off the recalcitrant radiator.
2. Unscrew and remove the bulletlike air valve from the side of the radiator.
3. Turn off another (healthy) steam radiator in your apartment. Unscrew and remove its air valve.
4. Replace the valve from each radiator with the valve from the other.
5. Turn on both radiators.
6. If one air valve is defective—which is usually the case—the radiator that wasn't working will now flame passionate. The radiator that had worked and had warmed to the touch, will now, alas, grow frigid.

To clean a faulty air valve:

1. Use a commercial valve cleaner. Or let the valve soak for a few minutes in either gasoline or soapy water mixed with ammonia.
2. Shake the valve vigorously to dislodge any glop that might not have been affected by the cleaning or soaking.
3. Rinse the valve well.
4. Allow the valve to dry.
5. Using a small piece of wire, clean the little hole on the radiator into which the valve fits.

Should you discover that when the cleaned valve is replaced on the culprit radiator, the radiator still does not heat up, the valve is probably corroded beyond hope. A quick trip to the hardware store for a new air valve should guarantee an end to chilly days and freezing nights.

To Get a Hot-Water Radiator Hot

Check to see if air is trapped within the radiator, as this is the most common ailment that afflicts hot-water radiators. If a radiator is filled with air, hot water is unable to enter the heating unit. So let's get the air out, the water in, and the apartment warm.

The procedure:

1. Hold a cup under the "valve," or vent, on the side of the radiator. The purpose of this valve is to release air trapped within.
2. Using the key that fits your radiator valve, open the vent.*
3. Trapped air will rush out. As soon as all the trapped air has escaped, water will come out of the valve and go into your cup.
4. Turn the key at once to close the valve.

Your radiator will now be as filled with water as it should be. The water will heat up, keeping you and your apartment warm.

At the beginning of each winter you should follow the above procedure to free trapped air from each of your hot-water radiators. Certain radiators require this care every month or so.

* Keys can be purchased at any hardware store.

"The Clang! Bang! Screech! of a hammering steam radiator"

Remember: Be good unto your radiators, and they will be good unto you.

Rattling Radiators

Have you ever had a pleasant dream brought to an abrupt conclusion by the Clang! Bang! Screech! of a hammering steam radiator? The experience can be nerve-racking. Well, relax. You need never again be rattled by rattling radiators.

The noise is most often the result of water trapped in or near the radiator. To quiet the din:

1. Put small blocks of wood (or old paperback books) beneath the two legs of the radiator that are farthest from its shutoff valve. This tips the radiator unit so that trapped water can flow back to the boiler.

If Step 1 doesn't solve the problem:

2. Put blocks of wood (or a couple more unread paperbacks) beneath the radiator's other two legs.

By raising the entire radiator, you also raise the pipe under it—and release water that may be trapped in a bend of that pipe. One of these two steps should eliminate the rattle and clatter. In case it doesn't, the problem may be that the radiator shutoff valve is open halfway only. This valve should be either fully opened or fully closed at all times.

When your radiators are finally made to work efficiently, check Chapter 5 for tips on getting the most warmth for your money. After doing all of the above, and thanks to a bit of patience and understanding, you'll never need suffer from Radiator Rebellions.

THE HAPPINESS OF HANDINESS

What a pleasure! You can relax and enjoy life in your apartment! With this chapter as a reference, and with the knowledge you've gained from it, you'll never again be horrified—or even over-annoyed—by perverse plumbing, erratic electricity, problem portals, or radical radiators.

Happiness, it seems, is a little bit of household handiness.

CHAPTER SEVEN

THE EXODUS

So you're moving again! What's the matter? Did you actually like Chapter 2? Couldn't you figure out some way to stay put?

Well, I guess you'll just have to return to Chapter 1, and trek this trail a second time.

But before you do, consider the following:

1. Find a SUBLESSEE early if you plan to leave before your lease expires.

   Remember to have the new tenant approved by the landlord.

   Be sure to have your sublessee sign a lease. (Most stationery stores carry standard leases. They cost about fifteen cents.) No matter how nice or how friendly the new tenants seem, it must be clear—on paper—that they are financially and legally responsible for your former apartment. A lease assures you, among other things, that they will not suddenly decide against taking the apartment. Or, if they do, that it is they who remain responsible for the rent.

2. Do not pay the last month's rent (see Chapter 1).

   If you are subletting, be sure to get an advance on the last month's rent from the sublessee.

3. Notify all UTILITY companies, two or three weeks in advance, that as of a particular date you will no longer require their services.

   If the sublessee wants to have the utilities continued, ask the various companies to switch accounts from your name to his. Even though these accounts will be switched a day or two before you leave, the arrangements should be made two or three weeks earlier.

   The telephone is especially important. If the company does not disconnect (or change) the phone on the appointed day, call the business office and tell them: "I'll tear the damned thing off the wall if you don't come and disconnect it today!" Not doing this is asking for phone-bill troubles.

   Other utilities—electricity, water, gas, and oil

—should be taken care of with equal decisiveness and promptness. So should other services, such as newspaper delivery and laundry.

4. Addresses: Notify your post office, magazine subscription offices, insurance companies, draft board, lawyer, creditors, relatives, and friends of your new address. Every post office can supply you (free!) with handy change-of-address forms that you can send to everyone you know.

   Leave your forwarding address with your landlord; a copy should also be taped to your mailbox in the apartment building from which you're moving.

   Records: Ask that your medical and dental records, legal records, and bank accounts be transferred to your new neighborhood.

5. If you plan to store possessions with your former landlord—or in his basement—while you're away, get a written statement of items left and under what conditions.

   No matter how friendly the landlord, verbal agreements are of little value. Make a list of those things you're leaving, how much (if anything) you're paying the landlord for storage, and how long he is to be responsible for these items. Make sure one or both of you has insurance to cover your property in the event of fire, theft, or flood.

6. Read Chapter 2 on moving.

7. Be sure to clean your apartment thoroughly, after you move out. If you don't do it, the landlord may hire professionals to do the job at your expense. Remember: fifteen cents worth of Spackle (Chapter 3) will protect you from the landlord's wrath.

8. Arrange to be present when the landlord or realtor inspects your apartment to assess the damages. This precaution should eliminate the possibility of unjust or arbitrarily high charges for damages.

9. Finally, be sure to leave your keys with the proper party—be it sublessee or landlord.

Having accomplished the above, thereby assuring yourself a smooth exodus, please turn to page 1 . . . and start this book over again. Ah, how history repeats itself!

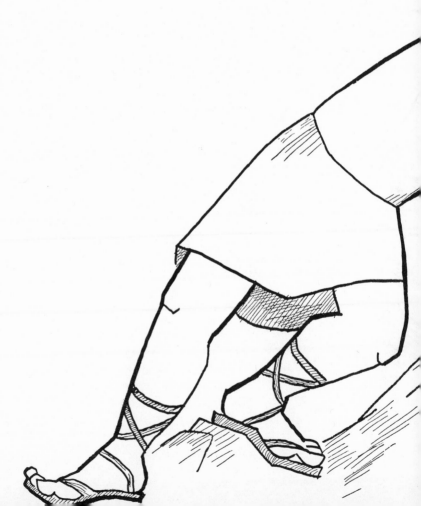

Sisyphus and his boulder: "Ah, how history repeats itself!"

INDEX